Calling o1

Choose a color on t[...]1, and imagine this color flowing [...] head and body. The color you chose is the most healing for your body right now. As this color flows into your body, it brings the energy of the healing angels.

If you chose rose, you are drawn to the healing angels of divine love who heal discouragement, bring cheerfulness and new energy, and evolve your circulatory system.

If you chose yellow, you are drawn to the healing angels who clear and balance your mind so that you can think with greater clarity.

If you chose green, you are drawn to the angelic healers who heal glandular problems, strengthen your immune system, and dissolve stress and excess tension.

If you chose blue, you are drawn to the angelic healers who heal high blood pressure, infections, and other illnesses.

If you chose violet, you are drawn to the healing angels who vitalize your physical body, repair cells, and accelerate the healing of any injury or disease.

If you chose gold, you are drawn to the Solar angels who work from higher cosmic planes of light to bring the healing angels to you.

A Note From the Author

Regardless of how brilliant and compassionate our outside healers are, we are ultimately responsible for the body we have. Only we can listen to our soul and glimpse its divine plan for our lives. Only we can clear the space for the healing angels to help us create a finer physical instrument so that we can live in the joy of our highest destiny.

A forty-one-year-old psychotherapist who had painful, swollen joints took the workshop Healing Yourself With Light. She was on full disability and had little hope that she would ever get better. She was there to try to keep from getting worse. When she returned the next year to take an advanced seminar, this woman showed no signs of her agonizing five-year disability. She sat up straight, walked gracefully, and appeared quite healthy, even radiant. Her changes were so dramatic that others asked her to tell them everything she had done. After a moment, she said, "I have done only one thing differently; I have gone on healing journeys with the angels every night for one year without a single exception."

Many other people are also connecting with the healing angels on a regular basis. They are using the Healing Yourself With Light course for a variety of goals—to lose weight (more than one hundred pounds for one account executive), to cure illnesses, and to heal and upgrade their bodies so that they can develop their spiritual sight and serve more effectively in their work.

It is because of the success of hundreds of people in evolving and healing their bodies—and in lightening their lives—that I have put this system of angelic healing in book form to make it available to everyone who needs it.

Healing Yourself With Light

How to Connect With the Angelic Healers

Books by LaUna Huffines

The Awakening Life Series

Book I: *Bridge of Light:*
Tools of Light for Spiritual Transformation

Book II: *Healing Yourself With Light:*
How to Connect With the Angelic Healers

Healing Yourself With Light

How to Connect With the Angelic Healers

LaUna Huffines

H J Kramer Inc
Tiburon, California

Published by H J Kramer Inc
P.O. Box 1082
Tiburon, CA 94920

Editor: Nancy Grimley Carleton
Cover Art: Copyright © 1995 by Ki
Cover Design: Jim Marin/Marin Graphic Services
Composition: Classic Typography
Book Production: Schuettge and Carleton
Manufactured in the United States of America.
10 9 8 7 6 5 4 3 2 1

Library of Congress Cataloging-in-Publication Data

Huffines, LaUna.
    Healing yourself with light : connecting with the angelic healers
/ LaUna Huffines.
        p.   cm.
    ISBN 0-915811-56-1
    1. Healing.   2. Vibration—Therapeutic use.   3. Angels.
I. Title.
RZ999.H84   1995
615.8'52—dc20   94-41667
                                                              CIP

*I dedicate this book to the healing angels,
who are here to heal, regenerate, and rejuvenate
all who connect with them.*

To Our Readers

*The books we publish are our
contribution to an emerging world
based on cooperation rather than on
competition, on affirmation of the human
spirit rather than on self-doubt, and on the
certainty that all humanity is connected.
Our goal is to touch as many lives as
possible with a message of hope
for a better world.*

Hal and Linda Kramer, Publishers

Contents

CONTENTS

Preface

I invite you to be among the pioneers who are healing themselves with light—the light of the soul and the light of the angelic healers. You can become a powerful healer as you learn to work with the healing angels. You can create a healthy and energetic body, build light into your cells, and rejuvenate yourself so that you can fulfill your dreams. Vitalized with the light of the soul and the healing angels, you can have the energy and the freedom to do whatever has the highest value to you.

Many of you will be drawn to this book for different reasons. You may wonder why you have experienced illnesses or other physical challenges when you are doing all you know to stay well. You may be coping with headaches, bronchial problems, muscle aches, allergies, insomnia, digestive problems, a stiff neck, an aching back, or other aches and pains. You may have periods of feeling so tired when you awaken in the morning that you have to talk yourself into getting out of bed. You may be catching colds and viruses every winter, or you may worry about your memory and your bright, sharp mind beginning to diminish.

You may have a serious illness or life-threatening disease that requires medical assistance or surgery. If so, the work of the angelic healers can complement the medical help you need. The healing processes given in this book show you how to regenerate and rebuild health and vitality regardless of any obstacles in your life.

Or you may be perfectly well and want to rejuvenate your body and raise the light in your cells so your body and mind can hold more light. You may want a clear, focused mind so you can reach higher states of consciousness, be more creative, and become a source of strength that enables others to grow. This method of working with the angelic healers, with your Solar angel, and with your soul shows you how to build a new body that can hold a higher vibration of light.

This system of healing yourself is not mine. It has come to me as a gift from a highly evolved angel named Jaiwa and a group of other healing angels who are dedicated to assisting those of you who want to bring light into the cellular level to heal and regenerate yourselves. Through the years when people came to me who were sick, I would sit quietly, and then move into the higher frequencies of these angelic teachers. These angels would use beautiful colors and pulses of sparkling light and sound to heal. Whatever they touched gained this sparkle of light and energy. They showed me how to help others create a new blueprint for their body, upgrade the systems in their body, and work with their inner healer.

Many people began coming and asking to learn how to connect with the angelic healers. Over the years the healing angels showed me a complete system of healing and rejuvenation as I continued to assist more people. Some of these methods are ancient, and some are quite new. In each chapter of this book, I have presented the teachings of Jaiwa and the angelic healers as faithfully as possible. I have taught these methods of angelic contact and healing in seminars and on tape since 1988 to people from all over the world.

The initial group of students came and participated in a series of seminars. They came from a wide variety of backgrounds, age groups, and educational levels. Their careers and lifestyles ranged from professional musicians, teachers, city planners, bank examiners, bookkeepers, psychological and physical therapists, secretaries, and jewelers to small business owners, homemakers, mothers, writers, real estate agents, opera singers, waitresses, and corporation consultants, among many others.

Hundreds have graduated from the Healing Yourself With Light training. They are pioneers in demonstrating with their own lives how profound changes in the physical body can be when one is connected with the healing angels. Some changes were rapid and dramatic. Other changes were subtle, yet they also created profound healing. After consistently working with these tools over a period of time, the graduates look and feel much younger. They are dynamic and enthusiastic. They feel better, sleep better, and think more clearly.

I hear many inspiring stories from those who have brought their body to a higher level with the healing angels. Each story is unique, describing the wide range of healing that can happen with this method for evolving the body. Some find that the healing happens so easily in one area that they quickly begin thinking of other areas to heal or upgrade. Others experience a step-by-step transformation, with unexpected healings happening before the healing they are seeking. Some are still in the process of treating a life-threatening disease but have already lived much longer and with more vitality than their doctors predicted.

The effects of physical and cellular healing with light reach beyond physical health and vitality. A few people were about to give up on life when they came for healing. They were successful in the outer world, but their weight, fatigue, or another physical challenge was holding them back. Using this system of working with the angelic healers, they removed the obstacles to their success. As they received the colors and higher light their body needed, they focused on their new future, creating more fulfilling careers, relationships, and friendships. Some began teaching classes on healing using these processes. Others have begun writing books, composing music, writing poetry, and developing as excellent artists in other fields. Each time they returned to the Healing Yourself with Light group, we all rejoiced at the compassionate love and light of the angels of healing.

During the classes, the healing angels were aware of all of you who would someday be using these techniques. We included you as a part of our group, sending light and preparing the way for all of you who would be joining us in healing with these special angels. I am deeply grateful to them–and to you who are ready to rejuvenate your body and your life with light. May you experience more energy, joy, and love than you have ever known as you work with your soul and the healing angels to heal and evolve your body.

LaUna Huffines

Acknowledgments

I offer my heartfelt thanks to Sanaya Roman for her inspiration and assistance on many levels, and for her excellent ideas that are woven throughout this book.

I am also deeply grateful to my sister, Jean St. Martin, of Dallas, Texas, an outstanding healer/therapist, for her support of this work and her valuable input on guided imagery.

My appreciation also goes to my publishers, Hal and Linda Kramer, who have awaited this book for five years with keen interest and enthusiasm, and who wholeheartedly believe in the importance of this system of healing and regenerating oneself.

I am especially grateful to Gloria Crook, founder of the School of Ageless Wisdom in Arlington, Texas, for our discussions about the Solar angels and their true identity, and to Orest Bedrij of New York City, for our discussions about creating a God-like balance in body and mind.

I want to thank Carol Gerson, John Enright, Tim Read, Anita Dittman, and Edward Alpern, who read parts of this manuscript and offered valuable comments. And my appreciation goes to Anita Dittman and Naomi Jarvie for efficiently managing the office while I have been writing this book.

I am grateful to Ki Fujinaka, of Honolulu, Hawaii, the talented artist for the cover painting depicting the triangle of golden light that is at the heart of healing in this system.

My appreciation also goes to Nancy Grimley Carleton, my editor, who steps lightly, yet with discernment and clear thinking.

ACKNOWLEDGMENTS

And my heartfelt thanks to the hundreds of people who have already taken this course on healing with light through tapes or in seminars and are holding a focus for all of you who will be learning to heal and rejuvenate your body with the angelic healers.

Introduction

You are living in the midst of dramatic changes in the way people live and relate to one another. Humanity is taking heroic steps forward through an awakening spirit of love and goodwill. Now the angelic healers can approach more closely to help those of you who are ready to transform your body and mind to hold more light. People in every country are calling upon the angels and meeting together in groups to heal themselves and one another through the powerful work of the angelic kingdom.

Higher frequencies of light and energy are flowing into this planet from the cosmic planes. They are more intense than ever before, and they will continue to become brighter for many decades. As the Earth's magnetic field is charged with this higher frequency of light, you can learn to enter into its powerful healing frequencies. The healing angels work with this Solar light, which carries tremendous healing power and offers you an unprecedented opportunity to heal and evolve your physical body.

You can use these processes for any area of your life. If you seriously practice these spiritual connections, they will heal and evolve much more than your body; they will change your life. These are also the processes of awakening to new dimensions of the light within. They give you a finer sensitivity to expand your consciousness. Practicing these methods will awaken and develop your spiritual sight and show you how to use your energy, your time, your talents, and your creativity where they will truly make a difference.

The purpose of this process of healing is to free you from having to put excessive emphasis on your body. At this advanced stage of human evolution, you won't need to focus on your body once you revitalize, heal, and upgrade it. You can turn your attention to more important work in your life. This book will teach you the way to heal from the higher spiritual planes and will help you connect with the healing angels. It will help you heal and rebuild your body–and your life–to hold more light. From a sacred place of healing, the angelic healers will come and work with you. They will help purify and clear your energy body (also called the etheric body). Your etheric or energy body is an invisible web of golden light surrounding and interpenetrating your physical body. By following the methods given in this book, you will strengthen your etheric body so that it can rejuvenate your physical body.

Through this system of healing, you will learn to draw to yourself higher frequencies of light that bring the finer molecules to your cells that resist disease, and that clear out anything that stands in the way of angelic healing. You will learn how to respond to this divine assistance by doing all that you can to supply what your body needs.

Perhaps you already realize it is time to take charge of your body. You may experience an inner desire to change or improve your diet, to find an inner stillness, to release undesirable tensions and pressures, or to heal a chronic problem. You may have an illness that is a warning signal to bring something in your life to a higher frequency, a signal that a relationship, a career, or a belief is unable to hold the finer light pouring into you. Any illness prompts you to find out what is needed and how to supply it. You can do this and more. No matter what your existing physical symptoms are, you can create a more pain-free, energetic, and younger body than you had before. As you practice the guided journeys, you will be freeing the dense particles from your body and building the body you need to enjoy your life. Working under higher direction, you are not only becoming healthier and gaining new vitality, you are raising the vibration of your whole body. You are learning to know yourself as you exist in the higher dimensions. As the spiritual stream of light flowing into you grows stronger, you can clear all obstructions and bring this higher light into every cell of your body.

The purpose of the angelic healers is to help humanity create a healthy, vitalized body, to transform the human body so that it radiates with light. These angelic healers offer you permanent healing. As you open your mind and heart to them, you help open the door between the angelic kingdom and the human kingdom.

This dramatic transformation of humanity is possible because the vast creative intelligence of all life is bathing this planet in a greater intensity of energy than ever before. Some call this creative intelligence love, and others call it light or God, yet no words can fully embody its awesome majesty and magnitude. In the past, the higher frequencies of light have been shielded to protect humanity from receiving more intensity than the body can handle. Now these shields are gently lifting. As powerful spiritual energies move closer to humanity, they bring building blocks of a finer subatomic substance to those who want to create a body of greater vitality and longevity.

Evolved souls are especially sensitive to this radiant light flowing into the planet. You may or may not be meditating or praying each day; either way you may be extremely sensitive to these finer frequencies of light. You may have suffered because you did not realize the importance of upgrading your body to keep up with the increasing light. Many symptoms of ill health arise because of a higher sensitivity and a greater refinement of the body. You may now require a better quality of air, food, and exercise than many people you know.

Whether you have minor physical complaints or major ones that you want to heal, physical problems do not mean that you have failed! They are not caused by a lack of faith or trust or love. They are areas where the radiant light is somehow blocked from reaching you. You may need new receptors at the cellular level to hold this light. As you bring in more light, you will need to keep upgrading your body and the way you treat it. Your skill in handling the light that is pouring in determines how high you can go. The condition of your body *determines how far you can progress* on your path and how much soul joy and love you can handle. As you evolve your body, you become more responsive to this light, and even greater opportunities can open before you.

With the healing angels you can develop the ability to get well and to stay well, to detect subtle imbalances and prevent illnesses that are just beginning. Radiant light can move freely through your energy circuits, clearing areas that were blocked from receiving the energetic charge your cells needed. Each system grows stronger as magnetic currents flow into your cells. The transformation of your body makes it possible for you to ascend into higher spiritual planes.

As you go through this book, you will discover that there is a divine order in creating a healing environment for your body. When higher frequencies of the angels circulate through your energy field, they may first open your mind to new priorities. Or they may first heal an emotion that has been blocking your soul's light. Many have discovered that the area they initially focused on was not always the area where the next healing occurred. When one man decided to heal his eyes, for example, he discovered that his digestion improved first. His digestion improved only after his fears were calmed. Try not to create expectations about changes. If you find expectations about your healing creeping in, trust that the divine order of regeneration frequently lies beyond the wisdom of the personality. Acknowledge every positive change in your life as a sign that healing is happening in divine, perfect order.

You are not simply working with mental or emotional energy to heal and evolve your body, although it is a useful part of healing. Permanent healing is not brought about just by thinking about health or by affirming divinity or eliminating errors in the way you think. The changes you can make are not the result of hiding from problems or suppressing symptoms. The healing and rejuvenation you can create by using this system are the results of working with highly evolved angelic healers who direct streams of light and color into your body. They will bring a new substance to your body so that it can use the finer energies you are drawing to yourself. These energies contain the higher frequencies of your soul and your Solar angel.

In Part One of this book, you will learn who the angelic healers are and how they work. You will discover that you have a very important reason to get well, and you will find the deeper purpose in evolving your body. You will travel to the Island of Regeneration, where you will begin your journey of healing and rejuvenation. You will create a meter that shows you how strong your will is to heal and evolve yourself. In Part Two, you will go to the Temple of Healing and meet your Solar angel and soul. Through this higher connection, you will learn how to draw the healing angels to help you in the Room of Inner Stillness, the Room of Light, the Room of Love, the Room of Colors, the Room of Sound, the Room of Wisdom, and the Room of Images.

In Part Three, you will meet and work with the directors of the systems in your body to bring new images of a truly fit body into the physical dimension. You will find out what is needed to heal your systems. Part Four, Becoming Younger, will show you how to change programs for aging into programs of rejuvenation and how to raise the light in your cells. You will learn how to use an illness to evolve your body, how to reverse damage that has developed from the past, how to reverse an injury by acting immediately, and how to make the choices that keep you young. You will learn how to stay in touch with and to raise your will to be well.

Healing in the future will be based on light, vibration, color, and sound. It will correct the originating cause of a disease rather than just erasing its symptoms. Even today, medical science is at the threshold of discovering the unseen healing energies of the angelic healers. The twenty-first century will bring precise scientific ways to use color and sound with these angelic agents of healing. Gradually, healing with light, color, and sound frequencies will become widely available. Scientists are already studying how the physical body responds to different colors and why color and vibration are such effective healing agents. Medical intuitives are being trained to work with physicians to help with difficult diagnoses. A few medically trained intuitives are already assisting physicians with remarkable success in diagnosis, frequently before any symptoms are present. The healing angels are happy to work with all forward-moving science, even if they are not always recognized consciously as part of the healing team.

How to Use This Book

This system of healing yourself is invaluable to your dreams, your goals, and your future. The way to experience the power of this system is to decide on a wholehearted approach. A half-hearted effort yields only partial results. A full-fledged effort inevitably brings profound results, and these results are nearly always permanent. They can generate extraordinary changes in other areas of your life. Even a small change is a catalyst for shifts, just as a pinch of baker's yeast added to dough causes it to rise and become light. You cannot be too young or too old to receive great benefit from your contact with the healing angels. As you take the time to practice the principles and methods of healing yourself with light, you will be giving yourself the gift of lifelong health and vitality. Imagine the support that a healed and evolved body can give you in creating a wonderful life that fulfills your highest vision and purpose.

Creating Your Healing Center

You can make the most outstanding healing shifts by selecting a room or a small area in your home and making it your temple of healing center. Imagine how you can make this room a beautiful place in which to receive the angelic healers. Fill the room with soft angelic music, a fresh flower or two, and a fragrance that you enjoy. Set a candle on the table in front of your chair and light it each time you work. All of these preparations help bridge the human world and the angelic kingdom. When you use the same location to work with the healing angels, they build light within and around this area. It becomes your sacred healing space. This essence light protects you from outer distractions and helps you to make angelic connections more easily. Gradually, you will be able to bring in the angelic healers almost as soon as you close your eyes.

Guided Journeys

The guided journeys at the end of the chapters provide you with the steps to transform your body with the angelic healers so that you can put into practice immediately what you have learned. Each journey and exercise is designed to assure your success, and each one builds on the one before. The exercises speak to your higher mind rather than your conscious mind and work best when you take time to put yourself in a very quiet, unhurried state before you do them. Familiarize yourself with the steps before you take each journey. Try reading one step, closing your eyes while you take that step, then opening your eyes to read the next step, and so forth. You can also have a friend read the journeys slowly to you, or you can make tape recordings of the journeys. If you prefer professional recordings, we have produced tapes to go with the chapters with similar yet more in-depth journeys than the ones here. Each is about twenty minutes in length and takes you farther than a written exercise can do. The tapes are listed in the back of the book.

Your Healing Journal

If you get a loose-leaf or spiral-bound notebook and title it *My Healing Journal,* you will have a place to make notes about the ideas and the information that come to you as you read. Honoring all ideas that come to you opens the door for an abundance of insights and inspirations to enter. By recording these ideas, you can examine them thoughtfully at a later time. Higher insights are like dreams – they are so clear at the moment you are in harmony with a higher wisdom and so quick to flee the next moment. The act of capturing them by writing or drawing a picture or symbol acts as a magnet to pull in other ideas that lie just beyond the reach of your mind. Describing them in your journal helps you to string these ideas together and see the brilliance and logic behind them. This connected string of ideas, like a strand of pearls, forms your path to outstanding health and vitality.

You can divide your journal into four sections, Part One for the Angelic Healers, Part Two for the Temple of Healing, Part Three for the Directors of Your Systems, and Part Four for Becoming Younger. Information from your soul and the angelic healers does not always come in outline form. It usually filters into the mind in a nonlogical manner. By placing the information in the section or sections where it best fits, you will soon have an excellent healing manual, specifically created for your body by the angelic healers and your soul. You may be amazed at how much knowledge about your body and healing continues to come to you once you have created a way to organize and put these ideas into action.

Answers to questions you asked the day before may come when you least expect them – perhaps when you are taking a walk or drinking a cup of tea. You may suddenly recognize a habit you want to change and build a new habit in its place. When you are in this process, write and post the new habit in prominent places in your home. Its positive energy will impress your unconscious mind every time you see it. When you look at the new habit, you are immersing yourself in its energy and drawing to yourself the circumstances, the people, and the information that will help this new way of thinking and acting become a natural and spontaneous part of your life.

As you read, the angelic healers are teaching you on a level beyond the words in this book. Slow down and let the words touch your heart as well as your mind. Honor the healing and the ideas that come to you by putting into practice all that you know in your heart will help heal you.

Part One
The Angelic Healers

About Part One

Your healing begins as you go through your body and decide what you want to upgrade, heal, or regenerate first. You will learn what the angels can heal, how they heal, who they work with, and how they work. You will learn how to measure your will to heal yourself on a special meter, what could stop your will, and how to raise it. You also will learn how to get the most from an illness and to embrace all that gives your life meaning. You will then be taken to the Island of Regeneration to become sensitive to the angelic presence here and to begin exploring the sacred space where the healing angels work.

Part One will set the success of your healing journey. You will have the opportunity to bypass your usual thinking and see the obstructions that could prevent the angelic healers from healing you. Your honest inquiry about the hidden benefits from an illness will allow you to see other ways to get these same benefits. You will begin to recognize just how much power you have to clear the space for angelic healing to happen and to give thanks for the unrecognized moments in your life when the angels have touched you in a time of need.

Chapter 1

The Presence
of the Healing Angels

Your healing is ready to begin! Before you go any farther, stop and think of what you want to work on as you heal and evolve your body. This way, you can start your healing immediately. Do you want to heal an illness, an infection, or an injury? Do you want to heal a chronic problem, such as your digestion? You can work with any problem as you begin your healing.

You can choose more than one problem to work on as you meet with the angelic healers. If you are facing a serious physical problem, you might choose a small problem to work on at the same time. In each guided journey, work with the small problem first and then the big one. This way you can become more confident as the smaller, "practice" problem improves and you open to receive healing with the bigger problem.

If you are not sure which problem to choose, stop and tune into your body. Mentally travel through your body, beginning with your head and face and moving down to your feet. Notice which areas feel out of balance, less alive, or weaker than the rest. Check your eyesight, your hearing, your skin, your heart, and your mental sharpness. You may choose to upgrade a system in your body, such as your respiratory,

3

circulatory, nervous, or immune system. You may want to improve your vision, hearing, or memory. You can ask for assistance in developing greater vitality and energy or in raising the light in your cells. Or you can work on rejuvenating your whole body and all of its systems.

Anything you choose is appropriate to work with, from the smallest problem to a life-threatening illness. It is possible that an unexpected healing will come first, even though you are not focused on it, but by focusing on a specific change in your body, you can begin right now to work with the healing angels. Rather than reading about *how* it can be done, you will be *doing it* as you read. Your ability to work with your Solar angel and soul and the healing angels can become so natural that gradually you won't need any healing. You can remember how to heal yourself the moment you sense an illness hovering on the horizon of your life and catch a potential problem before it develops into anything serious.

Stop here and make a list in your healing journal of everything that you would like to heal or upgrade. For about three minutes, write as rapidly as you can without censoring anything that comes to mind. Even though you think you know what you should do about a problem, if you haven't been able to make yourself do it, include this problem on your list.

Next, go over your list and review it, adding to it, combining items, or changing the list as you refine it. Look for the basic or "root" symptom that might heal some of the others on your list if it were healed first. Give each symptom on your list a priority number. You may get completely new insights about healing that symptom as you go into each room of the temple in future chapters. Releasing cravings and ad-

4

dictions, for example, might heal other physical symptoms on your list. Healing a sugar addiction might precede healing a thyroid problem. Getting angelic help to clear up candida might precede working on chronic headaches. The combination of all your symptoms will give you the clues to know which one to choose first.

On a fresh page in your journal, make another list with the problems in order of priority. Beside each symptom on your list that calls for a diagnosis or medical help, include finding the right healer or physician, the right level of medical intervention, and the right kind of therapy that will be most effective and the least invasive to your body. Healing angels frequently work through a doctor or other evolved soul to help you.

You are now ready to begin. Select one or two areas of healing and upgrading, and keep these in mind as you read about the angelic healers and their true work and then learn to create a meter to find your higher will to be perfectly healthy.

What the Angels Can Heal

The healing angels can transform any illness. They can work with major diseases, such as cancer, or with smaller annoying problems, such as sensitive gums or sore shoulders. They can clear up infections and heal diseased tissue. They can reverse degenerative diseases, such as arthritis or heart disease. They can subdue or eliminate pain and heal some problems that human medicine cannot reach. They can reverse pain from headaches or heal injuries from an accident. You can work with the angelic healers to clear up skin

rashes and other chronic problems, such as digestive, bronchial, and throat problems. They can eliminate nervous tension and dispel anxiety and fear. They can help you discover
and eliminate the true cause of an illness, or they can heal
a potential disease before it even affects your physical body.

Angelic healers not only heal; they can rebuild and
regenerate your body. They can give you energy and lift
chronic fatigue. They can rebuild systems in your body that
are not working well, such as your circulatory system, respiratory system, nervous system, or immune system. They can
stimulate your glands to function better, including your master
pituitary gland and your thyroid, adrenal gland, thymus, and
pancreas. They can also work with your organs, such as your
kidneys and eyes. They can rebuild your lungs and restore
your heart and arteries.

The angels are here not merely to bring your health and
vitality up to "normal," but to go beyond normal to bring you
a finer quality of cells than you had at birth. They can help
you to evolve your body and bring the high energy you need
to fulfill your true purpose. They work by regenerating your
body at the cellular level, transmuting your cells and bringing them to a finer frequency of light.

As you rebuild your body with the angelic healers, you
are building light into every system, gland, and cell. You are
evolving the body you have now into a body with a higher
frequency of light. The healing angels don't seek to replace
medical assistance and technology. They willingly work with
whatever medical assistance you choose. They can accelerate
recovery after surgery or add angelic light to any medicines
you need. If you are taking medication that has undesirable
side effects, they can help offset these side effects.

How the Angelic Healers Heal

The angelic healers work with group awareness. Even though they have individual consciousness, they blend their energy and draw from the entire group of angelic healers. They always assist when you ask for help in creating a body and mind that can handle more light. To do this, the angelic healers work under the direction of your soul and Solar angel on the soul planes. They follow laws that supersede the known physical laws of the Earth plane to evolve and strengthen your physical and emotional body. As they help clear and purify your body, they are clearing the way for you to build a stronger relationship with your soul.

The healing angels use tiny particles of light and color that activate the codes in the center of your cells to heal and regenerate your body. These particles form waves of love, light, vibration, sound, and color as they reach you. They bring sparkling light to your cells and systems. The angelic healers know exactly how intense these waves should be for your individual healing and cellular evolution. At times you may sense these currents as gentle. At other times they seem like strong, forceful waves of energy flowing through you.

As the angelic healers move closer in order to share their knowledge and healing power, they see what kind of healing and regenerating you need, and they wait for you to clear the space to receive their healing. They work first in your energy field with your etheric body. Your energy field consists of the subtle energy around your body; it is made of a refined substance that few people can see. It is fluid and changes from moment to moment as other people come into your energy field or as your own thoughts and emotions shift.

7

You may be able to feel this part of yourself, which vibrates at a higher frequency than your physical body, by placing your palm a few inches out from your body just above your navel and slowly moving your palm toward your body and out again a few times. Notice a shift in the energy around you as your palm comes in contact with the energy field surrounding your body. You may also notice yourself feeling calmer, and you may even spontaneously take a deeper breath as your palm presses on your energy field. As you play with this energy, you can develop a finer sensitivity to your etheric body.

The angelic beings assist you in bringing the finer substance of your spirit into your body with light, color, and sound frequencies. As they help clear your energy field, your body begins producing young and vibrant cells that enhance your mind. First, the angelic healers read your energy field and see which of the higher colors and vibrations are missing or off-key. Then they provide the finer matter of light and color that fills in what is missing. Since these angels are the embodiment of beauty on the spiritual planes, you become beautiful in the most profound sense. Your energy body gradually becomes more radiant as you continue to work with the angels.

You may not fully understand how the angels heal, but your heart knows. Long before your mind can fully accept the reality of the angelic world, your heart senses the angels as powerful agents for pure spiritual energies. Ask your heart what it knows about the angelic beings and trust its response. Heart knowledge is true knowledge. It has not been influenced by the prevailing beliefs of this age. As you work with the angelic healers, your mind learns to listen to your heart. When *both* your heart and your mind desire to work with these highly evolved angelic workers, the doors open and an extraordinary opportunity stands before you. The angelic healers recognize the desire of your united heart and mind, and they are drawn to you to fulfill your desire. Their presence alone evolves you as well as your body.

About the Healing Angels

The angelic healers are master architects of creating beautiful forms through vibration and color. Their evolution includes master angels, the archangels, who are acknowledged and described in almost all religions. Although there are recorded references to the angels dating as far back as ten thousand years, certain angels are only now drawing close to all of humanity. With the blessing of the archangels, highly evolved healing angels have come to heal and teach all who want to learn how to build a body with a finer vibration and immunity to disease. The essential quality of the angels is joy. Angels evolve through serving the plan of evolution; they depend on human evolution for their own evolution. Their consciousness is immersed in serving humanity. One of the major differences between angels and humans is that for humans much suffering stems from the illusion of being separate from the soul, from spirit, from God, and from other human souls. Fear, separation from their source, or resistance to higher evolution does not exist for angels. They do not ever withdraw from the light as humans do.

The angels are not tied to space or time. They have a body of light rather than a dense physical body made of the minerals of the earth like the human body. Because the angelic body filters light with transparent colors and patterns, it is sometimes possible to see angels as shining beings. However, their body is not truly physical. It is of a finer substance than ordinary physical matter. They are completely visible to one another and frequently to those people who have etheric vision and can see on a higher plane than the physical one. Many people have had a brief moment of this vision when they were able to see the healing angels for a few seconds.

The highly evolved healing angels work solely with human evolution. You will meet these angels on the Island of Regeneration. The most highly evolved of the angels who work with human evolution are the Solar angels of the white and gold hues. Their work is with your soul. They help build your spiritual body, which is the home of your soul. The Solar angels bring the other angelic healers to you. Your Solar angel calls in healing angels to assist in upgrading your physical body, your emotional body, and your mental body to a finer frequency of light and energy. You will meet your Solar angel in Chapter 5, in the first room of the Temple of Healing.

You will also meet groups of angelic healers who work with vibration, sound, colors, and light. These angels facilitate the cosmic plan of higher evolution as they work. They provide a protective mist of light that surrounds all of you who are working to build love and light on the planet. The angels of the green and orange hues of color rebuild diseased or damaged tissues through sound and vibration. Those of the violet colors build vitality into your body from the energy of the Earth as well as from spiritual planes. They assist in vitalizing your energy body, which surrounds your physical body. They can also heal your physical body. If you are fatigued and have low energy, or if you are prone to catch colds and other respiratory diseases, the violet angels may be your healers. Angels of the yellow bands of color assist in building, reconstructing, and healing your nervous system and your memory, giving you a clearer mind. They help your higher mind and brain communicate.

You will also meet the angels of divine love, who embody a finer love than is known in the human evolution. This love has a highly refined vibration that builds the will to live and heals discouragement and depression. They help lift the weight of worry, anxiety, or despair. The angels of divine love bring healing energy to your physical body as well as your emotional body. They bring energy to your heart and circulatory system. These angels give freely from love that has no restrictions or limits. They are the essence of love, connecting you with the greater light that gave birth to your soul. Since these angels are composed of a substance made from the essence of love, they transmit the unconditional love of spirit to you.

There are other angels, such as those who guard and protect the sacred places of the Earth and those who work with the animal kingdom, the vegetable kingdom, and the mineral kingdom. A very large group of angels creates the beautiful places of nature and work with non-human species of life on this planet. Other groups of angels watch over, heal, and evolve the vegetable kingdom. They furnish the subtle substance for trees, plants, and flowers. Many flower, herbal, and homeopathic healing remedies are gifts to humanity from various groups of angels.

Recognizing Moments of Angelic Assistance

You may have met the angels during an emergency. When time seems to stop and you are aware of what to do to get yourself out of a difficult situation, a group of angels may save your life even if you do not consciously recognize their presence. In a fraction of a second, you may be lifted out of a potential life-or-death situation or be taken out of time and suspended in air to prevent an accident. Rarely do you have any idea that this is happening; you may feel as if you are making brilliant decisions that provide all the right moves to save you. You may feel inspired and clearheaded when only a moment before you had no idea what to do. Or you make a split-second decision to run, to jump, or to turn around abruptly that later shows you were sensing events that were about to take place. Angels frequently take action just before an accident that would have taken place without their intervention or their warning you to be more alert.

Angels often put new ideas into your mind when you feel trapped in a situation or an illness and can see no way out. Think of a time when you were really low or sick and suddenly you were able to turn things around—as if something changed within you and you knew just what to do. This is the work of the angels. They leave you with free will to choose, which is the basis of the human evolution, yet they offer you choices that you didn't recognize before. They open a higher way out of an entanglement or an illness.

Seen and Unseen Angelic Healers

Sometimes the healing angels work so quietly that only later tests confirm their healing work. When the daughter of a Healing Yourself With Light student needed eye surgery after an accident, the family grieved when the surgeon gave them little hope to save her eye. The family linked together and called for help from the angelic healers, and when the time came for the surgery, her eye was already healing so dramatically that no surgery was necessary.

At other times you may get a glimpse of what these healers are doing. One woman with a chronic glandular problem asked for help from the angelic healers. To her complete astonishment, she could see the angels come and pull some substance out of her energy field as if they were vacuuming invisible cobwebs off her. They followed this cleansing by bringing in beautiful colors to that area, and then they were gone. Her glandular problem is now healing rapidly.

Angelic Healers as Awakeners

The angelic healers can send you a charge of life energy when you least expect it, or they can awaken you when you have forgotten that you have the right to create a wonderful life. The angels' mission is to guide and assist you in evolving your mind and your body. The healers can work even while you are sleeping. An eighty-year-old woman was awakened in the middle of the night when "lightning" struck her just above and between her eyes. She was so startled when it "hit" her that she jumped up from a sound sleep to close the windows from the storm. Suddenly she realized there was no storm. The sky was clear, with the blinking lights of stars everywhere. The brilliant flash of light had to come from another kind of electric fire. She then realized that an angel had come to awaken her ability to sense her divine self.

You can call in the healing angels if you awaken in the night with a common illness, such as a stomach virus. These

13

healers come and begin eliminating the virus infection and the discomfort. Many people have done this. They know the healing shift has happened when the pain leaves and they feel at peace. Soon they are comfortable enough to fall asleep again.

How Angelic Healers Work

A forty-six-year-old engineer called on the angelic healers to help with a shrill, continuous ringing in his ears that had resulted from a scuba diving accident in deep water. The doctors had told him that nothing could be done, yet the noise was beginning to interfere with his concentration. He asked a clairvoyant friend who had etheric vision to observe and see what happened as the angelic healers came. She saw tiny workers arrive, under the supervision of a higher angel, and work as a group. They appeared to be rapidly mending or sewing. In less than five minutes, they were gone. The ringing in his ears became softer immediately and changed its shrill tone to a softer, lower, and more pleasing tone. In later sessions, the angels softened the ringing in his ears even more, until now it is hardly noticeable.

An accountant described his healing journey this way: "It has been two years since I began to learn how to heal myself with light. I am now more than one hundred pounds lighter, and my mind is extraordinarily clear and alert. My body and mind are now purified enough to receive clear impressions from my soul. When I first began opening to the angelic healers, I was ready to die. My fifty-sixth birthday was approaching, and I weighed close to three hundred pounds. Diets did not work. I had seriously worked with all of them.

I lived with the healing angels at work, in my car, and in the gym. I am truly living in the light. People tell me I glow with light, but they have no idea why."

A young artist had one cold after another. Her respiratory system seemed to break down every winter and never fully recover. After working with the healing angels, she rarely ever has a cold now, and if she does, it only lasts a day. You, too, can heal yourself and eliminate annoying colds or viruses you may have taken for granted as part of living. Before you check your will to be completely healed in the next chapter, begin thinking about the joy that healing and regenerating your body will bring to your life.

Chapter 2

Raising Your Will
to Be Healed

In this chapter, you can get in touch with your will to heal
yourself and raise the light in your cells. You can learn how
to raise this will higher, not through affirmations or imagining it to be so, but by discovering where the conditions are
that hold back your will and releasing these. Once your will
to be healed is free from any conditions, this creates a magnetic energy to attract the healing angels, who will work with
you and give you the energy to do all that you can to assist
in your healing.

Your will to be well and vitally alive is the key to your
success in being healed and in upgrading your body to hold
more light. Free will is the basic law of the human evolution.
No one is allowed to interfere with your free will. The angels cannot
come and heal you unless you are fully committed to being well.
If some part of you is holding back, they must respect this and
wait until you are ready. When you are ready, they will help
heal, regenerate, and rejuvenate your body – but not until then!

Creating Your Meter

To measure your will, you can create a meter that by-
passes your conscious thoughts or beliefs. This meter mea-

16

sures your will to create a finer body that is vitalized and healthy throughout your life. The needle on this meter measures your will on a scale of 1 to 10. You will be measuring how clear your unconscious mind is to allow healing to happen.

You are learning to connect other dimensions of yourself that know the answers that you can't quite reach. Later, you can also use this meter to answer your questions about creating the body that can serve you best. It can show you how well any of your organs or systems is functioning, or if any potential problem exists. One woman also used her meter to see which activities in her life had the energy of her soul behind them and was very surprised at the answers. The higher the number, the stronger the yes for that activity.

Creating a Meter to Find Your Will

1. Imagine a meter with a dial and numbers from 1 to 10. Create the style of meter that fits you—a small, modern meter, a speedometer type, or another style. Give your meter a definite shape and color. See if the meter can fit into your hand, or if it is a larger model that sits on a table. The needle on the meter can register accurately whatever you ask. Make the needle and the numbers on the dial luminous so that you can see them easily in the dark. Take a moment to sketch or describe your meter in your journal.

2. Now ask your meter to show you how strong your will is to create perfect health. Decide that you want an honest answer and will not try to influence the needle.

3. The needle will move to one of the ten numbers. Watch where the needle lands, and write this number in your journal before you read further. If you don't get a number at first, build

your meter with more detail, painting each number with thick paint and creating your needle with a sensitive magnetic point. Then ask the question again.

Scoring

Meter reading 1 to 3: You are not yet ready to make significant changes. Look for the benefits that make this problem worth all the trouble and discomfort it is bringing. There is something you are still learning or gaining from having this problem. For example, someone may treat you much better when you are feeling ill. Your family may seem more understanding and assist in taking care of you. Your boss may allow you to take extra time off. You may get sick leave, or you may be able to stop doing something that you don't want to do. Others may not expect so much of you. Sometimes getting a headache, a backache, a virus, or a cold is the only way you let yourself have a chance to rest. Once you are sick, when you think of how your life will be when you are well, you may not have any real reason to get well. It's very difficult to get well if your life seems easier when you are not too healthy. As you identify the reasons your will to be well is between 1 and 3, take these reasons with you and work on releasing them as you meet with your Solar angel and soul and the angelic healers. You can receive divine inspiration about your future and your inner power to create that future. Knowing what holds you back from being healed is valuable information. Ask for angelic help. It holds the key to your freedom.

Meter reading 4 to 6: There are some definite advantages right now to staying right where you are. In this middle range, you have established a balance between being well and being sick that is working for you on some level. You may need time out to reflect on what you really want in life. Your soul may be using this time to come closer to you. Your personality may be in transition between being centered around the material world and being centered around your soul. You can uncover the advantages and look at them to see how you can get the same benefits that an illness gives you while you are perfectly well. There is nothing that can be gained from an illness that you cannot *also* have when you are well. You may not realize this until you think about it, but it is so. To free your will to rise above this middle range of 4 to 6, use your will to be vitally healthy in the guided meditations and ask for assistance from the angels in healing your will. When you free your will to become a 10 on your meter, you *free yourself* to live with the full force and creativity of your soul—and you may discover that your body is fully healed in the process.

Meter reading 7 to 10: You are ready to begin healing yourself or upgrading your body with the angelic healers right now. You are willing to change just about *anything* to heal and create a vitally healthy body that can hold more light. The angelic healers have permission to work with you right now. If your will is a 7 or 8, you will also benefit from examining what is holding your will back from reaching 10. As you work with the angelic healers, ask for insight and help in freeing the energy that is held beneath your will until it is free.

Why Your Will Is So Important

Healing can be exceptionally rapid when your will to be well is strongly influencing you. Angelic healing requires your active cooperation. Your commitment to do *everything* it takes to create a body that vibrates on a higher frequency sets the space for the healing angels to work with you. The healing angels automatically respond when your will to cooperate is unwavering and clear. You cannot expect positive results if you ask for healing and regeneration one week and block healing the next week by going against the guidance you receive as you work with the healing angels. They only have permission to build healing colors and frequencies into your body when you show that you are ready to build them into your life. If you don't make the changes that you know are wise, the illness may return or another one may take its place. As your higher will becomes strong, nothing can stop you from fully supporting the healing you are receiving.

If you cannot bring yourself to cooperate fully right now, it may be that a part of yourself is holding out until you have learned all that you can from an illness. You may need to learn to say no to someone or to eliminate an activity that drains your energy. You may need to say yes to your hope that a wonderful life can be yours. You may need to stop criticizing yourself and recognize your courage and willingness to get the most benefit possible from the experiences that physical problems bring. Once you learn all you can from a physical problem, you will find your will rising to heal whatever is not working properly in your body.

Freeing Your Will to Get Well

1. If you want to free your will to heal yourself, read these questions and write in your journal the first answer that comes to you. As you ask yourself these questions, give yourself per-

mission to answer with total honesty. Your heart knows the level of your sincerity, and your honesty increases your body's trust in you.

- Is there some part of me that is resisting making a genuine commitment to creating perfect health?
- Are there some advantages in my having this physical problem? Even if there is no obvious advantage in being sick or having low energy, is there a hidden advantage that I am not aware of?
- Is there anything I would have to do if I were in perfect health that I don't want to do? If there were something I would have to do if I were in perfect health that I don't want to do, what would it be?
- Is my illness just serious enough to allow me to do a few things that I enjoy (like reading, relaxing, watching television, and talking with friends) and not have to do what I don't really want to do?
- Is there something someone expects of me that I don't really want to do and am now temporarily relieved of doing?
- Is my will (or someone else's will) pushing me into a project or relationship that feels more like an obligation than a shared purpose?
- Am I involved in something that my heart and mind are both rejecting? (Trying to meet personal goals or someone else's goals for you that are not in line with your higher purpose can create an illness that wakes you up to make changes.)
- What would make it worth the effort to be truly healthy and to rejuvenate my body?
- What would happen if I were totally vitalized and regenerated and did what I feel is most important in my life?

- How could today, next week, and next year be different if I were totally well right now?
- What would I do if I had abundant energy and good health right now? Is there something I have often thought about, or something that I am already involved in, that I would do if I had the energy to do it?
- What would happen if I realized that I don't have to be sick to stop doing the things that I get out of when I feel tired, nervous, or sick?

2. Review your answers to these questions and make note of any patterns you observe. When you can find and appreciate the advantages of being sick, you are on the way to freeing your will to be well—and on the way to a rapid recovery.

Raising Your Will to Be Perfectly Well

Getting the Most From an Illness or Physical Problem

Whatever physical problem you are working on can offer you much more than you may know, but it can only do so if you know how to get the gifts from it. You can get these hidden gifts through any illness—whether an annoying allergic reaction or a life-threatening disease—that opens the space for your higher will to move into your life. Illness is not a preferred path for anyone, but if illness comes for any reason, you can use it as a springboard to gain a finer quality of life than you have been able to develop previously.

You don't have to be sick to receive these gifts. You just need a strong desire to raise the light in your cells so that you can work with enthusiasm and high energy throughout your life. Think about these possibilities as you read them, and

22

give yourself permission to open the pathway to a wonderful sense of compassion, humor, and wisdom along the way.

In deciding which gifts you want, you can move through an illness much more rapidly. Select the ones you want the most. These changes will be the easiest to make, and they will be the most fun. Take one of these at a time and begin drawing it to you as you do the exercises in future chapters.

"What Ifs" Move Your Needle Higher

Let your imagination soar. Ask: What if the next twenty years could hold for me a healthy body and a bright, clear mind? Imagine outrageous possibilities and begin them with "what if." Ask yourself: What if I had more joy and peace during the next month than I have ever known? What if I made such a powerful contact with my soul that it would guide me into the wisest decisions all year—decisions that create the kind of life I truly desire? What if this year turned out to be the most valuable year of my life? What if, over the next few months, I gained the skill to heal myself and stay well? What if I were healthy and fit for the rest of my life? What if my life could bring light into someone else's life—or into many people's lives?

You can also play this game in a group of two or three people, and let each one be "it" while others create "what ifs." The light spirit that overflows into this kind of creative play comes from an awakened love in each person's heart. Together, you create energizing pictures. These pictures can accelerate healing many times over. The energy from positive pictures about your life builds the enthusiasm to create a body you can count on. Enthusiasm generates the action to take care of your body's simple needs. These pictures can guide you—lead you, dare you—to be more resourceful than you think you can be. They enable you to accept angelic help and use your new vitality with a sense of joy and higher purpose.

Embracing What Gives Your Life Meaning

If you knew that a dynamic and powerful energy was stored inside you waiting to be released, would you want the key to release it? The key is hidden in an extraordinary wisdom that lies within your heart—something that has great value to you, something that makes you breathe deeper when you think about it, something that gives you delight when you work on it. This might be a certain hobby, or it might be a major shift, such as moving to a beautiful area, becoming a healer or a wise teacher, or joining a group of people like yourself for a shared purpose. Or it could be spending time in a beautiful setting, writing, drawing, speaking, creating music, or exploring a new place. What matters is that you feel enthusiastic when you plan it.

Even if you are not sure what will bring this extraordinary wisdom out of your heart, begin creating a list of possibilities in your journal, and new ideas may start flowing into your mind. Embracing something you love opens your heart as a flower opens when the sun shines on it. The petals of light behind your heart begin to vibrate and open to become a radiant flower of light. As you embrace this "something," it can provide a tremendous healing assistance for you. It becomes your way to express that which is noble and beautiful and loving within yourself. It draws you to your intended purpose. When your mind is focused on this luminous "something," just thinking about it inspires and nourishes you. As you keep your eyes on this goal and concentrate on how you will shape it, changes begin to happen. Taking action, no matter how small, toward this goal strengthens you. Action forms a path for your soul's will to assist you and for your healing to happen.

You don't have to know how you will do it. Your creative self will begin working on the how and when. This part of you is active even while you sleep. You may not know this is happening, but it happens all the same. You may change or refine your list as your creative self goes into action. When you are touching this wisdom, it raises your will to be well. Even if you only sit and visualize how you might be able to take part in something that has great meaning to you, or what group of people you can link with who share the same goal, your will becomes stronger. Your will to express the wisdom of your heart also brings you a longer life. The two are very closely connected—your will to express the wisdom in your heart and the health and longevity of your body. As your will becomes stronger, you find the time and energy to do whatever supports the healing angels' work.

Make your list of possible goals in your healing journal. It takes courage to acknowledge in writing something so close to your heart. At the top of your paper, write: "Activities That Have the Deepest Meaning to Me." Write whatever comes to you, even though you do not know exactly what form it will take. Include the day, month, and year. Feel free to change or add to what you have written as you go through the exercises in following chapters.

If You Are Already Doing What You Love

You may already be devoting yourself to the area that has the deepest meaning to you and still have a physical problem to heal. You may be raising children, creating a business, educating yourself, or teaching or learning something important. Look around and see if your work is balanced with relaxation, play, and occasional laughter with friends. Brief spurts of stress and overwork are usually all right for your body to handle. But prolonged periods break down its vitality and wear it out. Check your schedule and see if you are trying to do work that is not your responsibility. Or you may be so inspired and creative that you are trying to do more than your body can handle, like an acrobat twirling plates while he turns somersaults.

Ask yourself: What could possibly be so important that it is worth ignoring the real needs of my body now and paying the price of illness, a weakened immune system, low energy, and a fuzzy mind later? Once you reflect on this question and answer it honestly, you will find it easier to make the time to create the body that regenerates itself year after year. If you really want a future in which you are strong and active and healthy with an extended life span, you can have it. Imagine how much more effective and joyful your life can be as you build this future. Imagine how a physical problem is teaching you to find and embrace the higher will of your soul and bring you new balance and joy.

Your next step is to acknowledge that there is a way that you don't have to be sick to have a better life. You may not know how, but there are many ways. By focusing on the prospect that it is possible, ideas come to you of how to bring your life into a new balance of health and higher vitality.

Now it is time to take a new reading with your meter to check your higher will to heal and bring finer frequencies of light into your body. Do this now, and note the number on your dial and today's date in your journal. The number will continue to change as you go to the Island of Regeneration and follow the path to your Temple of Healing.

Chapter 3

The Island of Regeneration: Home of the Angelic Healers

You are ready to be taken to a sacred place of healing. A very beautiful island, called the Island of Regeneration, has been created by the angelic healers to provide this place. This island exists on a subtle plane rather than on the physical plane. Its vibration is too rapid to create density and mass. The essence of the vegetable kingdom in its full glory exists here. The soul or essence of the trees and flowers sparkles in the sunlight. The colors of the flowers are much more beautiful than colors on the physical plane. It is as if the souls of the trees and the flowers on Earth are but small reflections of the angelic energy here on the Island of Regeneration.

The Island of Regeneration is shielded with strong forces of light, which surround and protect it from the merely curious—those who would come without a sincere desire to change. Since the Island of Regeneration exists on a finer and more subtle plane than the physical plane, the only way to find this island is to be taken here. All of those who are sincere in heart and mind will be taken to the island and welcomed. You are invited in response to your inner call that you are ready to meet your Solar angel and to receive from the angelic healers. Your deep desire to bring more light into your body, to create a strong, healthy, vitalized body, sends the signal for you to be brought to the island. You do not need to know how, or even where, to begin. You will be treated as an honored guest who is here by invitation, learning to see, sense, and hear on the subtle planes of reality.

Your Healing Partnership

The Island of Regeneration is the starting place to enjoy the greatest healing partnership that you could ever enter into – to meet and work with your Solar angel, your soul, and the angelic healers. The atmosphere is clear of dense thought forms, emotions, or toxins of any kind. While you are here, you can harmonize with the island and let its peace into your heart. The healing angels see you as a shining beacon of light in the world. You can help the angelic healers to unfold the beauty of your whole being, petal by petal, just as the petals of a flower unfold in the sunlight.

Whatever healing you visualize on the island can happen. Anything is possible. As you evolve your body on the island, your will to upgrade your body and raise your cellular vibration tends to become focused and strong. Each journey to the island creates another step in your regeneration. You are assisted again and again to transform your cells and systems to handle all the light flowing into you.

Honoring Your Sacred Space

This island is a sacred space because the healing angels are gathered here. It is important to honor their presence. The angels all work closely together – angels of vibration and sound, angels of beautiful colors, angels of divine love, angels of images, angels of wisdom, and angels of light. They refuse no one who is brought here. Their compassion is without limits. They vitalize your soul so that it can regenerate your life force to heal and to send incredible joy to you. You may not be aware of their presence at first, but your soul, your higher mind, and even your cells will know.

You can come to the Island of Regeneration any time you feel tired or discouraged. It refreshes you and relaxes you. It prepares you to meet with the angelic healers in the Temple of Healing. Come with a wholehearted desire to create a body that radiates with vitality, a body that is a good instrument for the soul to express its higher purpose. These healing changes are given as a free gift. To receive these gifts in their full measure, make an inner commitment that you will honor the healing here and explore its many uses.

A Journey to the Island of Regeneration

It is time to begin your journey to the Island of Regeneration. Think of the area or areas that you are going to work on and make an inner commitment that you are ready to learn how to heal yourself with light. As you bring your consciousness to this radiant center of healing, you are also leading the way for many evolved souls who will follow and learn to set up healing contacts with angelic beings as you are doing. Your own friends and family may be the first to benefit from the changes you make here.

Imagine yourself standing at the edge of a sandy shore beside the ocean. Send out the thought that you are ready to learn how to use light to heal the part of your body that you have chosen. Watch for a boat to appear on the horizon in response to your request.

As you look for the boat, set aside beliefs about how healing happens. It is not necessary to know how healing will happen, only to realize that you can receive healing on the island. First, you ask for healing and open to receive it, then you make the decision to cooperate with the angelic healers. Make a deliberate choice now to be open, and set aside questions about what lies ahead of you on this island. By letting go of expectations and entering the island in a spirit of adventure, you can simply enjoy the journey that awaits you.

In your mind's eye, imagine a boat appearing far out on the horizon, moving toward you. As it comes closer, two figures wave to you. The boat reaches the shore, and two smiling faces greet you in a warm spirit, calling you by name. They are here to take you to the island. Step into the boat, lean back, and relax. As the boat picks up speed, feel the wind on your face and in your hair. The ride is fast and smooth; your boat is traveling just above the surface of the water. When you reach the island and dock the boat, your hosts go with you. Step onto the grass, and fill your lungs with the fragrant air.

Harmonize yourself with the nature and the beauty on this island. Many mountain streams cascade into great waterfalls. These waterfalls charge the atmosphere with an electrical energy that accelerates healing. If you breathe deeply, you can almost smell the pure, fresh water of light as it flows over the falls. Explore one of these waterfalls in your imagination, and stand beside or underneath it. Swim in the large pool of crystal clear water below it. Bring its purifying energy into yourself.

To create harmony with nature, see the meadow, the trees, and the flowers as living forms of light and color. Every inch of ground is cultivated by special builders of nature. The entire island is dotted with flowers. Tiers of orange, gold, yellow, rose, blue, white, and violet flowers wave in the breezes from terraces that stretch as far as you can see. They create a bridge of harmony and connection between spirit and matter. Explore the gardens, and imagine the fragrance of the flowers. Walk among these flowers to get a sense of the perfect balance of sunlight, moisture, and rich soil that ensures that each flower reaches its full elegance and color. Notice the beauty of an especially radiant flower, its face to the sun, a gentle breeze moving it ever so slightly. Turn your face toward the sun the way an opening blossom faces the sun, and imagine yourself as a human flower, opening to the rays of the sun.

Groups of angels are all over this island. Imagine that you can sense them near the waterfall and in the gardens among the flowers. Your creative imagination helps you to connect with a higher part of your mind and to bypass any part of your mind that believes only the densest matter with a physical form is real. The healing angels are here to empower all who come to absorb healing energy and to be regenerated. They are here to evolve and heal your body so that it can receive and harmonize with greater light.

The angelic presence on this island adds sparkle to the air and to everything on the island. It creates tremendous beauty, colors, fragrances, and music. Linger among the tall trees and the garden of flowers. Make these images so vivid in your mind that you can visualize them anytime during the day. They give you energy, and they set the space for a true regeneration in your body, mind, and emotions.

A beautiful Temple of Healing is at the top of the highest mountain on the Island of Regeneration. You are ready to follow the path up the great mountain to find this temple and to begin working with the angelic healers.

Part Two
The Temple of Healing

About Part Two

In Part Two, you will find your Temple of Healing and go into each of seven rooms to connect with your Solar angel, your soul, and the healing angels. In each room, you will receive different modes of healing. If you do not need healing, you will begin raising the vitality of your body and heightening its vibration so it can handle more light.

As you connect with your Solar angel and soul and become receptive to the angelic healers, you will begin to recognize their presence and the effects of their work. You will develop a new power of visualizing and building a magnetic center within you that draws a far more joyful future to you. Learning and practicing these basic healing modalities will bring greater energy to your inner healer and prepare you to begin healing whole systems in your body in Part Three.

Chapter 4

A Sacred Healing Place: Your Temple of Healing

The Temple of Healing on the Island of Regeneration is dedicated to bringing human and angelic evolutions together. Highly energized with billions of tiny photons of light and color, this temple is the most beautiful sanctuary you can imagine. The temple provides a sacred atmosphere where you and the angelic healers can work together. Your imagination does not "create" the temple; it already exists and awaits you. Your imagination opens doors that have been invisible until now so that you can find the temple and explore its healing power. If you prefer to think of the Temple of Healing as a metaphor, use it as a pure and divine place for healing that exists in your higher mind. It is the act of imagining this sacred place all around yourself and placing yourself in its pure light that enables the angelic healers to work with you. The more frequently you come to this sacred space, the more easily the angels can regenerate your body.

Since your Temple of Healing exists on the subtle planes of a higher dimension, it is only available to those who sincerely desire to learn to heal and evolve with light. The temple is beneficial even when you do not have an illness or physical problem of any kind. You can come here simply because you recognize the importance of raising the light in

35

your cells so that you can move to the next level on your spiritual path

The Temple Rooms

When you enter the Temple of Healing, it will immediately begin broadcasting the frequencies of your Solar angel and soul. Your temple contains seven rooms, each filled with a different aspect of the Solar light that the angelic healers use. The first room is the Room of Inner Stillness. When you immerse yourself in the stillness of this room, you will find a profound silence within. From this place of silence, you can rise up to meet your Solar angel. In the Room of Light, your Solar angel will take you into the Solar light to meet with your soul. Your Solar angel and soul will form a special relationship with light to bring the angelic healers to you in the other rooms of the temple. In the Room of Love, you will make contact with the angels of divine love and open your heart to be healed through the unlimited power of spiritual love. In the Room of Colors, all the angelic healers will transmit beautiful colors into your energy field to help you heal. In the Room of Sound, you will find your soul's note and practice your own healing sound. In the Room of Wisdom, you will meet your inner healer. Your inner healer is the part of your spiritual self that is closest to the Earth plane and will show you how to take the practical steps in healing yourself that honor the guidance of your soul and the angelic healers. You will learn how to absorb all the healing the angels bring to you. In the Room of Images, angelic healers will help you create and energize the pictures that are most healing and rejuvenating for you; these will be the pictures you will create and energize throughout your healing process. They will help bring healing light, patterns, and colors directly into your physical body.

The healing angels from each ray of color will assist you at different stages of your healing and regeneration. All of the angelic healers work with color, sound, light, and love. Perhaps the angels of divine love, who are on the rose ray of color, will work with you this week, while next week the angels on the yellow or violet hues may be your primary healers. Trust your Solar angel to bring to you exactly the angelic help that you need. As you work with your Solar angel and the angelic healers, they will weave thousands of tiny filaments of healing light and connect them to you. These filaments of light will create new connections with all the dimensions of your being. They rebuild your body not simply by restoring weak areas, but by building a finer body that resists disease and becomes an excellent agent for the highest aspects of your being. Come to your temple with the wholehearted intention of making your life and body all that they can be.

A Journey to Your Temple of Healing

It is time to leave the meadow on the Island of Regeneration and go to the Temple of Healing. Imagine yourself climbing the mountain to reach your temple, following the path beside the expansive gardens of beautiful and fragrant flowers. Watch the giant monarch butterflies flying from flower to flower. Listen to the whirling wings of the hummingbirds. Inhale the sweet fragrance of the wild jasmine. Some people find their temple right in the meadow as soon as they step off the boat to the Island of Regeneration. If you do not sense yours here, begin

37

climbing the mountain to reach your temple. Follow the trail beside the mountain stream.

When you reach the top of the mountain, look for your temple. Let an image of it come into your mind. At first, your temple may be hidden by trees. There may be a beautiful lake in front that reflects the entire temple like a gigantic mirror.

Now look at the temple itself. What does your temple look like? Some see it with a large golden dome and a slender tapering spire of glistening white and gold. Its walls are translucent, as if lighted from within. Others may imagine the temple in entirely different ways. This is your temple. Notice what it looks like to you. It may be round with an inner courtyard. Notice how each room glows from within.

Walk around the temple, and notice that you can see the beach and the ocean from all sides. Look at the walls of your temple, noting their texture and color. Listen to the chimes and temple bells playing softly in the wind. Occasional chords of celestial music waft into the temple rooms. Your temple may change each time you come here. It is made of living energy that becomes more radiant each time you visit.

Your temple is the place of reverence where you meet with your soul. If your sacred space has transparent walls or no walls at all, this is fine. Use what is useful to help you create your ideal healing space. You can simply have a sacred space surrounded by flowers where you meet with your Solar angel, your soul, and the angelic healers. As you reach more confidently to the frequencies of light where your soul and Solar angel reside, your space or temple becomes more infused with light; it becomes a more powerful place of healing, a place of joy and profound peace. Take time now to close your eyes and picture your temple. You may want to sketch it in your healing journal.

Trust the cosmic laws of healing. Go through the rooms

in the temple with a sense of timelessness, free of the need to have healing happen in a certain way or timing. Let yourself experience the healing energy of each room. When you are in each room, angelic patterns of light are raising your cellular vibration, strengthening your heartbeat, and restoring a sense of play in life.

You may have a dramatic experience the first time you go into your temple. You may feel very serene and peaceful, or you may feel no difference at all. It does not matter what form your experience takes; the changes in your energy field happen either way. They happen as soon as you step inside the first room of your temple. Every journey to your temple adds to the regeneration of your body. Areas of your body that you may not have known needed healing may be touched and regenerated as well as those areas you are aware of. You can't consciously perceive each change as it happens—subtle chemical or glandular shifts, for example—but each one is restoring your cells and adding light to them. The healing will continue for years, long after you have visited the rooms.

The Shower of Light and Color

In the center of your temple, imagine an open circular courtyard filled with flowers and sunlight. As you enter this area, you might notice a variety of flowers in full bloom and the vines of fragrant honeysuckle and jasmine. In the center is a circle where the sunlight is pouring in. Walk over, and step into this circle. Feel the rays of the sun giving you a shower of light and colors. This shower clears your energy field of impurities from the physical world and prepares you to connect with the healing angels. Streams of colors are falling into a pool of liquid light around your feet. First, focus on gold and a pure white light flowing over your head and around your body. Next, imagine soft hues of rose flowing into you and around you. Imagine vivid, clear shades of yellow. Now focus on vivid shades of blue, green, and violet.

Let each color of the rainbow fall over your head and body like liquid light. Focus on one color at a time, and allow it to permeate your whole being. All the colors are transparent as a pure, clear light flows through them. Breathe these colors into your lungs. Feel them entering the pores of your skin, refreshing your brain, your eyes, your ears, and your throat. Feel the colors move through your shoulders and neck and down your body. Feel these colors clearing tiny cobweblike strands that are in your energy field. Imagine that all the dust and grime of years of walking down the dusty roads of life are being washed off your energy field. Let the colors clear all toxins that are clinging to your energy field. These toxins may be other people's anxieties, fears, and negative emotions, or they may be your own. Allow the shower of colors to clear whatever has been caught in your energy field. Notice how you feel after this shower. You may feel lighter, as if you have set aside heavy and unneeded luggage. Repeat the process, this time focusing on the area you want healed. Let the colors wash over this area, starting with gold and going through each color.

Now that you have cleansed your energy field, you are ready to enjoy the peaceful, restorative, and healing energy of the Room of Inner Stillness. Here, you will meet your Solar angel and experience its powerful energy flowing into you.

Chapter 5

Connecting With Your Solar Angel: The Room of Inner Stillness

The Room of Inner Stillness gives you the space to find a deep inner silence and to feel peace within yourself and around you. This is where you can set aside outside concerns and immerse yourself in this place of peaceful solitude. You can begin hearing with your inner ear and begin seeing with your inner eyes. This is the room where you will meet your Solar angel.

You may have been in a sanctuary in nature at some time or in a cathedral or church or mosque where you felt an extraordinary quiet and peaceful state. It may have seemed as if a part of some great cosmic creative force was standing in the center of your being. The Room of Inner Stillness gives you a similar feeling. Its energy takes you beyond a state of hoping to one of actually *receiving* healing. It takes you beyond thinking about healing or about anything that needs to be healed. You simply decide that you are ready to be in a state of pure harmony and tranquillity, and you are here.

Entering the Room of Inner Stillness

Before you enter the Room of Inner Stillness, allow your breath to come in more fully as you imagine the peacefulness of

41

the solitude here, its tranquillity and harmony. Take a shower of colors in the courtyard of your temple as you just learned. Now imagine that you are being guided to a special room. Look around and notice its peaceful atmosphere, its serenity and stillness. This room has a very soft glow, as if gently lighted from within. It may seem familiar, a special place you once knew well. Or, it may feel as if this is the first time you have been here.

The Room of Inner Stillness exists outside of time. As you enter this room, you can sense that you are in a special sanctuary, a safe place to look at what is most important in your life and to make your first contact with your Solar angel. Allow yourself to begin moving into a state of serenity, equilibrium, and stillness within. You are completely protected from outside energies in this sanctuary. It is a refuge and a retreat from the ordinary concerns of the world. Listen for a subtle inner voice that beckons you to be still and at peace. These sounds do not come through your physical ears. They come through your Solar angel. The quieter your mind, the louder these sounds can become in your inner ear.

Select a chair or mat to sit on, and when you are seated and comfortable, let the tranquillity of this room flow into you. A beautiful vase stands beside you. It holds a single flower with a beautiful color and a sweet fragrance. Notice the color and fragrance of this flower. It may be a different flower each time you come. Its purpose is to bring the fragrance and beauty that assist you in meeting with your Solar angel.

You are entirely in charge of how much stillness you find in this room. To begin experiencing the healing energy of this room, notice the energy flowing into your neck and shoulders and arms. They may feel heavier or lighter as the blood flows through more easily. Give permission for the muscles in your face to relax as you release the face you present to the world and let the face of your true self emerge—soft, gentle, and at peace. Think of the word *serenity,* and let yourself experience its essence as you slowly say this word several times. As you enjoy a deeper state of serenity, imagine a color and a texture behind these words as well: tranquillity, harmony, balance, composure. Softly repeat these words several times. Give permission for their essence to bring your body and mind to a state of poised stillness and awareness.

Let your breath flow naturally as your mind lets go of all concerns and your emotions become calm and still. Breathe into your heart, into your eyes, and into your throat. Pause between breathing in and breathing out. Let each breath tune your mind and body to the note of pure serenity. Let this serene state deepen as your breath shifts even more, becoming soft, gentle, and almost imperceptible. Bathe in the stillness here.

Your Solar Angel

You are now ready to meet your Solar angel, who has assisted your soul and you since your soul ventured out from Spirit to become a separate entity. Your Solar angel is not the same as your guardian angel. Your guardian angel is a dim reflection of your Solar angel. Your Solar angel will stay with you to guide your evolution until you are liberated from taking a physical body and work only from the higher dimensions. Your Solar angel identifies with your life and all that is going on. It helps you to find and cooperate with your divine purpose, to see if you are at cross-purposes with it, and to make any adjustments needed. Your Solar angel weaves your soul's body of light and colors. This angel amplifies your soul's call when it is ready to create a physical body and, through vibration and sound, calls forth the appropriate grade of molecules for your life here. It helps you to be more fully conscious as your soul releases the physical body at death so that you can move into your soul's radiant body.

Solar angels work for evolution. Your Solar angel never can be induced to bring anything that goes against your evolution. Every message, intuitive insight, and healing you receive here moves you forward on your path toward enlightenment. This angel brings the subtle spiritual substance that creates the connecting bridge between your mind and your soul.

A Relationship of Pure Love

To get an idea of the relationship between you and your Solar angel, think of how deeply you can love a child. The child may depend upon you to evolve, even to exist. When you have a deep love for a child, you use infinite patience in teaching and training him or her. You accept the limitations of the child, who can only communicate with limited thoughts and ideas and who has a limited ability to grasp the greater world that you live in. On a far higher frequency, your Solar angel is a teacher for you, one who has even deeper love for you, the love that lifts you into higher dimensions of yourself.

When you call your Solar angel into your life, you receive an opportunity to be filled with the spiritual energies that give you the capacity to become vibrant with life and to be filled with love beyond anything you have known. You will be bringing this angelic presence into your mind and heart. The Solar angel brings you as much light as you can possibly use and express. Nothing on Earth, no illness, pain, or other situation, can prevent you from making a connection with your Solar angel.

You can only sense your Solar angel after you have created the right space around yourself. Setting the space to make this contact shows your deep will to heal and transform your body. The space you set for the Solar angel determines how much it can help you. To create this space, set aside all pictures of how you expect to experience this angel and drop your images of what the Solar angel will be like. Don't expect to see an angelic face with a flowing white gown or to hear an angelic voice. Most people who come here do not see, hear, or feel anything unusual, although this may happen. What counts is not an experience of seeing or hearing, but your ongoing commitment to cooperate with your Solar angel, to let this connection clear any obstructions in your body or mind so that your Solar angel can work more closely with you.

A Relationship of Pure Light

Only when you silence the many voices of your personality and the environment can you feel the presence of the Solar angel. Your Solar angel approaches you on a different frequency than your intellect. You will be going beyond the intellect to learn the language of spirit. Your angel may send such an intense ray of light into your mind that it releases you from worry, gives you hope, and opens a new path for you. This may happen immediately, or it may happen gradually over a period of weeks. Some people feel the Solar angel as a gentle crown of light around their head or body. Some people hear a very gentle and high tone in one ear for a few seconds. Others see or hear nothing unusual, yet the shifts in their bodies and their lives are as profound as in those who feel or otherwise sense the contact. These shifts may not occur immediately, but they will happen during the next weeks, months, and years.

One woman in our seminar experienced her Solar angel as a golden star. Another woman didn't see anything, but she felt an extraordinary peace in her heart that lasted for several hours. Some wondered if they had really made a connection with their Solar angel the first time until they realized that they were able to think more clearly and to handle their work with a greater sense of ease and pleasure. A fifty-year-old man acknowledged that he had been thinking of finding a way to get out of life, to end it, because he knew he was just drifting without a clear sense of direction. By imagining how his life would be different when he was vitalized and healthy, he got a glimpse of new and better possibilities. Each time he connected with his Solar angel, he felt more energy and a stronger sense of vitality. He joined a group who shared his love of nature. He began helping to clear some beautiful mountain trails that had washed out and realized that he had moved into these possibilities that made him appreciate life as very precious.

When your Solar angel can come more fully into you, it will have a very real presence. It will bring a current of force to you that pulses in a certain rhythm and is on a certain note and color. You may bring in only a little of this energy now and then bring in more as your body adjusts to it. Even being touched by the Solar angel for a brief moment starts the process of healing and expansion.

Meeting Your Solar Angel

1. Move into the serene state that you developed as you sat in the Room of Inner Stillness, and let slow, deep breaths come and go. Imagine that your past is moving away from you and clearing the space for a new future.

2. Open your mind and heart to your Solar angel. Ask for the veils to be dissolved that have separated you from knowing your Solar angel. Think of how your life would be if the love and peace of your Solar angel could shine through your mind and body. Imagine the power of your Solar angel to regenerate you and your body. Allow yourself to believe that you can be healed. Give permission for your Solar angel to come closer to you. Open to the higher energy that this angel has for you.

3. Focus your eyes upward and call the Solar angel to you. High above your head is the golden light of your Solar angel. Imagine the light of your mind opening the door for your Solar angel to come closer to you. Imagine this living energy form slowly descending toward you. The Solar angel will come to the "you" that is beyond the passion of your heart and the searching of your mind.

4. Create a picture in your mind of the light of your personality being centered in your head. See it rising up above your head to meet the light of your Solar angel, which is radiating like a sphere of golden light. The Solar angel brings a brilliance to the air around you.

5. Watch this sparkling golden sphere descending to meet the light of your mind, which is ascending until they meet above your head. Give yourself time to fully sense the point where the two lights meet, as if an electrical energy is charging the atmosphere and filling the room with a vibration of harmony, tranquillity, and the healing power of this benevolent force.

6. Let the Solar angel come closer. Its strands of golden light can touch your head and become anchored in your energy field. Give permission for your Solar angel to bring its light into the thoughts circulating around your head. Imagine new channels of golden light being brought into the space around your head and adding light to your beliefs and thoughts.

7. Imagine a subtle halo over and around your head. Your angel is sending tiny pulses of light to open new pathways for it to reach your mind. Through this pulsing light, the angel is transmitting healing energy to the spiritual receiving center at the top of your head.

8. Ask the Solar angel for help in the area you chose that needs healing. The Solar angel directs healing into this area as you briefly focus on it. Beyond this, there is nothing you need do; the wisdom beyond your conscious mind will direct this energy into areas where it is needed. Stay a few minutes in silence and stillness while you absorb the healing energies that are flowing into you.

Your Solar angel works in many ways to show you how to reach the higher dimensions where it lives. Assume that you are making contact even if you don't experience anything unusual. After several visits to the Room of Inner Stillness, you will develop a sixth sense as you become more sensitive to these frequencies. You will notice a new sense of balance between the outer world and your inner self. You may also feel much more optimistic about your future. In your healing journal, describe anything that you feel or observe in the Room of Inner Stillness. Even if you didn't consciously observe anything, your new knowledge is recorded in your higher mind each time you reach up to your Solar angel. Gradually, this knowledge is transmitted to your conscious mind.

Now you are ready to go to the Room of Light to learn how Solar light transforms and rebuilds your cells. Your Solar angel will assist you in reaching the higher frequencies of your soul and forming a powerful triangle of light that draws angelic healers to you.

Chapter 6

Creating Your
Golden Triangle:
The Room of Light

The Room of Light is filled with a glowing light that is vibrant with life energy. This is the room of transformation, of opening to receive more than you have ever imagined receiving, of sensing your soul as the source of true intelligence and wisdom and love. In the Room of Light, your Solar angel will connect you with a very fine light called Solar light. This Solar light comes from the Heart of the Sun rather than the physical sun itself. This essence energy of the sun stands as an aura within and around the physical sun. The rays of Solar light that shine on you in the Room of Light are the source of your true life energy. You can learn how to absorb some of the powerful healing energies of Solar light at the Heart of the Sun. Even though these rays are not readily visible, you can clearly experience their effects as a powerful spiritual energy of regeneration and rejuvenation.

After you experience the Room of Light, your Solar angel will take you to meet your soul. You may think of your Solar angel and your soul as two aspects of the spirit within you; from the human perspective, they can seem like two parts of one shining entity. With your soul and Solar angel, you will learn the most important healing process in this book. If you learn nothing else, when you use this process to bring in the healing angels, you can begin healing anything.

Entering the Room of Light

Imagine the Room of Light now, and get a sense of the wisdom that awaits you. If it has been several days since you journeyed to the Island of Regeneration and to your Temple of Healing, go by boat to the island and travel to the Temple of Healing. You can also return to the temple by touching your fingers to your forehead.

Take a shower of light in the courtyard of the temple. Bring the colors of your shower of light over you one at a time, as drops of liquid light in orange, gold, yellow, and rose. Next, use shades of green, blue, and violet. When you feel light and clear, you are ready to enter the Room of Light. Your Solar angel awaits you.

Enter the Room of Light, and take a seat in the center. As you enter this room, notice the inner glow of everything in it. Everything in this room is luminous, but the intensity of the glow will be brightest in the place where you are to sit. Your chair or mat, the low table in front of you, and even the tablet to make notes, all glow with a white light. As you look around, let its luminosity flow into you. The light is a living light, a living intelligence that is offering you new knowledge and understanding. Some people have discovered a mirror in this room, and when they looked into it they could sense their Essence Self in place of their body self. This is the gift of Solar light—to sense the essence that stands behind the form.

You can sense the essence of whatever you think about in this room. Find the tranquillity that you learned in the Room of Inner Stillness. When your mind is no longer talking to itself and your emotions are quiet, imagine the radiance of your Solar angel. Absorb the radiance it brings; sense its presence within your heart and its essence love surrounding you.

The Power of Solar Light

The Solar angel brings Solar light into this room from the Heart of the Sun. Its rays bring elements that are necessary for your life. These elements are tiny beings of healing. After they bring you their light, they go back to their source to be recharged and purified before returning again. As you work in this room with Solar light, be aware of and open to these living beings who are bringing you these finer rays of light.

You can tap into the greater wisdom that Solar light brings. Begin by imagining the rays of Solar light around your head in the Room of Light. To the degree that Solar light can enter your mind and heart, you receive illumination. You can think of a spiritual quality, such as nobility, courage, or wisdom, and experience it immediately. Solar light is also an agent of rejuvenation. To the extent that Solar light can come into your body, it heals and rejuvenates it. Solar light evolves your cells. It dissolves toxins as it filters into your cells and transmutes them.

The connection you can build to your Solar angel and soul in the Room of Light draws this regenerating energy into your cells. Through this column of light, you begin receiving frequencies of Solar light that restore your body and cells year after year.

You have a small sun within yourself. It radiates with the combined light of your mind, your emotions, and your body. As you connect this inner sun with Solar light, the two lights merge and distribute light throughout your body. To receive the Solar light and brighten your inner sun, it is necessary to

51

prepare yourself. As you breathe, imagine that you are drawing healing light into your lungs, your heart, and your bloodstream. Each morning, look at the sun's rays lighting the Earth and think about the presence of Solar entities in these rays who can help you solve any problems of health for that day. Visualize these Solar rays spreading into the cells of your body, strengthening them and giving them new life. The living energy within these rays strengthens and evolves your body. Let profound feelings of gratitude rise from your heart for the help that is coming to you.

Healing With Solar Light

It is time to work with the Solar light and your Solar angel to heal your body. Think of the area of your body or your life you want to heal. Begin breathing in such a gentle, natural way that all tension dissolves. The Solar angel will focus upon Solar light and bring its rays to you and raise the vibration of your body and mind. Imagine your Solar angel drawing rays of Solar light toward itself and transmitting these rays to you now.

Solar light transforms whatever it touches. Let this Solar light form a mist of light around you so that only the finest frequencies can come through. Your Solar angel directs a stream of Solar light to the part of your body that you are working with now. Let yourself breathe in this energy and absorb it into your cells for a few minutes. Your Solar angel envelops you in love as it brings Solar light to you. Healing has now begun! It is happening right now exactly where you need it. It will continue to happen even while you are doing other things. Thank your Solar angel for its assistance, and open to receive all the healing that is being sent to you.

You are now prepared to meet your soul and to learn how to create a sacred triangle with your soul and Solar angel that will become your most powerful healing process.

Meeting Your Soul

Your soul knows you better than anyone else does. It watches your birth into this world. It watches you go through your childhood and teenage years. It watches as you become an adult. It exists independently of the drama of your life—always observing, always silent. You may have sensed this silent watcher in the space between thoughts, just before falling asleep, or when you successfully handled a crisis.

This silent watcher is in touch with the Universal Mind and Heart of the Sun. It does not belong to or identify with the physical world as you do, yet it is ever present with you. It does not belong to you, yet you carry its guiding energy within the center of your being. It watches as you develop higher consciousness and expand into your higher mind. It is conscious of your agony and your ecstasy as you go through all of life's experiences. This silent watcher does not hide from you. It is responsible for your ability to think, to create, and to live in a body. It is never sad or angry or discouraged. It does not suffer pain or loss. These are all experiences that the personality goes through while the soul looks on and guides.

The soul wants its love and vast intelligence to be expressed through you. It will respond when you turn your eyes upward and wait. As the soul touches you, your heart will fill with love. Your soul will flood you with light and energy.

The Love and Intelligence of Your Soul

Your soul is linked with the soul of humanity. It meditates with cosmic beings who are on the planes beyond the soul plane. It focuses on the cosmic plan to help humanity to evolve and to live in peace and love. When you are connected with your soul, it not only transmits healing energy to you, it gradually reveals some of this plan to you.

The love and intelligence of the soul are awesome. Only the soul knows your highest destiny, and it works closely with your Solar angel to help you fulfill this destiny. Once you realize yourself as an extension of your soul, you will know within that you are never alone and that your soul has the resources to bring to your life whatever is needed. Your Solar angel helps you build the connecting Bridge of Light to your soul by providing the substance for this bridge. You can learn about building this connecting link with your soul and bringing its radiant qualities into your life in Book I of the Awakening Life Series, *Bridge of Light* (HJ Kramer, 1993). (This book helps you to build a Bridge of Light and draw many rich soul qualities into your life, such as joy, courage, love, and truth.)

Your soul always responds when you build a Bridge of Light that links you with it. Only you can build this bridge. You build it by spinning a line of energy from your heart to your soul. When your bridge is complete, your soul can become the closest companion you will ever have. This companionship dissolves the loneliness and feeling of isolation that many evolved souls experience. The relationship with your soul strengthens your will to live your life fully. Your soul transmits its vibration to your mind and body. Your soul reaches down to you, and you reach up to it to build this connection. It can reach you when you build a Bridge of Light to it from your side.

Effects of Soul Contact

Your soul's vibration is so high and clear that it heals at the level of cause. It works with your etheric body, which underlies every nerve in your physical body. When the root of a problem is loosened and cleared out, that illness doesn't come back again. The vibration in your body that made the illness possible is gone.

When you contact your soul, you may recognize things in the past you did that you now wish you hadn't done and things you didn't do that you wish you had done. If this happens, you may be tempted to get caught in regret about the past, including how you have ignored your body's real needs at times. You may have eaten anything that was at hand, drunk whatever others around you were drinking, taken drugs, or created a lifestyle that overstressed your body. Whether you blame yourself or someone else, looking back is not the way of the soul. The soul looks only toward your future to see how you can assist in its long-range plan of evolution.

Soul insights may be brief, but no matter how brief they are, note them in your healing journal. The inspiration, ideas, and enthusiasm that come to you from the soul will increase as you take the time to acknowledge them. By describing the times when you feel that you are responding to your soul, you will increase your ability to receive more healing and your connection will deepen.

Soul Revelations

The light of your soul may reveal imbalances that have been covered and veiled from higher light. Physical symptoms from years back may come up, especially if the symptoms were originally suppressed by antibiotics and other medications. If you have physical symptoms as this clearing takes place, the symptoms are usually brief. Frequently they last only an hour or a day. You can help by lifting them out of your energy field with your fingers and tossing them away. Just knowing what is happening can keep you calm and centered. One man went to a retreat and meditated many hours each day for a week. The next day, he thought he was "catching" a virus. Then he realized that all the light he brought in was stirring up toxins that had been in his cells for years. He drank pure water, took a quiet walk, and decided to trust that these symptoms were signs of purifying his body. He gave permission for these coarser substances to be released without fear or resistance. In a few hours, he felt clear and well again. You can do this, too, if you sense a cleansing taking place. This temporary surfacing of old symptoms does not happen to everyone. The response of your body to so much light partly depends on how purified it already is. Most of the time you will feel more joyful, clear, and energized with each soul contact.

Recognizing Soul Contact

A small fragment of your soul is anchored in your energy field at birth. One strand of its light is anchored near your heart, and the other strand is anchored near your head. The soul's vast intelligence and love exist on the higher frequencies of Solar light. It is here that your body and your life can be transformed.

You may meet your soul easily, or you may wonder if

56

you are making contact. Some people have a dramatic experience, while others do not. Many people notice new ideas coming to them during the hours *after* they have reached up to their soul rather than during a meditation itself. Everyone's experience is different. Some people hear a very brief high and pure tone in one ear. Others hear the soul's voice. A very bright psychologist had tried to connect with his soul for a long time before he was convinced that he was successful. He had decided his intellect was blocking his soul's voice. One morning, as he reached within once again to make contact, he distinctly heard a silent voice from within himself say, "I am closer than you think." This voice was so clear and unmistakable that he knew it to be the voice of his soul. A mother of five children had a similar experience. She built a Bridge of Light to her soul night after night after her children were in bed, but she wasn't sure she was making a real connection. Finally, she asked the question "Are you there?" and the answer came back as if it were coming from inside her heart, "I am here." It came so quickly and unexpectedly that she knew it to be real. In both cases, the soul contact was a significant step along the path of healing and spiritual awakening.

You don't need to hear a voice to be connected with your soul. Your soul heals without words. Its presence is the healer. Some people feel a sense of deep peace move through their body as they make contact, while others feel a stimulation near their head or heart. Some people see or sense the light of their soul. Others feel joyful. All joy accelerates healing; it is a quality the soul specializes in. Sometimes an image may come to mind during soul contact. One woman described seeing a tiny figure of herself sitting in a lotus position and rising rapidly on a golden column of light that extended as far as she could see. Her soul seemed to exist in different dimensions up and down this column of light. Many people have found that by reaching up each day for a period of time to meet the soul, they can eventually span the distance to its sacred space almost as soon as they close their eyes.

You are ready to meet and to begin working with your soul. As you read the following steps, you will be developing an ability to contact the energy of your soul and receive its healing energy.

A Journey to Your Soul

1. From the Room of Light, communicate your sincere desire to your Solar angel to know your soul and its purpose.

2. Merge with the higher love and wisdom of your Solar angel. Your Solar angel will weave a luminous Bridge of Light to your soul. As you practice, your bridge will become stronger and you can rise with more assurance to the soul plane. You will feel freer to communicate with your soul.

3. Imagine that your Solar angel is bringing a golden stream of Solar light toward your head. See this golden light coming all the way down to the top of your head and opening the path to your soul.

4. Imagine this light forming a bridge that leads to your soul. When the bridge seems steady and strong, go with your Solar angel into the Solar light where your soul resides.

5. Notice the increased beauty and brilliance of the light as you move closer to your soul. Sense the radiant energy around your soul as you move into its light. Move as close as you can into the energy of your soul now to feel its love and compassion and wisdom. If you can sense its voice, it will be

like the voice of a long lost, beloved friend. Open to feel the dynamic energy of your soul.

6. You are now in the energy of your soul, a master on its own plane. It sees you clearly. Invoke its healing energy. Invite it to focus on your life and to prepare your body to receive more of its light. Surrender to this loving and radiant being of light. Be fully receptive of your soul's healing energy. Your soul's vibration will touch your mind first. You may feel as if you are awakening after a long dream. Next your soul is touching your emotions. This may feel like an in-breathing of love. Now your soul's vibration is reaching your cells and stimulating them to greater vitality. Let the soul's pure frequencies of sound and light spin out denser substances from your body.

7. Think of the area you want to heal. Feel your soul sending energy to this area. As you come back across the Bridge of Light, think about how you will keep strengthening this connection with your soul.

Your Triangle of Golden Light for Angelic Healing

You are now prepared to learn the most important healing procedure in this book. This is the basic technique for healing with light. You will be using it over and over to heal or rejuvenate your body and to build in finer matter. This process is simple, powerful, and profound. It goes beyond words, beyond affirmations, beyond hopes and dreams. It is a way of connecting with the healing and vitalizing energy of a much higher frequency of light than you live in. Everything else in this system of healing with light is based on the process you are about to learn. All healing with light—all transformation, all cellular regeneration, rejuvenation, and longevity—comes from creating a strong connection with your soul and your Solar angel. This triangle forms the connection for your soul and Solar angel – and for you – to heal and raise the vibratory tone of your whole body. It sets up positive shifts that heal your body at the molecular level. You will be using this triangle as the basis of your spiritual healing. If you learn nothing else, if you use none of the other procedures, this one process can bring you tremendous healings and positive changes. When you use it, you will sense what to ask for. You will recognize that you can open doors to great healing, and that your active, intelligent participation is vitally important. This is the process that opens your life to permit miracles to happen.

Creating Healing Treatments

Your soul and your Solar angel will work together very closely to make deep healing possible. All true healing with light is done with Solar light through the soul and the Solar angel. Other healing angels work under the guidance of your soul and Solar angel. Your Solar angel and soul can work effectively to help you when you join with them and learn how to blend your energy with theirs. You will learn to do this by creating a triangle of light with them and illuminating this triangle with their vibratory energy and colors. Through this triangle of light, your soul and your Solar angel can bring the other angelic healers to you. The triangle becomes more and more powerful as you visualize it. You can receive healing treatments many times a day through this triangle simply by getting very quiet and creating your triangle.

You are now going to be creating this triangle of healing energy. It carries such powerful healing potencies that its regenerative energy moves deep into your being to heal long-standing problems. It becomes the pathway for creating a physical body that is an excellent instrument for your soul. The triangle enters through the top of your head, and its golden light keeps flowing into your head and heart and all through your body as long as you hold your triangle in form. The cover painting of this book depicts this triangle.

Creating Your Triangle of Healing With Your Solar Angel and Soul

1. Sit very quietly in the Room of Light. Just in front of your eyes, imagine three bright points of light in a triangular position. Think of your Solar angel for a moment, and connect with its presence. Let your Solar angel be a point of light at the top of this triangle. Think of your soul now, and call in its presence. Let your soul be the second point of light at the top of the triangle. These two points of light sparkle with brilliance and radiant energy. The third point of the triangle touches the top of your head. The sun within you is radiating its light into the triangle.

2. Now a sparkling golden light is streaming from these two points of light, filling the triangle and pouring into your head. First, become aware of the beam of light that connects your Solar angel and soul in this triangle and of the two beams of light that flow into you. Open to receive the beam of light from your Solar angel. Next, open to the beam of Solar light from your soul.

3. Charged with this powerful Solar light, send a beam of light to your Solar angel and another to your soul. Each point of your triangle is now in contact with the other two points. You are receiving energy from your soul and from your Solar

angel. The energy you are sending to them is returning to you in a purer form after it circulates and blends with the energy of your Solar angel and soul.

4. Let the particles of Solar light become even brighter as your energy harmonizes with the golden light flowing into you. As it circulates around the triangle, it is sparkling with a brilliant and pure golden light, filling the whole triangle with golden light. Let the light circulate through the triangle many times until you can feel the energy simply by closing your eyes and thinking of it. You will be using this triangle as home base for all of your spiritual healing. It forms the connection for your soul and Solar angel to restore and to raise the vibratory tone of your whole body. Your golden triangle deepens your connection with your soul and Solar angel. It sets up positive changes that regenerate your body at the molecular level.

5. Now that you have learned this most important process, you're ready to begin healing yourself with light. As you focus on this triangle, think of the problem that you want to heal. Let the energy of the golden triangle flow into your mind, releasing any belief that would limit the power of your Solar angel and soul. Feel the golden light flowing into your mind and giving you a higher vision of how much is possible. Feel the golden streams of light reaching your mind and linking with your emotions, transforming any anxiety, doubt, or fear into a positive experience of the love and compassion of your Solar angel.

As the spiritual energy moves into your mind and flows into your emotions, it clears a pathway to reach the area you are working on. Sense the shift as the golden light touches this area and moves around it. Feel the area being charged with liquid colors and light. Now let your whole body become luminous as the golden light moves all through it. See your atoms transforming to hold more light. See how you are moving into greater energy and vitality through this triangle.

6. Every chance you get this week, practice making this triangle between your Solar angel, your soul, and yourself. Learn to feel its energy immediately and easily.

7. Over the next few days, notice shifts in how you see yourself and how you feel about yourself. You may begin breathing from a deeper place, you may sense more beauty around you, or you may experience a lighter feeling. You may feel more optimistic, and you may sleep better. Describe signs such as these in your healing journal. They are a part of the healing process.

In the next rooms of your Temple of Healing, the angelic healers will be empowering and enriching your golden triangle with love, sound, images, and other colors. You will then meet with your inner healer to find out what you can do on the physical plane to bring the sparkling light that is in your healing triangle into your body and cells.

Chapter 7

Healing With the Angels: The Room of Love

If you discovered that all the love you have known up to now is only a dim reflection of the love that you can experience with the angelic healers in the Room of Love, would you be highly motivated to meet them? If you heard that an unexplained sense of joy could bubble up from the core of your being, would you want to know how this happens? The Room of Love is the place not just to feel a little better, but to know love shining from your heart and to stand in wonder at the healing that the angelic healers of divine love bring to your body. This room shines with a warm rose glow. It offers a protective cocoon of energy around you, a place to discover the divine love that is already growing within you.

When the angelic beings touch the love within you with their loving energy, changes begin. You stop criticizing your body or telling yourself it is getting old or weak or sick. You stop resenting your body for aging, or feeling guilty for not taking better care of it. You recognize your body's valiant efforts to stay healthy and vitalized in spite of all the environmental and personal stresses today, and compassion flows from your heart. You also see how much light is already in your body and how much love is in your heart. You become aware of all the love that you send out to others with your thoughts.

The Angels of Divine Love

The Room of Love is filled with healers called the angels of divine love. These angels place a rose glow around your body and your skin. They place rose hues just above your head and heal nervous anxiety and worry. They place them just outside your heart to heal the heavy feelings of tension and pressure that drain your energy. Their presence dissolves depression and enhances your will to live.

The angels of divine love surround and protect your healing triangle of light with rose colors. You can get a sense of how they do this from the cover painting on this book. Your golden triangle with your Solar angel and soul provides the atmosphere for the angels of divine love to work through. The brighter and clearer your triangle, the more powerfully these healing angels of divine love can transform your emotions and your body. When you are closely connected to your Solar angel and soul through your triangle, they bring the angels of divine love right into your heart center. They offer you as much joy as you are able to receive at one time. They hover all around you and pour a healing energy of love into your whole being. You can become filled with a sense of lightness and happiness in the Room of Love as these angels free your emotions from the cobwebs of the past and open the petals of love within your heart. You may feel lighter long after being with these angels, happier and freer than before.

Dissolving Obstructions to Healing

The healing angels bring love to every atom of your being to help you transmute the negative emotions you have experienced into emotions that are healing to your body and to the people in your life. They do this by sending waves of love through you to dissolve coarse particles of energy that attract guilt, blame, or unforgiveness to your energy field. Wherever you have felt separated from others, they can lift the veils that create this sense of separation. They show you how to remove the veils that the personality builds to protect itself from the awesome experience of knowing the true Self, the soul, as pure love. Nothing can dissolve these obstructions to your higher will to heal yourself and evolve your body and life to the next level as quickly and thoroughly as the combination of your soul and Solar angel and the angels of divine love.

As you meet with the angels of divine love, you can hold any part of your life or body up to be healed. If there is anything that you feel guilty about, it will come to mind as soon as you enter the Room of Love so that you can decide how to clear it. Guilt blocks your ability to receive from the angels of divine love. Its voice would not allow you to know this healing state of love. In the Room of Love, you can find a way to correct whatever you have done in the past and release all guilt. If you have not forgiven another person for hurting you, you can do so in this room with the radiant angels whose love can permeate your very being. Before you enter this room, decide to clear everything that creates resistance to being loved with the assistance of the angelic healers. Then give permission for these angels to send their radiant energy into your heart.

Physical Problems That Shift First

The angels of divine love do not produce love; they reveal the love that lies at the core of your being. Their love is not sentimental, but rather a specific atomic frequency that heals. It cannot be reproduced with machines or through pills. It comes only from the soul planes into your body. The angels of divine love help release the powerful healing force of love that lies within your soul. This force brings in your higher will to live, to expand, to explore, and to make new discoveries about love. Depression, worry, fears, and anxiety lessen and begin clearing. You learn the right use of your imagination by bringing it through the filter of love. This helps spin coarser cells out of your energy field. As residue from the past is loosened, the problem you are working on now can shift and begin healing.

The power of divine love heals diseased tissue, swollen joints, aching bones, chest pains, breathing pains, and headaches. It can help with treating autoimmune diseases, such as arthritis, chronic fatigue, or AIDS. Other problems that respond well to the vibration of the angels of divine love include circulatory problems, heart disease, and problems with asthma, digestion, and insomnia. The thymus gland becomes more active and can help create immunity to diseases and viruses.

Loosening and Removing Clogged Cells

What has happened in the past to you is not important for your healing. Letting go of what has happened is crucial. Anger, blame, guilt, fear, and all the other negative emotions cannot damage your body or make you sick if you can acknowledge them and then let them go so they can pass through you. However, if these emotions are not acknowledged and released, they can weaken your natural resistance to disease and aging. They can clog up your cells, slow your metabolism, and wear out your heart. They can work underground long after you forget that you haven't released them from your energy field. Nothing that has happened to you—no hurt, abuse, cruelty, abandonment, or deceit—is worth the rapid aging and illnesses that these emotions cause if they stay in your body and crystallize in your cells. Whatever is already in your cells now can be loosened and removed. With your full cooperation, the angels of divine love can begin loosening old feelings that have settled in your muscles, organs, and glands. If coarser atoms from the past have settled in your arteries, joints, throat, eyes, brain, or digestive track, the angels can help you remove them and put finer atoms in their place. The angels bring the kind of love to your cells that makes your body flexible, strong, resilient, and immune to disease. All of this happens as these angels use colors unknown on the physical plane and sound frequencies that are only beginning to be heard here.

The Law of Love

As you make contact with the angels of divine love, you make contact with the law of love and begin realizing that this law is the essence of your existence—the most dynamic energy in the universe. The law of love brings order to your life and to your cells. It gives you an open mind and a wise and tolerant acceptance of yourself and others. Your mind and heart become broad, kind, generous, and benevolent. Your willingness to forgive, to overlook weakness, to accept errors, and to hold out your hand to those who seem to fall—all of these are the qualities that accelerate healing on all levels.

This doesn't mean you have perfected these traits. It means you understand how valuable they are and you are developing them in every way you know how.

As you learn about the law of love through the angels of love, you can build a powerful healing relationship with yourself and with the people in your life. You begin seeing the divine love within others. You begin sensing the beautiful energy of the combined love of all the souls in your family—sisters, brothers, parents, and children. You also begin sensing the shining sphere of love that your spiritual family has created, and you recognize their wonderful healing force pulsating in your heart center. This can happen even though you do not yet know the members of your spiritual family. You are linked with these souls through the law of love.

Distinguishing Personality and Spiritual Love

The angels of divine love bring spiritual love to you. When their love flows into your triangle with your Solar angel and soul, it becomes a great healing agent. As this love fills your mind and heart, you may experience any of several emotions—freedom from worry, reverence, gratitude, compassion for all who, like you, are evolving their minds and bodies. This love differs from romantic or family love, or what we define as personality love. Personality love introduces you to spiritual love. It focuses on one person or a family group and teaches you how to give to someone in a very personal way. Spiritual love is all inclusive—like the sun, it shines equally on everyone and everything. You love others because you are filled with love. Unhappy and unpleasant emotions lose energy because you are not feeding them with your

THE TEMPLE OF HEALING

attention. Soon they drop away; they die out for lack of energy. As fear subsides, the negative emotions do not receive enough energy to hold them in your energy field.

Healing Through Spiritual Love

With each treatment from the angels of divine love in the Room of Love you gain understanding from a higher perspective, as if you are looking below you at your old emotions. You may sense the sorrow and suffering that all people experience as they master Earth's lessons. You may feel compassion for the human race. Your own healing is stimulated by this compassion for others. Your compassion for others provides the release that allows you to forgive yourself for mistakes you have made in the past. This healing follows your forgiving the mistakes that others have made. Only through forgiveness of mistakes can you be bold enough to accept the increasing levels of the love that your soul and Solar angel hold for you. In spiritual love, you are not conscious of yourself as the lover or the beloved. You are not aware of giving love or receiving love – simply of being part of an energy that transforms whatever it touches. You can learn to touch this love every day.

As you see tendencies of thinking and acting that are blocking the radiance of your divine love, you may be able to sense areas of your body that need more love and less criticism. You are not criticized or judged by these higher beings who radiate with spiritual love. You are accepted just as you are – as a soul with a personality who is evolving and learning the power of healing and transforming each part of yourself. The angelic healers broadcast to the spiritual love that is already seeded in your heart.

70

A-El-I-O: The Angels' Sound for Divine Love

The angels of divine love use many sounds to heal. Here, we will use four key sounds that contain healing vibrations. They are A-El-I-O, pronounced ah-el-ee-oh. Each syllable vibrates with a different stream of healing love. The combined power of these sounds creates a sympathetic response in your cells as they begin resonating with the love of the angels. The sounds A-El-I-O fill your emotions with love. They fill your mind with thoughts that connect you with the angels of divine love.

These vibrations of love from the higher dimensions trigger healing on many levels. Together, these four syllables, containing four vowels, help you align yourself with the love of the great spiritual masters of the human race. Each vowel has a power of its own; it resonates to a musical chord that heals. When you repeat these syllables and focus on their meaning, your life can shift to a higher dimension. Each time you speak the word A-El-I-O, you are invoking the angels on the ray of love. Your cells receive this energy and use this vital life force to build a much finer body for you. Expressing these sounds from your heart brings your personality into a finer relationship with your mental, emotional, and physical selves so that they can work as a team, each sharing and supporting your highest evolution and happiness. The clearer the broadcast of your healing word of love, the more smoothly you can move from personality love into soul love.

Igniting Your Spiritual Flame

As you use the healing sounds of the Room of Love, the angels of divine love can ignite the spiritual flame that burns behind your heart in the golden web of light that surrounds your physical body. As this flame burns brightly, enthusiasm can emerge once again, and the joy of living can return. The divine spirit of your soul becomes enlivened; you feel taller, stronger, more graceful, and more confident. You can look at yourself—your life and your body—and see yourself through the eyes of your soul. Traits in others that used to irritate or intimidate you reveal themselves simply as symptoms of feeling fearful and unloved. Love from the higher dimensions filters into your energy field, and other shifts come; you now possess the freedom to act from a deeper place of honesty than before and the courage to offer this level of love to others.

After using the sounds of A-El-I-O and being with the angels of divine love during a seminar, one woman reported, "My unhealed child part was brought right up front in a painful way. It was empty, full of loneliness and pain—that invalidated feeling of not being seen for who I am. I have a wonderful husband. He's growing, too, but he's not in touch with the soul love part of himself, so he can't touch this part of me. I took the part of me that was in so much pain, and put it out here in front of myself and just held her out to these angels of healing like a child to be healed. For the first time, I loved her and understood her. It felt so good, and it couldn't come from anybody else. I could feel love pouring into this child, like a part of me. I have never before felt this kind of healing love come into the really painful part in my life." Several months later, this woman realized that she was not struggling so hard to get approval. The little child within her had become stronger and had begun growing up.

After working with A-El-I-O and the angels of divine love in a seminar, another person laughed and said, "Now A-El-I-O is singing inside of me with a full chorus of baritones, sopranos, and altos. This has gone on for three days. I feel wonderful. Every step is a giant leap. The energy is very deep and penetrating. Every cell is resonating in a deep and stabilizing way."

Healing in the Room of Love

1. Before you enter the Room of Love, give yourself a shower of colors. See these colors flowing over you and within you, glistening with liquid gold and rose. Let each color rinse the dense frequencies from your energy field.

2. Enter the Room of Love, and sit or lie in the center among the fragrant rose and white flowers. Breathe deeply, and you may be able to sense their sweet fragrance. They exude a healing angelic substance. Love is pulsating through this room. Your heart is already responding to the tiny luminous particles that are streaming into the room from the open skylight above. Give permission for any places in your body that need more love to open to these subtle frequencies of love.

3. Now create your triangle with your Solar angel and soul and yourself. This time, fill your triangle with a beautiful shade of rose. This is the key step for healing with love.

4. Your Solar angel will bring the angels of divine love to you now. They come through the energy in your triangle. Open to the angels of divine love here. Drink in their love as a rare and healing elixir of life energy. Ask that any emotion that has created a problem in your physical body be loosened and released. If you are working with a specific physical problem, focus on it as you sound the syllables of these healing frequencies of love with the angels. If you are freeing your total will to create a finer body, focus on the list you made of what prevents you from reaching a 10 on your meter.

5. Speak or chant the "Ah" of A-El-I-O, drawing the sound out to a very long and steady note. Open your mouth wide to get the full benefit. Let the sound vibrate through you until you feel its resonance in your chest. The stronger this vibration, the more your heart opens to give and receive love. Let this resonance become steady and vibrant. Stretch the "Ah" to a long, slow "Aaaaaah" as you exhale. Remember your rose-filled triangle with the Solar angel and soul as you do this.

6. "El" (as in *bell*) is a call to the One Creative Force. As you say "El" aloud, let this note travel up a column of light above your head. Then say or sing it aloud again. "E" draws serenity to you, and "L" is a cosmic vibration that uplifts the soul. The "El" vibration spins beautiful patterns of love around you. Keep sounding it as you travel upward on a stream of Solar light. The more peaceful your concentration, the more you are lifted above and out of your body to the angels of divine love.

7. "I" (pronounced "ee" as in *see*) takes you into the center of these healing patterns. Place this sound between and above your eyes and feel its vibration between your eyebrows. Let the "I" resonate with your soul. If you are singing the notes, sing the "I" on a higher note.

8. As you say "O" (as in *oh*) bring a line of lighted energy from above into your head and down your spinal cord. Imagine the angels of divine love bringing healing into every nerve in your body.

9. Now speak or chant or sing the full vibratory sound of A-El-I-O seven times, and imagine its sound ringing throughout your Temple of Healing. Listen for a resonating response in your heart. Each syllable brings in more angels of divine love to get you the full frequencies of spiritual love.

10. Feel the angels of divine love around you now, vibrating with the frequencies of love and joy. Bathe in their energy as they purify your heart and neutralize all past suffering. The

waves created by their vibration bring you closer to these healing angels. They recharge your cells with pure spiritual love.

11. See this love flowing as a river, through your body,
your emotions, and your mind, refining them, purifying them,
releasing them from all density of the past. Feel this energy
vibrating in your bones, muscles, and cells. Give permission
for your cells to become saturated with this higher healing love.
You may sense these currents as gentle or very strong and forceful, like waves flowing through you.

12. After singing, humming, chanting, or silently sounding these healing syllables, your cells will vibrate with love as
it is known in the spiritual dimensions. There is nothing you
need do now; the wisdom beyond your conscious mind will
direct this love into the areas of your body and emotions where
it is needed. As you complete this deep healing, give your body
time to absorb the energy. Simply sit quietly for a few minutes,
or surround yourself with beautiful music or pictures that help
you to stay in this serene and peaceful state.

Chapter 8

Receiving the Colors of Angelic Healing: The Room of Colors

The Room of Colors acts as a prism to separate Solar light into more than two hundred distinct colors. Being in this room is like being in the center of a kaleidoscope of color. When you enter this room and build your triangle of light, the first colors that flow through it will be the colors that are already woven into the body of your soul. The Solar angel weaves these in as the soul gains new experiences on its own plane and through all of your Earth experiences. The next colors you will sense in this room are the new colors that the healing angels are bringing to regenerate you through the prism in the center of this room. These are the colors that you do not have, or that you need more of, in your energy field. They will bring to your body the frequencies that it lacks to heal itself completely. The colors the healing angels use are far more beautiful and radiant than the colors on the physical plane. These colors are vibrant, frequently mixed with silvery or golden hues. They sparkle with light. They are iridescent, even the deeper colors. You can know these colors only by sensing them with your inner eye. They can't be reproduced on the physical plane.

Your Healing Colors

The angelic healers use many colors as a primary source of healing and evolving your body. They have worked to heal you many times with color when you have asked for help, even though you may not have been aware of their presence. You don't have to see the physical color to absorb and merge with it. The angelic healers bring the frequencies of the colors you need for healing into your body. You can receive a beautiful blue or green hue and observe your pulse slowing and your blood pressure improving. You can observe a sense of discouragement dissolve and a serene and lighter mood take its place as they bring the right colors to you.

The angels in this room know which colors will bring balance and new life force into your cells. They bring these colors to the area where there is a problem. They bring a beautiful shade of rose that gives you energy when you are suffering from chronic fatigue or when you are simply worn out after a long day's work. They use a soft yellow to improve weakened kidneys or adrenal and thyroid glands. They use blues and greens to heal high blood pressure, fevers, and certain infections. They use orange to clear the cobweb-like, sticky substance in your etheric body from the atmosphere. Where there is congestion in your body, such as in your eyes, sinuses, liver, or joints, the angelic healers use a special tone of orange.

Color Baths

When the healing angels are helping you heal, they embody these colors with their vibration. They weave new colors into your energy field to offer you protection from further disease or illness. If you need vitality, they use rose or orange hues. There are many hues and intensities of these colors. The color depends upon the quality of energy that is needed. In one part of your body, you may need a rich, deep rose, while in another part you need a pastel rose. If you have congestion in your lungs, you might receive clearing as the angelic healers bring an iridescent orange into this area. For infections, you might get help through sapphire blue, which acts as a disinfectant on the physical plane. Poison ivy or other rashes may also be relieved and healed with sapphire blue. A clear hue of green is helpful for general healing needs. It cools down the center of the atoms (rather than exciting them, as red would do) in order to bring them back into balance. If you have an inflammation, observe the angels using a rich green or a green tinged with yellow. For higher energy, they use stimulating colors—bright orange, golden orange, and yellow. The exact shades vary for each person. So long as you work from within your triangle with your Solar angel and soul, you will be in alignment with the best healing angelic forces and will receive the hues that are most beneficial to you. As you begin perceiving which colors the healing angels use, you can give yourself color baths with these colors simply by imagining these colors bathing you with their transformative light.

Healing Emotions With Angelic Colors

You can produce happy feelings, playful feelings, a serene and tranquil state, a sense of positive expectation, or whatever emotion you sense is the most healing to you now, simply by focusing on the color that creates the state you want.

When you want to feel more cheerful, more confident, or optimistic, you can do this by using different hues and tones in yellow, gold, orange, or rose. Every positive state you produce through the frequencies in a color goes directly into the cells of your body as nourishment. To discover what color to use to shift an undesired emotion, experiment with several colors. Notice how intense the emotion is before you begin to use the color and check the intensity again after you permeate it with healing colors. If you are feeling unloved or unappreciated, hues of rose—from a rich deep rose to a soft pale rose—can transform this feeling. No matter what the reason for these feelings, they can change when the correct frequencies of colors are in your energy field.

Healing Your Thoughts With Angelic Colors

You can add light to your thoughts in the Room of Colors. To calm your mind so that it can provide the space for your soul's creative energy, you can surround yourself here with a luminous green. For clear thinking and stimulating your mind, bring a shower of bright yellow over and around your head. You can get out of a mental fog so that you can create with your soul by using a beautiful tint of yellow-orange. You can become sensitive to the ways that each color affects you and develop the intuition to know and use the correct shade of color in any situation. If your will to live is not really strong, use rose. Two or three shades of rose will build your will to live.

This is how one student described his experience in the Room of Colors as he worked with a negative and unwanted belief: "A golden stream of light from my Solar angel came in and merged with a sapphire blue light from my heart. I was focusing on an area where I've been having a lot of resistance to healing, and suddenly I saw that this holding was being time-released. My illness has built up over years, and its healing must be a gradual releasing process. My experience was very gentle and natural."

Your Soul's Color

Your soul has its own color and its own sound or note. This color and this sound are like your soul's signature. Your soul's color is sparkling and iridescent as if silver is mixed with it. Your soul's color is one of the celestial colors that has no earthly counterpart. The beauty of this color signifies your soul's state of evolution. The radiance of this color proclaims your soul's success in learning from all of its Earth experiences. The angelic healers use your soul's color as your dominant healing vibration. You can find the Earth color that is closest to it and bring this color into your life. If more than one color comes to your mind as you meditate with your soul, select the dominant color that you feel most drawn to at this time.

The color of your soul gives you an expanded feeling. This is a color that your body is calling for and most easily responds to. When your soul's color is in your mind and body, you will tend to start breathing more freely and easily. This color will energize you when you are tired and calm you when you are tense. This color will bring your mind and body into harmony with your own soul and your Solar angel. Imagine how you can bring this color into your life, your clothes, and your home. Get a square of fabric in this color or paint this color onto poster paper. You can use two or three sheets of different colors that seem to radiate with the color of your soul if you are not sure of the exact shade. As you look at these colors, you will find the one that is most balancing to your system. Soon, you can recall this hue simply by thinking about it and bringing the vibration of your soul to you.

Finding Your Soul's Color

Your soul's color resonates to a specific vibration of Solar light. In the following journey, you can find your soul's color and use it to energize or purify your body, clear your mind, and calm your emotions. Later, you may take a specific problem to infuse with the soul's hue. For now, simply experience the profound sense of serenity, love, and balance that your soul's color brings to you.

1. From the Temple of Healing, take a shower of light and sit in the center of the Room of Colors. The colors on the etheric plane are incredibly beautiful and healing. Observe where your chair or mat is in this room so that you can see the display of these colors as they move over and then flow into your body.

2. Imagine a great crystal above this room, which is open to the sunlight. This crystal acts as a prism to separate the seven bands of colors into many tones or shades of each color. Let these bands of colors swirl over your body. Note the difference as you imagine orange moving over your body for a moment. Then shift to yellow for another moment. Note what happens to your mood as you bring in an iridescent rose and let it play over your body. Let green hues, blue hues, orange hues, and

yellow hues bathe you in their frequencies. Note the shift in your body as you change colors.

3. When you have some experience of the changes these colors make in the way you think and feel, create your triangle with your soul and Solar angel.

4. Ask your Solar angel to strengthen your soul's color flowing through the triangle. Keep focusing your eyes upward to your triangle. The color that comes to your mind may be very subtle—sparkling with tiny bursts of light. It may be translucent, or it may have a texture like velvet. Open to experience the energy of the color flowing into you.

5. Imagine your soul's color flowing as liquid light. Let this color become a river that fills the room. Bring it over your skin. Let it create a mist of color around your body that allows only the finer frequencies to enter your energy field and move into the atmosphere.

6. Let this soul color flow into your mind and help spin out worry and other repetitive thoughts. As the substance of new ideas is drawn to you, you may sense these ideas as tiny bursts of light sparkling with the color of your soul. They carry the iridescence of your soul's color.

7. Let your soul color spiral over and around your whole body as a liquid light. Your Solar angel is weaving your soul's exact color around you so that it will flow into your mental, emotional, and physical body and cells. Make this color bright and clear.

8. The Solar angel is now forming a mist of protection around you that matches the color of your soul and strengthens your will to be well. This protective mist breaks up undesirable conditions around you before they reach your energy field. This mist contains the nutrients for which your heart and your mind and your body thirst. Let yourself bask in this radiance and absorb these nutrients into your whole system.

9. Play with the mist. Imagine it protecting you from all disease and negative influences. Bring this hue to any area that feels lacking in vitality. Immerse your will to be well in this color. Imagine your will to overcome all barriers to its freedom being increased now. If your body is already purified and you are heightening its vibration of light, imagine this color streaming into the central core of your cells.

10. Sit for a few minutes to let the energy of your soul color come into you more deeply. When you focus on this color, you are calling your soul's presence. Use its color to heal and vitalize yourself throughout the day.

Visit the Room of Colors again later to become more sensitive to the difference the color of your soul makes when you allow it to play over your body and mind.

Healing and Evolving Your Body
Through Angelic Colors

You are now ready to work with the angels to heal and evolve various areas of your body. The angelic healers will use the colors that are most healing and regenerating to you now.

There are different groups of healing angels, and each group works with various types of physical problems. You will work with all the angelic healers at different stages of regenerating and evolving your body. Some of the colors they use release toxins from your tissues and cells, while others bring in a sparkling substance for new cells. Some colors give you physical energy; others calm your emotions; and still others clear your mind. As you work with these angelic healers, you can become more sensitive to what each group is doing to add to your inner harmony and health. You can

83

train yourself to consciously sense which colors they are using so that you can supplement their healing work with these colors as you go through the day.

1. Go to the Island of Regeneration and to the courtyard of your Temple of Healing. This time take a shower of white light to clear yourself to receive from all the different groups of angels.

2. Be seated in the Room of Colors. Create a triangle of light with your Solar angel and soul as you prepare to regenerate and evolve your body and mind. Add the color of your soul that you worked with in the preceding exercise, and let this color become solid in the triangle. If you don't yet know your soul's color, fill the triangle with white light for now.

3. The Solar angel now calls on the various healing angels to work with you, beginning with the angels of love. These angels are bringing several shades of rose—deep, rich shades and pale, transparent ones. Draw these colors into your heart. Let them flow over your face, softening the lines around your eyes and mouth, relaxing the tension in your lips and forehead, rejuvenating your skin. Angelic healers of divine love are working through this color to regenerate you. Be very still within as these angels assist you.

4. Next, your Solar angel brings in several shades of yellow—a rich, deep yellow, a golden yellow orange, and a pastel shade of yellow. The angelic healers who belong to the yellow hue are working with your mind as you focus on this color. They are also working with your brain and nervous system. You may notice a shift in the energy around your head as these shades of yellow spin around you.

5. Your Solar angel is now bringing in green—first green with hues of yellow in it, then an emerald green, and finally a silver green. Feel tenseness leaving you as a very calm and

relaxed state of awareness moves in. The angelic beings on the green hues are working up and down your spine and over your body. These angels clear headaches, tense muscles, sore shoulders and neck. Imagine that they are painting your body with a healing green.

6. Your Solar angel is placing sapphire blue over you to call in the angelic healers on the blue ray of color. As they come, they are moving slowly through specific areas of your body where healing is needed. You may feel the shift as this shade changes to electric blue, sky blue, and silvery blue. Relax to sense this healing treatment.

7. Become aware of a medium and then a pale shade of violet as the violet healers enter. Let these violet healing angels permeate the air around you; breathe them into your lungs. They are healing any physical problem that you have.

8. The angelic healers will now bring the combination of colors that have the frequencies that are missing in the area where your physical problem is located. These are the colors that can heal it. See if you can sense the colors they are using now flowing over your whole body. Or you may feel the effect as a shift in your energy.

9. Notice if one of these colors stops at a certain place in your body other than the problem you are focused on. This will be an area that is somehow out of balance and needs regenerating.

You have now finished working in the Room of Colors. Take a moment to notice how you feel, to examine any new insights about what color you could direct to the illness or problem in your body that you are working on. Several times this week, use this color for a few minutes to further the healing that has begun. Come to the Room of Colors whenever you want to heal, evolve, or regenerate your body.

Chapter 9

Receiving the Vibrations
of Angelic Healing:
The Room of Sound

The Room of Sound is filled with the harmonies of cosmic healing. The healing angels sing songs that are unknown on the physical plane. No instruments are needed. Their songs come through vibration rather than through the physical plane. As you enter the Room of Sound, imagine that you are exquisitely sensitive to these tones. The wind chimes on the island are tuned to them. Your heart is tuned to them as well.

Beautiful cosmic notes are playing throughout the Room of Sound, each absolutely pure. These notes are subtones of the cosmic vibration and sound that created the universe and continue to create it. They are so powerful that they hold the Earth and the sun in a perfect spin. This spin arises in response to the vibration that was produced by sound and light. All vibration produces a response in matter that matches the vibration. It attracts and calls together the atoms out of which molecules, cells, and organisms are gathered, and finally a form is built—from a planet and sun to a human body.

Your Soul's Note

These sounds bring life to all beings. One of the notes on these subtones created you and your soul. This note is one of the strands in the great song of the universe. Every time this note is played or sounded on a musical instrument or through the human voice, it vibrates the cells in your body into harmony with your soul. You can learn this note that created your soul and use this sound to accelerate your healing and regeneration. This creates harmony between the vibration of the cells in your body and the vibration of your soul.

In the Room of Sound, your soul's note is vibrating its special tone into your mind and body. You will chant A-El-I-O, the higher vibration syllables for love, and the sacred word AUM on the note of your soul. As the sound of AUM pulsates into your body, this note raises the vibration of your cells. Be it in the key of C or G or A or any of the other musical notes, it is *your* healing note! With your soul note vibrating in your cells, your body is gradually purified until it becomes vibrant. Your whole personality spirals upward into a finer frequency of light.

Even though the actual range of the soul's note is above your physical hearing, it is heard and embraced by your heart. As you sound this note, you may feel calmer, more serene, and more optimistic. When this vibration reaches your head, it rings with the truth of your identity as a divine being. When it reaches your cells, they listen—and they respond by absorbing new light and dancing to this healing sound. As your cells vibrate to this sound, they are nourished. This vibration evolves your cells to greater consciousness and light.

When you are working with your light body, creating triangles of light with your Solar angel and soul, or following any spiritual discipline, you are tuning to this note. Since all that is created is created through vibration, you are re-creating yourself and your body as this note sounds and resounds within you. Your soul's note will play its color over your cells to add light to them.

Healing Properties of Your Soul's Note

This higher vibration of light and joy can transform physical illness to physical vitality. It can bring your body to a finer note. You may have had physical problems or illness from time to time and felt that you had somehow slipped off your path. Rather than being off your path, you had probably brought so much light into your body that it created friction between the denser frequencies in your cells and the finer frequencies of your soul. The vibration of some group of cells was too slow to be able to harmonize with the finer frequencies of light. As your Solar angel builds more Solar light into your soul's body of light, you will need to continue raising the light in your cells to create the inner harmony needed.

Just as the sun does not make anyone sick, your soul's vibration does not make you sick. Both have the ability to vitalize, heal, and rejuvenate you, yet their tremendous power must be honored. Without enough sun, the human body suffers and degenerates, just as all living plants do. With too much sun, the human body is drained of energy just as plants are. Your body needs just the right amount of sunlight, no more, no less. The same is true of Solar light. With not enough of the soul's vibration, problems emerge; with too much of

88

the soul's vibration before the body is prepared for it, physical problems also may emerge. The vibration and note of your soul cannot cause a problem, but the dense and slow vibrating areas in the body could cause problems. When part of your body is vibrating at a very slow rate, it is not able to receive what the soul is sending through you, and this creates resistance. When you raise the level of vibration, this area can receive much more of the soul's light. Your body can become completely free from disease and the common afflictions that humans suffer.

Where to Begin

One spiritual leader was told by his soul that he could not go any farther on his spiritual path until his body could respond to the higher vibration of the soul. He needed to bring his body to a higher frequency. This often happens to those who have not acknowledged the physical requirements that go with spiritual work. Even if you realize the need to increase the light your cells can hold, you may not know where to begin. Rather than begin on the outside—by changing your diet or adopting a fitness program—you best begin with the inner changes and guidance of the soul and inner healer. Outer changes in diet or exercise can follow. Fitness and diet changes will then come from soul direction rather than from feelings of "should" or "have to." As you spin off or speed up the slower vibrations, your body responds quite naturally to the soul's note. You acquire a taste for the healthiest foods; you allow yourself to go to bed without resisting your natural sleep rhythms. You allow yourself to play, to laugh, and to be happy. You even allow yourself to just be!

Listen to beautiful music in the Room of Sound to continue the healing that the angels give to you. Find the music that feels especially healing. Such music brings a special nourishment to your mind and your cells. Let your body relax as you listen. Songs that are in the key of your soul or that have harmonies sounding this note can clear toxins, shake out denser matter, and bring in finer matter. When the artist playing this music is in harmony with the emotional and spiritual flow of the music, it becomes even more powerful. Music can connect you to beauty and truth in ways that words cannot. The irresistible beauty of certain music brings in the presence of your soul. The music can serve as an offering of love from which your soul receives energy and responds. When this happens, your deeper will to heal and evolve your body awakens. This music gives you joy such as the angels experience and leaves the breath of joy dancing in your mind and body for days afterward.

Two processes of healing follow. The first process prepares you to become familiar with the note of your soul and allow your healing to begin. The second shows you how to sound the sacred word AUM on your soul's note to loosen any dense or diseased matter and to accelerate healing with the finer matter that this note brings to you. As you begin these journeys, decide that you can find your soul's note. Even if you do not sense inner sounds or a specific vibration, if your intention is to contact and respond to your soul's note, this note will resonate through your nervous system and then move into your bloodstream to purify it. This healing note will vibrate within your whole body and begin rebuilding your body with a higher quality of light.

Healing With Your Soul's Note

As you begin, use the physical challenge you are working on in the Temple of Healing or think about something else you want to heal. Perhaps your metabolism is slowing down or your brain is not as sharp and clear as you would like it to be. You may want to heal a muscle ache or an area of pain. These may seem like personality goals, yet they are essential to create the instrument that your soul can use. Raising your metabolism may mean that you will process more oxygen with each breath, your cells will receive better nourishment, your digestion will improve, and your immune system will function better. Every system would benefit. Thus, you can be more focused and creative.

1. Bring the inner stillness that you received in the first room of the Temple of Healing and simply relax. As your mind becomes quiet, imagine that you can hear the sounds of temple chimes, birds singing, a distant waterfall, and the rustle of leaves as the breeze stirs them.

2. Take your shower of colors in the courtyard of the Temple of Healing. Then enter the Room of Sound and sit anywhere you like. You can close your eyes to sense the inner cosmic sounds playing through this room. Pause here and close your eyes while you visualize this room and the sounds around you.

3. Now create the triangle of golden light with your Solar angel and soul, and merge with their energy so that you can sense and respond to the sounds *within* this room. These sounds are playing on your inner ear. You may feel a subtle shift within your head and your body rather than hear anything with your ears as your body responds to your soul's note. They

91

are on a note of such harmony with you that you may feel happier and lighter, even if you are not conscious of the note vibrating your body. This note is your soul's vibrating note, revealing its identity, its evolutionary state, and its measure of love for you.

4. Your Solar angel will amplify the note of your soul. This note is very high, outside of the range of human hearing. Don't expect to hear this note the way you hear music. The note will be silent to your outer ears, although it will clearly vibrate in your subtle bodies. Ask your Solar angel to enhance this note to vibrate into your whole body and personality. You may sense it in your inner ear. Later you can bring it to your mind, your emotions, and your body.

5. Your soul talks directly to your cells. Imagine the note of your soul reverberating now within your heart and within your head. You will probably sense it as a wave of energy inside of your head or behind your heart outside your body.

6. Imagine what the soul's vibrating energy within your head might sound like in an octave that you can reach with your voice, and then sound this note audibly over and over. Use the vowel sounds you learned in the Room of Love, A-EI-I-O, as you begin singing your soul's note. If you are not sure which note to use, try three or four notes as you chant, and select the one that makes you feel in harmony with your soul.

7. Now you are ready to use this note to heal. Sound your soul's note, and bring its vibration into any area that you wish to heal. You may want to heal your emotions as well as your body—whatever is blocking your free spirit and natural joy.

8. Your Solar angel is directing the angelic healers. It isn't necessary to know which group of healers is rebuilding this area to bring it in line with the higher vibration of your soul. Sometimes more than one group of angelic workers come.

9. Visualize the angelic healers using the sound and vibration of your soul's note to heal and restore the area you are

working on. They shift the molecular substance to bring its vibration into harmony with your soul.

10. Imagine the vibrations of healing being broadcast into your bloodstream and through your pulse with each heartbeat as the angelic healers spin out cells of lesser frequencies and build new cells. Imagine your cells hearing this message and drawing on its power of regeneration.

11. When the work feels complete (it takes only a few minutes), let a surge of gratitude emerge from your heart. It will be well received.

12. Play with your soul's note, sounding it over and over throughout the day. Begin observing your body's response to this note and your emotional response to it. It stimulates your will to be well and to raise your cellular light to a higher level of freedom. Create a song or chant on this note, and feel the lightness of spirit emerging.

(You may use any keyboard to experiment with the sound that resonates with your soul's note so that you can easily find it again by striking that note. Or you could purchase a round pitch pipe from a music store and keep it with you to bring your soul's note into your body.)

Healing Through the Sacred Word AUM

Even though you may have used the sacred word AUM (or OM) for years, its vibration is much more powerful when it is sounded on the note of your soul. Sounded on the note of your soul, AUM has the power to loosen any density or disease in your body and emotions and mind. You will learn in this journey how to let your soul sound its note as you pronounce AUM.

1. Enter the Room of Sound, and lift your eyes to your soul. Let your soul sound its note through you as you breathe. Its vibration will begin harmonizing your etheric, emotional, and mental bodies with your soul.

2. Listen for the inner vibration being transmitted to you from your soul. An awareness within you will respond to this vibratory energy.

3. Now link with both your Solar angel and your soul in a triangle of light. Imagine you are breathing as your soul and that its energy is flowing into you now. Become a conduit to amplify this healing energy as it flows into you. Let your soul sound its note three times through your voice.

4. The first time, say your sacred word, AUM, on the note of your soul very softly, and direct it to your mind and thoughts. As you transmit the energy of AUM to your thoughts and beliefs, let its energy flow through your brain, from the left to the right side, to the back of your brain, and into your neck. Let its energy flow into your central nervous system on either side of your spinal cord.

5. The second time, say AUM a little louder and direct it to your emotions. Let its vibrations touch your emotional body and bring it into a harmonious serene state as these frequencies loosen and release any coarse emotional feelings that are blocking your path of healing and regeneration.

6. The third time, say AUM with more force, and direct it to your physical body. Decide to act as a conscious transmitter of the subtle vibrations of happiness to the cells in your body. Let these special healing frequencies flow into your physical body and start clearing any congestion, disease, or illness. Give permission for the sacred word that you are sounding on the note of your soul to permeate your cellular structure, loosen any coarse or diseased cells, and replace them with particles of finer light. Focus on the part of your body that you are heal-

ing for a second and imagine the soul's note moving into this area and transmuting it to a higher note.

7. Now let yourself just be—no goals, no expectations, no requests. If a thought arises, simply accept it as a passing thought, and let it go. If a thought lingers, repeat the soul's note. If a feeling arises, accept it as a feeling, and let it pass by. If a feeling lingers, repeat the soul's note again from your heart. Sounding AUM, your soul brings you into its energy so that it can move deeply into your whole self and restructure anything you want to evolve with more light.

Chapter 10

Engaging Your Inner Healer: The Room of Wisdom

In the Room of Wisdom, you will be connecting with your inner healer. This healer holds the wisdom of your body and serves as the director of all of your systems. This healer translates the patterns of light, color, vibration, and love into practical wisdom. It knows the timetable of your life, the needs of your body, and the areas that need more light and those that are receiving too much light. This healer is gentle, wise, understanding–and always practical. It holds a complete overview of your life and knows how far you have come and how promising and rich your future is meant to be.

A Storehouse of Wisdom

This healer is within you. It represents a vast storehouse of wisdom and experience inside yourself. It has answers to your questions about your body and can show you how to move through an illness and how to add cellular light. Your inner healer is always going about its complex tasks of directing and guiding the regeneration of your systems, glands, organs, and cellular tissue. It is responsible for your cell division as it transmits incoming energy to your body. Your inner healer is a superb healer, too diverse for you to fully understand, yet able to show you clearly and simply what you can do to assist. You may be surprised at how sound its advice is, how obviously correct once brought to your attention. If you are anticipating a stern father figure, judgmental and somewhat disapproving, or an old crone who is shaking her finger at you for mistakes, weakness, and lack of willpower, you will be surprised. Your healer will focus on the effort you are making now, on your willingness to listen and to act. Your inner healer not only accepts you; it respects and encourages you.

The inner healer coordinates the healing and evolution of your body, mind, and emotions as you begin working with your Solar angel and soul. It acts as a moderator between you and your soul, offering advice and suggestions from a state of clarity and vision. These suggestions can help with any kind of problem, whether it originates in your physical, emotional, or mental body. Your inner healer can tell you which rooms in your Temple of Healing will be most helpful and which systems to work with when you have physical symptoms or challenges. Its advice comes after it has made a series of multilevel computations. The inner healer's intelligence is superior; it has a great storehouse of knowledge to draw from and can handle billions of pieces of information at the same time.

A Treasure of Practical Advice

When your inner healer speaks to you, you feel valued and encouraged. You know that you are understood and loved. This healer speaks from a very deep part of your being that may have been concealed from you until now. At times its messages may be delivered with wit and humor, showing you ways that you had overlooked, dissolving fears that held you back, and renewing your overall delight in being alive. It does not threaten you with dire predictions; it calculates probabilities in a flash of time and shows you new choices. Its compassion and understanding are deeper than you may be accustomed to accepting. At times the advice you receive may be that of a sage; at other times it may be sprinkled with humor. Above all, your inner healer is practical, pointing out some of the most important things you can do right now—and on a long-term basis.

Since your inner healer is pragmatic, it translates the guidance of your soul so that it is practical and useful in your life. A man asked his inner healer how to get the right vitamins and food so that he could let go of a substance abuse addiction. His inner healer told him that he was getting adequate vitamins and nutrition. "What your body needs now is more oxygen. Your cells are oxygen starved. Walk, walk, walk at least once a day for an hour, and you will find the balance that your body is craving." When the inner healer tells you what to do, it does so through instant communication that comes to you telepathically from another part of yourself. It is important to know that the answers are nearly always right there within you, and it is a great relief and also a cause for celebration to realize just how much this wiser part of you knows.

Healing From the Inner Physician

Another student of healing with light kept having rashes and wanted her inner healer to show her how to get rid of them. Instead it conveyed this message to her: "This is your body's natural way of releasing chemicals from certain foods that you are allergic to. Be thankful that it has a way to get these out of your system. Find the foods that you are allergic to and avoid them. Then you won't have any more rashes." This student discovered that she was allergic to a few substances and gradually cut all the foods that contained these substances from her diet. Her rashes have disappeared as she identified these products and eliminated them from her diet.

One student of healing with light was easily fatigued. She spoke with her inner healer to get help. She was told that she was getting enough vitamins and nutrients from her food, but that she was not getting the deep sleep that she needed for the cell repair to take place during the night. With this information, she began setting up a regular pattern of sleep. She found music that helped her to relax and began stretching exercises before she went to bed. She created her golden triangle and imagined herself being linked to her Solar angel and soul throughout the night. She soon regained her original health and now has more energy than she ever had.

Another student asked his inner healer how to heal a backache. He was told that his emotions had created the problem and that he felt weighted down with too much responsibility. His inner healer suggested he plan some activity that brought him a sense of joy each day. He started swimming several times a week and recovered the joy he knew as a child. His new sense of joy enabled him to buy a better chair for his office. Now his backache is gone.

You do not need to sit back and wait for a problem before you meet and talk with your inner healer. It is important to establish a good communication now even if your health is perfect. By checking in periodically, you won't need to be surprised by an illness; your healer will alert you to any potential problem that looms in your future and tell you how to prevent it. Your inner healer can also give you suggestions about how to take your body to an even higher level of well-being and capacity to hold light.

A Journey to Speak to Your Inner Healer, Part 1

First, before you begin, place two chairs facing each other in the room where you are. You will sit in one, and your inner healer will sit in the other. Place a pen and paper or a tape recorder near your chair. This exercise has two parts. In Part 1, you ask questions of your inner healer. In Part 2, you move to the second chair and become the voice for your inner healer, answering these questions with a timeless wisdom. The timeless wisdom of yourself as the inner healer is worth recording. Record what you say (on tape or on paper), and listen to it or read it in a few days to see how very wise the inner healer's suggestions are. Many have discovered that the inner healer only tells them once about something they can do. That is why it is important to record what your inner healer says and to put it into action one step at a time.

1. With a touch of your fingers to your forehead, transport yourself to the Island of Regeneration. Imagine yourself strolling through the garden in the courtyard of your temple, breathing the fragrance of the flowers. Let each breath purify your mind as the air flows through your lungs. Recall the feeling of deep peace and inner stillness that you enjoyed in the Room of Inner Stillness as you clear your energy field with a shower of colors.

2. Enter the Room of the Inner Healer, and sit in one of the two chairs here. Reach up to your Solar angel and soul, and form your triangle of light. Fill the triangle with a beautiful shade of yellow to create a welcoming space for the angelic healers of the yellow ray to assist you in connecting with your inner healer.

3. Look at the chair opposite you, close your eyes, and imagine your inner healer sitting in front of you, listening intently to your thoughts. Tell your inner healer about some of the changes you have made in the past several years. Describe some of the steps you have recently taken to build a healthy and refined body. Speak of your deep and profound desire to be useful in the world and to be a positive force for friends and for society. Honestly acknowledge any resistance to accepting yourself as you are. Your inner healer has the wisdom to work closely with you, giving you all the insights you need to create a finer body. It is important for your inner healer to know how expanded your awareness is so it can build on your understanding. You will be told only what you do not yet know and understand.

4. Imagine that you are addressing your inner healer as follows, or use your own words. Be sure to cover the larger questions about your lifestyle before focusing on specific problems: "Honorable Inner Healer, thank you for your presence here. I offer you my deepest respect as my consultant and inner healer. I want to give you a voice and learn how to create a healthier body that can hold and express more light. Inner Healer, in your wise and gentle manner, please suggest the lifestyle for my healthiest and most creative life to be expressed."

A period of silence may follow while your inner healer considers this question. Allow plenty of time to get all the information that your inner healer will give. You can ask as many questions as you wish. Be direct, and speak sincerely from your heart. Trust that your inner healer is listening carefully to each question. Each question will be addressed. There is no question on which your inner healer cannot give you some added viewpoint or assistance.

5. Now, ask for other information. You will get truthful answers. Some suggestions follow, or use your own.

- How can I free my dynamic will to be completely well and to create a finer body?
- How do I heal this_____ (whatever you are working on)?
- What can I do to vitalize my body? Sleep, fresh air, exercise?
- What is this illness teaching me? What gifts of compassion, patience, knowledge, understanding, clarity, or change is it giving me?
- Do any of the systems in my physical body—nervous system, immune system, circulatory system, respiratory system, or endocrine system—need a boost of energy and light?
- Are my current nutritional needs being met by my diet?
- How can I enjoy greater confidence in my ability to heal myself and to recognize that I am progressing?
- If there is a situation or relationship that is draining my energy, will you reveal it to me in your nonjudgmental way?
- Which emotions are my greatest boosters of vitality, and how do I make these stronger?
- How can I find the friends who will support these changes?
- Are there certain fears that are draining my energy and vitality?
- How can I become more cheerful and confident?

- What thoughts will bring a greater level of balance and vitality to each day?
- What kind of movement and exercise would be most beneficial to me now?
- Are there one or two other things I can do right now?
- What is my part in supporting the healing of the angelic healers? (If you need medical assistance, ask about the best type of healer. Ask about where to find information on the various methods of healing for symptoms you have.)
- What is my next step in evolving my body and cells to hold more light?

6. You are now ready to move to the other chair and speak as your inner healer.

A Journey to Speak to Your Inner Healer, Part 2

1. With the angelic healers of the yellow hues clearing your higher mind, prepare to let your inner healer speak through you.

2. When you feel ready to take the role of your inner healer, move yourself and sit in the second chair set in front of you. As you stand and walk to the chair opposite you, begin to take on the expression of a wise healer. Imagine the energy of your wise healer is forming a cloak of light around you. As you sit in the chair opposite your original chair, let your posture become the posture of a wise and caring person. Look at your original chair, and imagine your other self still there and listening as you speak.

3. Bring your breath into the top of your head to link with your inner healer. Pronounce the sacred word AUM, and inhale fresh air to clear your voice. You may feel a tingling or warmth as you begin to speak.

4. As the wise healer, you know the answer to the questions you asked earlier. Begin to speak and answer each question. Let your voice become the voice of a wise and experienced consultant, with a richer quality than your regular voice. Your words convey a wonderful blend of wisdom and love. You may be amazed at the timeless wisdom and the practical help that emerges! Even so, be sure that you check all information with your logical mind before you take action.

5. Even if you feel that you are making up the answers as the inner healer, say what comes into your mind without censoring or changing anything.

6. If by chance a part of your personality should try to pretend it is your inner healer, you can recognize it immediately. It will have a rather nasal, shrill, or harsh voice, and it will be critical or judgmental. It may want to help you, but it represents only one small part of your past and cannot see the greater vision of who you are in the higher dimensions. Reestablish yourself as the true inner healer and continue your work.

7. When you have answered all the questions, move back into the first chair where you asked the questions. Think about the answers that were given to you. If you did not record what you said, make notes now on the suggestions that you gave as the inner healer.

8. Decide when to meet with your inner healer again, and make your next appointment. Mark it on your calendar and honor this appointment. Come as often as you like to speak to your inner healer. Every time you sit in the inner healer's chair, the connection will be stronger, and the communication will be deeper and richer.

If you do not feel that you got all the answers you wanted from your inner healer as you did this exercise, do not be discouraged. It may take a few sessions to find out everything you want to know. Ask a friend to sit with you as you connect with your inner healer and to record what you say as the inner healer. (Set three straight chairs very close together facing each other, one for you, one for your friend, and one for your inner healer.) Your friend is a silent supporter, carefully listening and recording what you say. It's important that you do not look at or speak to your friend once you begin, and that you focus completely on your inner healer's chair while you ask questions and on your empty chair when you become the inner healer answering the questions.

Chapter 11

Creating Your
Healing Hologram:
The Room of Images

The Room of Images is a room filled with one hundred life-sized mirrors – all reflecting your inner images back to you. As you enter this room, you see that each mirror is reflecting different images that you have about yourself and your body. You will be bringing your soul's note and color to fill this room and watching these mirrors change to reflect your soul's sparkling images of you. They show you how beautiful your life can be and how vitalized and rejuvenated your body can be. As you focus on these radiant images, they replace the images on the mirrors that were reflecting your old images of yourself. You cannot help but recognize how unimportant some of your own pictures were or how blurred they were. As you move into this room, decide that you will let the old images fade away as you embrace your soul's powerful images, which reveal its higher intention for your life. Let yourself see these images and embrace them, saying, "I am ready to understand the larger picture of who I am. I am ready to help create my soul's higher reality in my life and my body."

At this point you become a co-creator with your Solar

angel of the health and longevity that you will need to fulfill your true destiny. Your old images give way to the new ones every time you see yourself filled with the love and the joy and the radiance of your soul.

Your soul's images will be reflected to you in three dimensions, not two or one. These images become your healing hologram. They show you the self you can be—healthy, energetic, and full of life, with abundant energy and enthusiasm to do everything you came here to do and to have more fun in the process than you ever dreamed possible. Seeing and accepting your soul's three-dimensional holographic image for you increases the healing the angels and your soul can do. If your mind has a negative picture of your body, it can block your soul's images from their power to heal you. When the pictures in your mind sparkle with the light of your soul, all healing and transformation is accelerated.

The right use of your imagination helps you develop the skill to hold the higher images in your mind. It determines how you think and feel. As you develop your ability to energize your future, with your soul's images, you gain the authority to send an order to your body, such as to protect you from a virus, and your order is obeyed. (There is only one exception: If you do not keep the commitments you make with your inner healer, your body loses trust in your authority and stops obeying your commands.) With the right use of your imagination, and with your active participation to fill your body's basic needs for good food, sleep, sunlight, and exercise, you can visualize an illness being brief, and it will be brief. You can visualize yourself totally well in twelve hours or twenty-four hours (whichever you can imagine) and watch your picture come true.

Observing the Results of Your Thoughts

In the Room of Images, you are training your mind to perceive the reflections of your soul's vision for you. This is the most rapid way of recovering from any illness and of evolving your body because in doing so you are energizing the intended purpose of your soul.

The first step is to notice the results of your thoughts. Each thought you concentrate on will produce some result. Recall the thoughts you had when you first awoke this morning, and observe the results of these thoughts. What was the message these thoughts sent to your body? How is your body responding? Decide which thoughts you have had since then that sparkle with the light of the angelic healers and your soul. If you find you are unconsciously preparing for the worst rather than anticipating good outcomes, sit in this room frequently to let your soul's radiant images of you be reflected back to you from all the mirrors. By training your mind to embrace your soul's image of your intended destiny, you open the door for your soul and your inner healer to guide you in making these pictures a reality. All pictures that carry Solar light are incredibly powerful.

How Your Soul's Images Rebuild Your Life

Emotional Rebuilding

Your soul's images for you magnetize the best moments of your life and show you how to expand these. For example, when moments of joy you have known come to mind, the sparkle of the angelic healers starts building greater joy in your future. Your inner healer receives the energy of joy as patterns of vitality and sends these patterns all over your body. These patterns automatically filter into your cells to create healing and purification. Your cells rejoice with you, and miracles of healing can happen.

Mental Rebuilding

Soul images act as a funnel to draw ideas to your mind that build a finer body. These pictures reflect the light of your triangle and are imbued with spiritual power. They become your healing hologram. When they are charged with the energy of the healing angels, they command the tiny entities of disease to leave. They help refine the substance of your physical body and bring it to the next level. Each level means a more resilient, more energetic, and happier body. It means that you begin attracting lighted thoughts rather than attracting denser thoughts to circulate through you. You can begin in this room to build the soul's images into your mind and body that will make your life more enjoyable and your body more resistant to disease.

Physical Rebuilding

Your new image helps your inner healer and the angelic healers to build healthy cells into each organ, gland, and system in your body. Your soul's image of you—your healing hologram—broadcasts soul energy through your brain, your breath, your bloodstream, and your heart. Your nervous system receives and passes the energy of this image to your blood.

Your image-enriched blood delivers its message into your cells. Each system responds and begins to improve. Cells that do not fit into the hologram are transmuted or released. Your hologram is especially powerful when you breathe life into it by visualizing and energizing it frequently. Then your image draws in new building blocks for your cells that were not available when you were born. It helps clear impurities from your bloodstream. The chemistry in your blood alters to be in harmony with the image. Your body has had the ability to manufacture these chemicals all along, but it did not have the instructions to do so until it began to receive the new messages. These new blood cells are of a finer substance to match the quality of light in your three-dimensional picture.

Holograms and Angelic Healing

Building a hologram until it has a life of its own is one of the higher laws of angelic healing. A teacher at age thirty-five suffered from depression. (This is a common problem among evolved souls, who can sense so many possibilities that they feel overwhelmed.) She had thoughts of simply giving up and ending her life. Her thoughts were so strong that her health began deteriorating. The depression gave her the illusion that she wasn't progressing in life and wasn't able to make a difference. As a result of her pictures of a future without happiness or health, she would walk up a street lined with beautiful orange blossoms and miss their sweet fragrance. She would walk by a laughing child looking up at her father and miss sharing in their delight.

She decided to sit in the Room of Images until she could

embrace the images her soul held for her. She did this for ten minutes twice a day. Finally, her soul's living, vibrating image of her became clearer. It came to life and danced before her eyes. She began feeling more optimistic and started building her health with the angelic healers. Her healing hologram had provided a place for the healing angels to reach through to her. Her old images of herself are fading out, and she is gradually shifting her basic emotional state into one that is in harmony with her soul's loving wisdom.

If you would like to experiment with how your thoughts affect you, create an image of a pleasant surprise happening sometime today. Make the image vivid enough that you feel it in your muscles. Your heartbeat might speed up a little, the tiny muscles in your face might soften, and a hint of a smile might come over your lips. Place this thought in your triangle of light and forget all about it. At the end of the day, observe what has happened.

Making Your Hologram Magnetic

The more attention you put on your hologram, the more it can help you. Your hologram has as much energy as you build into it. You can build a hologram so magnetic that it will attract to you the experiences that match its vibratory energy. Old images of losing flexibility and grace or strength as you become older will fade away. When you are focused in the light of your soul's images, any thought that destroys health will die out for lack of attention. Congratulate yourself every time you use your creative imagination in this way. Soon, you can see outside evidence that your body is responding.

Each Picture as a Seed of Light

Each picture is a seed of light that draws more light to it. Your soul is the source of all inspiration. Your focused mind is the photographer. The pictures are printed in light. The camera lens snaps a photo of the image your mind has captured. These photographs are then printed where they are constantly on display to your subconscious mind. This part of your mind looks at the picture every few minutes, absorbs its patterns, and then goes out into the world to set up a match. Just as you can enjoy a brightly lit home without understanding electricity, you can play with the cosmic patterns of light in this room without understanding exactly how your soul's image of you can set these currents up.

Begin by deciding that, even though you don't know how this is possible, you are willing to play with activating your soul's higher image of you. When this image or hologram is stabilized on the subtle planes of mind and emotion where you gave it a form and energized it, it can then begin radiating energy in the physical plane. Its positive charge of electrons sends continuous waves of energy to you. The hologram gradually merges its perfect health and vitality with your body.

Patterns of Love

The patterns of love in your hologram will enter your heart and become you. Whatever you sense or invent in the Room of Images is amplified by your Solar angel. Your hologram will sparkle for as long as you energize it regularly. Even though you will be doing this from a sense of play, your mind and heart begin to move into a beautiful resonance with your soul and become an even better receptor of its light. Let your creative focus open to accept more than you have before. Whatever you imagine here concerning joy, health, and happiness will enter your mind and body and become "you."

One woman envisioned a benign lump on her breast shrinking and disappearing as the healing angels worked with her. In a few weeks, her doctor verified that it had already become very small. Another woman was overweight, even after years of struggling with diets. She went back to the Room of Images again and again to vitalize pictures of herself as slender and fit. Each time, she felt more hopeful and inspired. In moments of temptation to go back to old habits, she imagined seeing her soul's sparkling images of herself in the one hundred mirrors in this room. She could not rebel against this image. She began to exercise and eat in ways that dissolved fat. Gradually, her body began to match her image. Six months later, she was still steadily losing the pounds that would help her to fit the image of herself in the celestial mirrors of this room.

Come to this room frequently to refine your hologram so that it more perfectly matches your soul's image for you. It will help you restructure your body to respond to a higher vibration. It will affect the way you think, the way you experience emotions, and the way your body functions. It changes as you change. More is revealed to you. Your soul's image will finally reveal the image of yourself as a radiant and dynamic person. Honor your healing hologram; let it become a pure conduit that holds all the joy and love of your soul and the healing angels. Let it continually bring new energy into your body and mind. One day you may realize the images you thought you were making up, even the outrageous ones, were all given to you by your soul and are happening now. They become in actuality the expression of the angels' beauty, love, and joy. Many are finding it to be so!

Developing Visualization Skills

Some people worry that they can't visualize even though they skillfully visualize every day. You visualize your destination every time you go out of the house to the store or on an errand. You know which streets to turn on because you are making pictures of the store and where it is. When you think of someone tossing a ball to you and your reaching out to catch it, you get an immediate feeling and picture of what that is like. When you think of throwing a ball to someone else, you also have an immediate sensory experience of the ball in your hand, the pressure of your fingers around it, raising your arm to throw it, and aiming with your eyes and mind as you release it.

You don't need to actually "see" an image on the screen of your mind. Very few people do. Rather, simply imagine what your body might look like if it were healthy, vitalized, and regenerated. To give your picture more energy, imagine what it would feel like to be living in *that* body, how you would spend your time, what you would do, and how your life might be different. Practice by visualizing yourself walking on a beautiful beach, curling your toes in the sand, splashing in the edge of the warm surf, feeling the surf on your body. Now add a sense of delight and well-being. Shift the scene to walking in your neighborhood with the same sense of confidence and pleasure. The positive energy of a picture you create and energize with your imagination talks to your cells with more power than a thousand words.

You will be surprised at how clearly you can impress images upon your mind and how long you can hold them in your mind. Here are two practice skills that can make your experience in the Room of Images a more powerful healing.

Visualizing Colors and Geometric Patterns

1. Think of a blue circle about three feet in front of you at eye level.
2. Place a gold triangle inside the circle.
3. When you can sense this gold triangle inside the blue circle, add a point of white light in the center of the triangle. Hold this image steady in your mind. If it wavers or fades, open your eyes to clear the screen of your mind, close them, and begin again. As you gain more skill, add a green diamond around the circle and practice holding these colors and shapes in your mind at once.

Visualizing Numbers

1. Visualize a five-number series, such as 37293, boldly written in chalk on a blackboard. Use any number you prefer. Make the chalk thick so the numbers stand out from the blackboard.
2. Add another number, and see how many numbers you can visualize at once in your mind.
3. Now read the numbers backward. By training your mind to hold a focus of patterns and numbers, you are increasing your ability to focus on and receive healing from your soul's image for you.

Your Healing Hologram: Your Soul's Image for You

1. On the Island of Regeneration, stand in the center court-yard of your Temple of Healing, and let a shower of light and colors fall over your body.

2. Enter the Room of Images, and look at the mirrors. There are hundreds of mirrors in this room, all reflecting back to you the images that you hold of yourself now. Take a few minutes to look at the mirrors and imagine that you can see the reflections of your images about your body and its health and vitality.

3. Build the triangle of light with your Solar angel and soul, and bring its golden light into your head and heart. Let this light fill the Room of Images. It will change the reflections in the mirrors to images that your soul holds for you. These will be three-dimensional instead of two-dimensional. They will have depth as well as form.

4. Let your soul show you one image it is holding of your intended destiny. It will be a higher destiny than any that you have previously imagined. These mirrors reflect images of you in full color. Look in the mirrors, and see their images of your-self fully vitalized and healthy—your face radiant with an in-ner smile, your muscles firm, your body flexible, and your posture straight and tall. Look at more images that are reflected in these mirrors—images of yourself with perfect health, strong and resistant to disease. Build in colors and sounds—from na-ture, music, or voice.

5. If you are working on healing an area in your body, let your soul show you how this area will be when it is fully healed. Visualize this area as healed. See what you would do differently if it were healed. Add the frequencies of love. Breathe deeply, hold your vision, and capture these images on the film of your mind. They are your first images to start physical changes.

116

If you are working on freeing your will to be completely healthy and regenerated, let your soul's mirrored images reveal to you how dynamic your life can become when your will is free.

6. Imagine you can see in the three-dimensional mirrors pictures of your evolved body that can hold more of your soul's light. Engrave these images on the screen of your mind to keep with you—filled with grace, poise, and a light spirit.

7. Next, look at your face in the mirrors—confident and relaxed, with an inner smile. See your face glowing with love; see the beauty of your divine self shining through your eyes. Capture other images of yourself—loving someone, playing with a pet or a child, stretching your body, creating something, exploring something new, and feeling very happy and healthy.

8. Look into the mirrors again, and let other images come that would be energizing and healing. Now let these images merge into one three-dimensional image that carries your soul's full image for your future. Imagine that you can see this one powerful image of the soul's image reflected over and over by each mirror. This three-dimensional hologram is made of light and beautiful colors.

9. Bring this hologram close to you. Notice the light shining from the eyes of your future self and the gentle smile on your face. Imagine walking around it to see it from all sides. This living form of yourself is a radiant symbol of yourself in the future. We will call this your healing hologram.

10. Acknowledge this hologram as your incoming self. Let its energy flow into your body. Ask your Solar angel and soul to refine it in greater detail over the next few weeks according to your highest possible potential.

11. Place your healing hologram over your heart and connect with it to receive its purifying and healing energy. Gradually your mind, emotions, and body will absorb every detail of this living image of your soul's vision of you.

Each time you think of your hologram and visualize it, you are adding energy directly to it—and indirectly into yourself. Use it when you want extra motivation to stay on a healing diet, when you feel discouraged about anything, when you want ideas on how to best use your energy that day, and when you want to accelerate overall vitality and strength. If you want happiness or joy, focus on the face of your hologram, and let the radiance and smile on this face flow into you.

Turn your hologram over to your soul as you go to sleep, to be refined in more detail during the night. Give it a sharp focus so it leaves an imprint on your cells and ask to awaken with ideas about how to manifest the vitality and beauty and health of this hologram in your body. Decide to act on one idea to bring this image into reality. Mark a date to begin making the arrangements, and take the first step. The light within your healing hologram will grow more magnetic and powerful. Take action on whatever ignites the flame in your heart. This is the action that is the most healing and regenerating for you now.

You have now worked with all the frequencies of spiritual healing. You may not realize how much you have learned since you began this book. As you think about the Room of Inner Stillness, you are already there. You can feel the release of tension as a quiet stillness comes into your mind and body. You can sense the golden light of your Solar angel flowing into you. When you think about the Room of Light, you are there, bathing in Solar light, meeting your soul. You have used your key spiritual process many times and bathed your body in the golden light from your triangle with your Solar angel and soul. When you think of the angelic healers in the Room of Colors, the Room of Love, and the Room of Sound, these healers are with you. When you think of your inner healer, this healer is present. When you think about your soul's healing hologram of you, you can feel its energy flowing in your heart and head.

When you want to work on a physical problem, your inner healer may suggest the rooms where the angels can best help you. Or you can simply choose the room where your soul or the angelic healers feel closest to you. One room may consistently lift your spirits and become your favorite. If you are working with a special physical problem, a regular rhythm of coming to the Temple of Healing—twice a day, twice a week, or once a week—may serve you best.

Every journey does not produce a miracle. But every journey will give you *something valuable* that is part of your healing process. One journey might give you a serene sense of inner peace. Another might give you a new insight or break up a pattern of fear and anxiety. Every question you ask is answered with practical solutions immediately or at another time. Be prepared for new and deeper levels of healing as you meet with the directors of your systems and learn what they need to match your soul's healing hologram for you. Your journey is just beginning!

Part Three

Healing and Evolving Your Systems

About Part Three

Now you are ready to work with the directors of your systems to heal and regenerate any system that has a problem or is not truly efficient. Each system of your body, such as your circulatory, nervous, respiratory, immune, and endocrine system, has a director who works from your etheric body, or energy body, where many energies come together. You will be using your triangle of light to bring the angelic healers to these directors to heal and to purify their systems. The directors will in turn show you what they need from you. You can find the answers to questions so that you can bring this director the material it needs. Once you make a connection, you can simply think of the director, establish communication again, and ask what you want to know. When you complete this section, you will have begun bringing each system in your body to a higher level.

Through colors, sound, and light, the angelic healers will help bring your systems into alignment with your soul, and with one another. They will work with your directors and your inner healer to upgrade the cells in these systems, to cleanse any toxic debris in the cells, and to distribute the energy flowing into your etheric body so that each system receives all that it needs.

Chapter 12

Connecting With the Directors of Your Systems

As you received the healing light of the angelic healers in Part One and Part Two, you have probably been working with a specific problem in your body. Now you are ready to work from a deeper level to assist in healing and regenerating the whole system where this problem begins. The director of each system holds the intelligence that oversees that system. The directors are responsible for all the cells that work under them. They train, guide, and direct these cells.

The directors work from your etheric body, the golden web of light that surrounds and interpenetrates your physical body. When your etheric body is healthy and clear of obstructions, the dynamic energy of your soul and Solar angel can flow freely to the directors of your systems. Your directors can handle everything that comes up without needing any attention from you. When your directors are receiving and sending the appropriate nutrients for their systems, they can correct imbalances, repair injuries, and rebuild anything in their system.

Your etheric body is not merely the source of your life energy and the home of your directors. This web of light is actually a part of the cosmic or universal web of light that connects all souls through its webbing. Its tiny threads of light connect you to everything and everyone—from the slowly vibrating mineral kingdom, to the plant kingdom, to the animal kingdom, to the human kingdom, and to the rapidly vibrating angelic kingdom and the kingdom of God or Universal Love. Your etheric body connects you to the Heart of the Sun and the great intelligence and love that shines from billions of stars and other planets in our solar system. You are most strongly affected by the etheric energies of the people you associate with. However, as you evolve your body and mind, you can receive great illumination from the higher kingdoms also.

Your Etheric Body: Where Healing Begins

Your directors are entirely dependent on the energy they receive from your etheric body.

Your etheric body is the framework for your physical body. Its tiny fibers of light underlie your nervous system and create the connections that form this energetic framework. It holds the blueprint that creates your physical body. A healthy and refined etheric body keeps your systems strong and healthy. It takes all the energies that come in from your soul, your thoughts and words, your feelings, the air you breathe, the food you eat, and energies from other people and the environment—and converts them into substances to feed your physical body. All of these are carried on different vibrational currents of energy. Your health and vitality are decided in your etheric body. Disease begins here as well. If your etheric body is devitalized, your physical body will be devitalized too. If your etheric body is vitalized, you will have all the energy you can use. The place to start your healing and the evolution of your physical body is in your etheric body rather than in your physical body. All healing must happen here first, with the loving help of your soul, your Solar angel, and the angelic healers.

Irina Tweedie, a highly respected Sufi leader in London, described her subtle energy body in a way that may help you to imagine your own etheric body. As you read her description, visualize the millions of tiny fibers of light underlying your nervous system and nourishing your physical body:

> At first I thought my blood was getting luminous, and I was seeing its circulation throughout the body. But soon I became aware that it was not the blood. The bluish-white light was running along another system which could not have been blood vessels. For I could see the blood vessels too; they were pulsating with every beat of the heart, doing their work of supplying blood to the tissues. But they were not the carriers of light. This strange, unearthly light, clearly seen in a semi-transparent body, used other channels. But of course! I suddenly understood. It was running along the nerves! The whole nervous system was clearly visible, and the light was circulating in it just as the blood does in the blood vessels. Only the circulation of the blood stops at the skin, but this light did not stop at the skin level; it penetrated through it, radiating out, not very far, say about nine inches. (It fluctuated, increasing and diminishing with some kind of flares.) It came out of the body and re-entered the body again at another place. There were points, like vortices of light in many parts of the body, and light

came out of one of them and re-entered through another one. As these points seemed to be countless, it looked like a luminous web encircling the body, inside and outside. It was very lovely, the Web of the Universe, I thought, and I was fascinated by the unusual and very beautiful sight.
[From *Daughter of Fire* (Nevada City, CA: Blue Dolphin Pub., 1986), pp. 127–28.]

Even though you may not see your energy body the way Irina Tweedie did, you can learn to be sensitive to its energy and recognize when it needs more vitality or is out of balance. You can learn to sense where the distribution of energy is off—with too much energy congested in one area and not enough energy in another area.

All the energy that comes into your etheric body is circulated and transmitted to the directors of your systems. This energy flows from your spiritual stream of light, your mental stream, your emotional stream, and your physical stream of energy. All four streams of energy make up the quality of your etheric body and also determine how you see and experience your world. The flow of these currents of energy is affected by your experiences, memories, and beliefs. An illness or disease occurs when the energy from one of these four streams is somehow blocked.

The etheric body you have now is the result of all the choices you have made in the past and the thoughts and feelings you have through the day. The etheric body you will have next year will be different, as a result of the choices you are making today, and tomorrow, and all year long. Your choices come from your thoughts and emotions, and each thought or feeling flows in with a color and its own vibration or sound. The colors and patterns in your etheric body have shifted since you began this chapter. They will shift again as you read this page. Each moment is unique and new. The thought in your mind or the underlying emotion that is in your heart at this moment is bringing in its own color and sound. The thoughts that are infused with sparkling light add beauty and strength to this body. The emotions that are infused with love add vitality to it. You increase the vitality and the intelligence of your directors in your etheric body by bringing greater light into your thoughts, and emotions. You bring them essence life energy through your triangle of light with your Solar angel and your soul.

Your Major Energy Centers

The directors of your systems work from centers of energy in your etheric body. Each center is formed from a vortex of energy and serves as a vital part of your whole system of energy. You may be familiar with these centers as the base, sacral, power or solar plexus, heart, throat, brow (also known as the ajna center, or third eye), and crown centers. They are located outside your spinal cord with the exception of your brow center, which is located slightly above and between your eyes an inch or so out from your body, and the crown center, which is located just above the top of your head. Each spinning vortex of energy has a color and a frequency of its own. As these energy centers develop, they begin harmonizing with your soul's color and frequency. It is this harmony that heals you, evolves you, and protects you from disease or other sickness. The harmony in your energy centers empowers the directors to upgrade their systems. Your physical body naturally reflects this harmony with health and vitality. You can play a major role in upgrading your systems by responding to your directors' needs under the guidance of your soul and inner healer.

Your Higher Energy Centers

Healing with light focuses on your four higher centers. These are your heart center, throat center, brow center, and crown center. These centers receive light directly from your Solar angel and soul. As your higher centers develop, they can handle more light. The higher centers begin awakening after you have been through so many experiences that you are filled with a passion to give your life meaning, to learn about the greater truth of who you are, and to fulfill your intended purpose. As your higher centers develop further, they transmit greater light. They develop as you begin to express the loving spirit and creativity of your soul, regardless of what form that might take. This might begin with relating to your family with love or learning about something that you love. You might return to something that you once were very interested in learning about until you were told that you had to grow up and earn a living. Your higher centers further evolve as you develop a spirit of goodwill, understanding, right living, right relationship, and other important character traits inspired by your soul.

As your higher centers evolve and can handle more light, they help your lower centers to evolve. They can then automatically correct problems that originate in areas of your body that are nourished by the lower centers (solar plexus, sacral, and base). When you have an illness that comes from a system

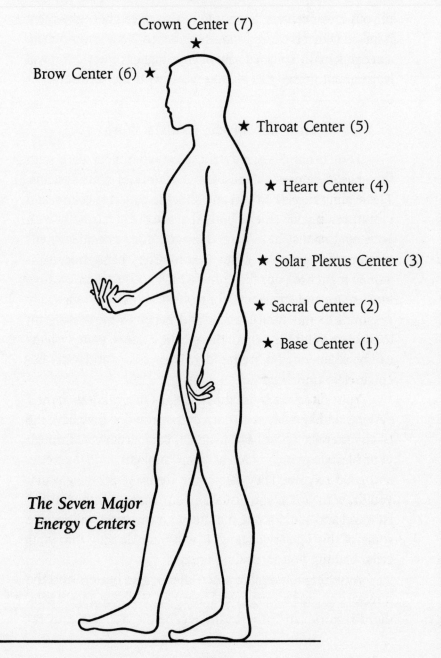

Crown Center (7)

Brow Center (6) ★

★ Throat Center (5)

★ Heart Center (4)

★ Solar Plexus Center (3)

★ Sacral Center (2)

★ Base Center (1)

The Seven Major Energy Centers

in your lower centers, it tends to heal as the higher center that is linked with it is cleared and strengthened. Your lower centers can drink in the spiritual light of your higher centers. You will learn about these links as you work with the directors.

How the Angelic Healers Work

Your healing is steady and sure when you work with the angelic helpers to assist the directors of your systems. The healing angels come in and shift the patterns, colors, and vibrations in your etheric body that are out of harmony with your soul or that have been damaged due to accidents, environmental stress, or other factors. They bring finer subatomic matter to your directors, which adds to their creative intelligence and efficiency. Your physical body automatically responds to this nourishment and becomes more resistant to disease. With the help of the angelic healers, your systems can be regenerated more rapidly. Their colors and tones become clear and beautiful.

Your directors sense the first signs of weakness in their systems and know how to correct it—provided they have the basic materials. These basic materials come from you, through your lifestyle in areas such as sleep, sunlight, food, exercise, and good oxygen. They also come from the Solar light that you draw to you. If you visualize your triangle with your Solar angel and soul for one minute, your directors will receive some of this light right now. It will filter directly into your cells, bathing you in healing energy.

Anything is possible when the angelic healers and the directors of your systems work together. With the angels' help, the directors can then repair, regenerate, rebuild, and rebalance their systems. They can make continual adjustments to your thoughts, feelings, and activities on the physical level. They learn to share extra energy with another director, to cooperate with your inner healer, and to upgrade their systems. In a sense, each becomes a superdirector in healing and evolving the system for which it is responsible.

How Your Inner Healer Helps

Your inner healer is the master director who teaches and coordinates the directors of the various systems. The director for each of your systems – circulatory, nervous, respiratory, immune, endocrine, muscular, skeletal, digestive, reproductive, and urinary – works under your inner healer. The inner healer holds your entire blueprint, while the directors focus on the parts they are responsible for creating. Your inner healer can bring specialized instructions and suggestions to you as you work with your directors.

Your inner healer is also the master director of your glands and organs. It is aware of everything going on in your body. It will work with you as you read these chapters to show you what is needed for your complete healing and regeneration. After you connect with each director, your inner healer can show you the practical steps to take next. It also may call on the angels to assist while you are sleeping.

Playing Your Part

Your part in creating healing is to learn to sense what each director needs to energize, heal, and evolve its system. Usually, these needs are very simple, such as what to eat, how to exercise, how much to sleep, and how to create the serene state of mind that heals and evolves this particular system. Don't expect complicated instructions. Most of the ideas that come to you will be so simple that you may wonder if you made them up. Sometimes you will get an idea that is meant just for that one day. You may get a sense of using a certain color that will help that director to balance its system, or you may simply be directed to call on an angelic healer and make your triangle with your soul and Solar angel. If a director needs outside professional assistance, you can get ideas on how to choose the best doctor or healer and what therapy will be the most helpful. You will want to draw to yourself good books and articles about the needs of any system you are working with. Your directors and inner healer can bring important data to you, but all intuitive information needs a landing place. Your open and educated mind about that system provides this landing place.

Preventing Physical Problems

When there are obstructions or an imbalance of energy in your etheric body, one of your directors needs your help. It may be working hard, but although it is an expert in running its system and knows what to do, it may not be getting the source material to do its job. Your directors can override stress, turbulent emotions, toxic overload, sugar, and parasites for a day or so, but their systems will break down if any of these continue for too long. Before any symptoms appear, your directors will need assistance from the healing angels and from your inner healer. You may not know about these problems until they are reflected in your physical body as a disease or weakness. But since problems in your physical body actually begin in your etheric body, they can be stopped there before they are reflected in your physical body.

There is much you can do to help. You can surround the director with the angelic healers, who transmit spiritual love. You can assist the director in receiving the translucent colors it needs, and you can work with the angelic healers to change the frequencies and sounds that are off-key for this director into those that are in perfect pitch and tone. You can show your director your healing hologram and find out what this director needs to match this hologram.

If you have a weakness in one of your systems, this director needs assistance to create a healthier, stronger, and more resilient system. If you want to evolve this system, learn what that director needs in order to work from a higher frequency of light. As you become familiar with the functions of each director, you can sense a problem before symptoms come up and find out how to prevent any tendency toward illness or disease. The earlier you catch a potential malfunction, the easier it is to stop it. You can send a higher blueprint of a healthy, strong system to each director, and this director will do everything in its power to match your vision. If something essential is missing or creating an imbalance, you can become sensitive to this and respond with what is needed before any symptoms appear. Since the directors are dependent on each other, when one is strengthened all the others are strengthened, too. When a malfunction in one system clears up, other systems get healthier. Each success means a healthier body and a lighter spirit. As a result, you can think better and feel better—psychologically and biologically.

Catching Ideas Sent to You

When information is sent to you, it may come for only a second or two. You can learn to "catch" these pictures as they flash across the screen of your mind. In your healing journal, write all that you *sense* even if you feel you are making it up. Make notes when you sense information from one of your directors of a system. Success comes from writing everything, and then checking later for its usefulness and accuracy. As you write, more details come to mind. The act of writing what you receive, even if only a few words or sentences, triggers the release of more information. If you are not clear, meet with the director again and again until you get a clear sense of what it needs. Some of the changes may seem obvious after you get them, but perhaps you did not know about them before. Such changes can open paths for healing to take place. No matter how simple the changes and ideas, write them in your journal. Stop to reflect on them, and check each one with your inner healer. If a system is not functioning well, you can benefit by checking each week or so until the repairs are complete. Excellent information may also come to you in the form of articles, books, and other people. Pay attention to your dreams. Sometimes your inner healer and director can show you through the drama of a dream what the next step is in upgrading a particular system.

Creating a Brighter Blueprint for Each Director

You will be creating your healing hologram in greater detail as you meet your directors. You will develop a blueprint for each system and hold this up as a new model. Once you know what you need to supply, change, or eliminate, and you do it, the director of the system can do the rest. It will call for the chemicals or hormones needed, and they will appear on the spot—enzymes, proteins, and other elements that match the light in the blueprint that is part of the hologram vision from your soul.

Every time you think about your healing hologram, the light from it flows into your etheric body to nourish the director of each system. When the director of any system is stimulated in this way, it immediately begins to set up higher standards for its system. Whichever cells are at the bottom of the group in color and vibration are spun off, and the cells in the top quality are raised to a higher level of light.

When You Are Doing All You Can

If you are doing all that you know to do and a particular system is still not functioning well, check with your director to see if there's some kind of emotional obstruction. The problem may stem from a painful memory or a chronic sense of self-criticism or other negative emotion. Take an honest look to find the emotion that is creating a problem in this system. Your emotions greatly affect the directors. Worry, fear, and anxiety handicap the directors. Positive pictures, gratitude, feelings of love, humor, laughter, delight, and anticipation help the directors. This is so important that even if you have to go back ten years to remember something you feel gratitude for or something that makes you smile, it is well worth it to strengthen your directors. For example, one woman who had chronic sore throats realized the problem in her throat arose from holding back what she wanted to say, even when she wanted to express a loving experience. She practiced speaking out many times while she was alone, and as she learned to speak out with others, her sore throat cleared up. Soon, she found many occasions to speak with others about the subjects that meant the most to her. Now she uses rare sore throats as a message that it is time to speak out more clearly or to establish her higher priorities over lower priorities. Listen to the words you are saying to yourself. Each word has the power to heal or to harm your body. "These people are driving me crazy; that group is eating me alive; this situation makes me sick; seeing this child makes my heart ache; I can't stand this situation; this air is poisoning me." These are examples of automatic phrases, which, when repeated, are taken seriously by your directors and your body.

Your Will to Be Well

You are dependent on your systems for a healthy body and a clear mind. The directors are dependent on you for success in their continued existence and power to carry out their purpose of building and regenerating their systems. This is where your will to be completely well comes in. It gives you the persistence to stay with your commitment to assist this director in rebuilding its system and regenerating itself. If you are tempted to fall into old habits of mistreating your body, at the moment you feel tempted, let your hologram stand in front of you and send energy to you. Your healing hologram becomes more powerful as you think about it, supporting the directors.

136

Small Changes – Big Difference

Much knowledge is available through your directors, too much to put into action all at once. Be patient as you plan the action that you will take. By moving on one change at a time, you move steadily forward. For example, all you may need is to get more sleep at regular hours to ensure that the rebuilding process is completed each night. Deciding to get more rest shows that you are serious about healing yourself. If you feel tired in the middle of the day, you can give yourself a break right then and there, even if it is for only ten minutes. Congratulate yourself for establishing one new habit. If your director needs special foods to regenerate its cells, you can learn what foods would be most helpful. Go to a health food store, a bookstore, library, or a computer health network to search out the best knowledge from all over the world for that system. Look for good information written for the layperson. One or two small changes can make a great difference.

Which System to Heal or Evolve First

Respiratory System

Your respiratory director needs help if you have sore throats, a hoarse voice, difficulty swallowing, goiter, bronchitis, coughs, asthma, allergies, a stiff neck, or frequent colds. Earaches, toothaches, gum problems, flu, and sinus problems are other signs that the director of your respiratory system is overworked. If you do not have any problems, you can upgrade this system. The director can show you what is

needed as you bring the light of your triangle with your Solar angel and soul over it. By upgrading this system, you can
change your breathing to put you in contact with your soul
all through the day. At the same time you can become more
creative. Those things which you have only dreamed of doing may become possible as your level of creativity gets higher
and higher.

Circulatory System

The director of your circulatory system needs help if
you have heart disease, high cholesterol, or atherosclerosis
that blocks your circulation. Other symptoms stemming from
this system that you can heal and regenerate with angelic help
are poor circulation, cold hands and feet, lack of stamina,
weakness, chronic fatigue, low immunity to disease, and aging. The director of your circulatory system needs a very clear
channel to receive from the angels of divine love and from
your soul to heal and upgrade its system. When your heart
center begins receiving the vital life energy it needs, your entire circulatory system is revived and regenerated. If you do
not have any problems in this system, you can evolve this
system and heal heartaches and heartbreaks, expand the reach
of your love, and transmit healing love to others. The angels
of divine love may come to help.

Nervous System

The director of your nervous system needs help if you
have headaches, nervousness, pain, or memory loss or if
you feel spacey, confused, tense, jumpy, anxious, or if you over-

react to everyday problems. Other signs for you to work with this director are poor eyesight or other eye abnormalities, multiple sclerosis, difficulty in concentrating, sleep problems, epilepsy, or pituitary or pineal gland problems. Some symptoms may require the help of two or more directors to be cleared up. Again, you will work with your inner healer and the healing angels to assist the nervous system director. If you have no problems to heal in these areas, you can begin evolving your nervous system. This means that you can reach your Solar angel and soul more easily, think with greater clarity and focus, see your higher purpose, and develop higher intuition.

Immune System

The director of your immune system is not able to protect you enough if you have an infection anywhere in your body, or if you have recurrent infections, incomplete recovery from illnesses, pneumonia, herpes, or fungus infections. This director needs attention if you have cancer, candida, tumors, frequent colds, acute illness or fever, chills, AIDS, chronic fatigue, or tuberculosis. If you have an autoimmune disease, such as MS, lupus, or arthritis, this director needs completely new patterns of light and color. If you do not have any problems in your immune system, you can begin evolving it to cleanse toxins from your cells, clear your skin, and create even more resistance to diseases and aging.

Endocrine System

The director of your endocrine system needs assistance if you have problems with your pancreas or with overactive or underactive pineal, pituitary, thyroid, thymus, reproductive, or adrenal glands. Other signals that this director needs help are any tumors affecting a gland, a disorder of the pituitary or hypothalamus that control many other glands, endometriosis, diabetes or low blood sugar, low metabolism, dizziness, sweating, irritability, and weakness. Your endocrine system director works from your seven major energy centers with its hormone-producing glands. Even if you don't have any problems with the endocrine glands, by evolving the endocrine system and thus evolving your glands, you can gain an even temperament, calm emotions, more energizing metabolism, and a cheerful, calm, and optimistic spirit.

Digestive System

If you have gas, bloating, gallbladder, liver, stomach, digestive, or colon problems, or if you have an overstressed pancreas, insulin imbalance, unstable blood sugar, elimination problems, fatigue, or high blood pressure, the director of your digestive system is overworked. Fears, anxieties, and repetitious worries are also signs that this director needs some relief from too much energy pouring in. If you want to upgrade this system, you can use your meter to calculate how much cleansing is needed and then work closely with the healing angels, your director, and inner healer to purify this system.

Skeletal System

If you have osteoporosis from a lack of bone density or insufficient red blood cells produced in the bone marrow, a broken bone, aching bones, or joints, or an aching back, the director of your skeletal system is overworked and needs assistance. This director works from your base center. If you have no problems in your skeletal system, you can evolve this system to be sure that your bones can always support your body and provide the basis for a perfect posture all your life.

Reproductive System

The director of your reproductive system needs help if you have problems with ovaries, testes, conceiving a child, menstrual or menopausal problems, uterine or prostate cancer, herpes, or other inflammations in the reproductive organs. This director works from your sacral center. If you have no problems here, you can evolve this system by bringing some of this energy to your higher creative center, the throat center. You thus empower your creative self to be expressed and to be heard in the world.

Urinary System

The director of your base center needs help if you have problems with your kidneys or bladder, general weakness, pale or frequent urination, kidney stones, kidney damage from high blood pressure, infections from obstructions or from drugs, bloating, or bladder infections. These symptoms are this director's call for help. If you have no problems in this area, you can upgrade the system with the healing angels so that your blood clears and excretes all waste products perfectly, thus keeping your energy high and your body youthful year after year.

Muscular System

Go to the director of your muscular system if you have problems with tight, sore, and aching muscles, muscle weakness, muscle spasms, tight jaws, back aches, or with a chronic stiff neck, shoulders, or hips. By evolving this director, you can build this system up to keep your muscles strong and flexible enough to fully support your skeleton and your whole body so that you can participate in exercise activities and have a flexible body regardless of your age.

Benefits of Upgrading Your Systems

Imagine the kind of body you can have by healing, evolving, and upgrading all of your systems! Imagine the power of having a body that is so responsive to angelic and Solar light that you can reach higher states of awareness and receive your soul's messages more clearly. Imagine new pathways that bring the angelic healers into your brain to build finer matter into these cells. Imagine having the calm, poised emotions that conserve your focus and energy and bring greater light to every cell. These are the steps that create a longer, more joyful, and productive life. They give you the sensitivity to know when your systems and centers need more light, when they need healing or regenerating, and when they are ready to link up with one another and build new pathways of connection with your Solar angel and soul.

You are now ready to begin working with your soul, Solar angel, and the angelic healers to upgrade and heal each system in your body. You can choose the system you want to work on first, or you can go through and work on each one. Choose the one first that you see can create the most change as the healing angels help draw out the director's highest intelligence to bring you vibrant health, rejuvenation, and greater light. Rather than working with every system at once, spread these chapters over several days to get the most benefit. You might begin Part Four while allowing more time to upgrade each system.

Chapter 13

Bringing Angelic Energy to Your Circulatory System

Your circulatory system (also called your cardiovascular system) lies the closest to your soul. It is the heart of your life, controlling your heartbeat and circulating life blood to every cell. The director of this system sees that all your body tissues and cells get a fresh supply of oxygen and nutrients every single second of your life.

The director of your circulatory system works from your heart center to purify and enliven your bloodstream. This director needs a steady flow of light from your Solar angel and soul to be vibrant and strong, to clean your arteries, and to keep regenerating your cells. As the angelic healers work with this director, they activate your thymus gland and thus strengthen your immunity to disease and aging.

This director knows its next step in evolution: to transmute the vibration of your soul into a substance that completely heals and rejuvenates your body. This director longs to send the life-renewing energy of love into the heart of every cell in your body.

Evolving Your Heart Center

Evolving your heart center evolves the director of your circulatory system and all its cells. As your heart center holds more light, not only does your circulatory system work more efficiently, but heart aches, grief, loneliness, sadness, and depression can be healed. You begin experiencing the higher love of your Solar angel, which carries healing energy. You can bring this love into your eyes and hands to become a healing agent for yourself and for others. You can relate to friends with more understanding and compassion. Each thought and act of love, no matter how small, helps to balance your blood pressure, end angina pain, reduce stress, heal heart disease, prevent aging, and open your life to greater happiness and joy. Just as you can develop muscles through lifting weights, you can bring new life energy to your heart and arteries by reaching out to something or someone with love. Every time you do this in your mind, you improve your director's ability to regenerate this system. When you act from this higher love to assist another person, group, animal, or plant, you are stepping up this director's vibration. Even love for the stars, the sun, and the mysterious living universe will evolve this system.

Some of the diseases that stem from weaknesses in this system are heart disease, high blood pressure, angina, shortness of breath, high cholesterol, and blocked arteries. Other problems are strokes, poor circulation, cold hands and feet, lack of stamina, weakness, chronic fatigue, liver disease, low immunity to disease, and premature aging. (For chronic or acute circulatory or heart problems, as with all serious problems, get a professional diagnosis and work with the medical community as well as with the angelic healers.)

The following journey will give you a sense of the miraculous nature of your circulatory system. It will also help open communication with this system's director.

A Journey Into Your Circulatory System

As you read this paragraph, pretend you are taking a journey through your circulatory system to enjoy the miracle of this system's efficiency and to sense where some part of the system needs more light or love. Start by experiencing your heartbeat renewing your life—each pump giving you life. As your heart receives oxygen from your lungs, travel through its left ventricle as it pumps blood into the arteries. Go all through your body into the network of tiny capillaries into the tissues and cells of your chest, up your neck, into your head, and down your arms and shoulders. Follow this energy down your trunk, into your stomach, into your pelvic area, past your hips, legs, and down to your feet. Sense this new life energy reaching to more than 60 trillion cells every second. Observe how fully each cell receives this life-giving oxygen and how quickly it releases all the wastes built up since the last heartbeat about one second ago. Now journey back through the veins carrying the carbon dioxide to your heart and into your lungs for a fresh supply of oxygen. Feel the rhythm of this system—receiving, sending, resting—receiving, sending, resting. This is the ideal rhythm for your body and for your life.

Clearing Your Heart Center to Strengthen Your Circulatory System

Your heart center is the anchor for your soul. You can evolve this center until every heartbeat carries your soul's clear tone and vibrancy to your body. If you have closed your heart because of something that happened to you—a time when you were hurt or mistreated—you may accidentally have built a shell of protection around your heart that obstructs the soul's

146

energy from reaching it. If you feel that you have closed or partly closed off your soul's life force from your heart and circulatory system, take a long look at the situation that caused you to do this. Decide if anything, no matter how serious, is worth cutting off *your own vitality* or *closing you off from your soul's light.* Shells that are built to protect the heart center also block you and the director of your circulatory system from receiving your full share of unconditional love from the healing angels – and from all the people you know. Once you recognize the places where your heart center is constricted by a protective shell, you can make the decision that nothing – no fear, no hurt, no anger – is worth the price you are paying. Both hurt and anger may be vital steps on the way to healing, but it is your willingness to release these feelings, once experienced fully, that raises your will to be well and to receive more from the angelic healers.

Healing and Regenerating Your Circulatory System

1. Touch your fingers to your forehead, and take yourself to the Island of Regeneration and the Temple of Healing. Take a shower of light, and let the drops of color permeate your entire energy field, cleansing it, refreshing it, reorganizing the patterns, and adding color where it is needed.

2. Go into the Room of Love, and take a moment to experience an inner stillness. Meet with your Solar angel and soul, and create your shining triangle of light.

3. Let this illumination flow into your heart center and the director of your circulatory system. As this golden light touches your heart center, feel the gentle pulsing of your soul's powerful love.

147

4. Imagine your heart center as an opening flower with petals made of light and color. Sound the word for angelic love three times, pronouncing each syllable of A-El-I-O with care and attention. Imagine these sounds vibrating, causing the petals around your heart center to begin to open.

5. Your Solar angel is bringing the healing angels of divine love in response to this call from your heart. An angel (or several angels) will come through your triangle and hover around your heart center to help dissolve any shells around it and to empower your circulatory system director. Give permission for them to cleanse and purify your heart center with their love. Let this love flow in now to bring strength and power to your circulatory system director. Imagine pulsing waves of love moving into your heart center, each wave beginning very gently and rising to a crescendo of lighted energy as it clears your heart center. Feel these waves vibrating the petals of light around this center and causing them to open even more.

6. The angels of divine love use a beautiful hue of rose to regenerate and evolve your circulatory system director. Imagine this color flowing all around you and to your director to repair any weaknesses or problems that have built up through the years. They may also use a second color, tinged with gold, to evolve your heart center and empower the director of your circulatory system. You may feel an openness and lightness in your heart center as these angelic colors are added to it.

7. Angelic sounds are being used now by the healers to loosen and dissolve obstructions. The obstructions are the result of anything that has separated you from your soul's love. These sounds are followed by celestial music on the inner planes that is raising the vibration of this center. Imagine all the grief or pain that has ever touched your heart being dissolved as these notes are played. You can deepen the effect of their healing by sounding the sacred word AUM as you learned in the Room

of Sound. Imagine that you are sounding this word over your heart center director. This might feel like a substance is being vacuumed out of your heart center and being replaced by a new energy.

8. As your heart center is cleared and energized, the director of your circulatory system is empowered to heal and evolve this system. If you have a specific healing or upgrade in mind for your heart, arteries, veins, circulation, or the quality of your bloodstream, think of what you will feel like when this is healed. Even if you are accustomed to the limitations of a heart that isn't pumping enough blood with each beat and thus has to work harder, even if you are used to the empty feeling in your heart when you recall certain memories, you do not have to live with these. They can be healed! Make a picture of what you can do with a strong heart that will always serve you— and of what your life will be like with a young and healthy heart, arteries, and circulatory system. Imagine having more energy as your bloodstream becomes purified and filled with Solar light. Imagine being filled with the joyous love that the angels bring. Show these pictures to your director and inner healer. They are your blueprint for a perfect circulatory system and a beautiful, evolving heart center of love.

9. Ask what you can do to assist. Bring in your inner healer, who is the master director. Your inner healer is wise, understanding, and very practical. It has a complete overview of your life and knows how far you have come and how rich your life is meant to be. This healer represents a vast treasury of wisdom and experience. It answers your questions and shows you how to move through an illness or to evolve this system to a finer light. Together, your inner healer and the director of your circulatory system can place the answers to your questions in your mind. They perceive your questions before you even ask them; they hear the questions as you formulate them.

149

Their answers may come before you finish stating your questions, or they may come tomorrow when you least expect it. Resolve to provide whatever the director of your circulatory system needs. Here are some areas you might want to address.

- Ask for new ways to express love, gratitude, and appreciation throughout the day and to sleep so soundly that your heart can regenerate itself more fully at night.
- Ask about several forms of exercise and aerobics training or walking to strengthen this system. Get information on how frequently and how long a session will be beneficial.
- Ask which vitamins or other supplements will fortify this system for you.
- Ask which foods you need to add or eliminate from your diet.
- Ask to learn how to express the love that your soul and Solar angel are pouring into you.
- Ask to see and seize every opportunity to dissolve fears—the fear of rejection, the fear of failure, and the fear of past errors—through radiating the love of your soul and the angelic healers.
- Ask for assistance in relating to your own self and your body with love and gratitude.

10. Imagine the angels helping your director cleanse and rejuvenate your heart and circulatory system. Visualize healthy arteries that bring an abundance of oxygen to vitalize your cells. Visualize your blood being healthy and balanced. Visualize a web of light creating a pattern for the blood cells to be vitalized by your Solar angel. See your blood cells sparkling with Solar light.

11. See your whole body with an aura of health and vitality. The changes you are visualizing are being received as

you send them to the director. These changes will continue to unfold over a long period of time.

12. Your circulatory system evolves as you circulate more freely in the higher dimensions of love and compassion. Imagine a way that you can circulate this higher love when you are with friends. Imagine making a heart connection this week with one or two new people. Think of one loving act you can do today that is completely unexpected.

13. Develop a shorthand code with this director. Decide that you want to know when you are being overly serious and forgetting to circulate love through your body and to your friends and associates. Ask to be reminded of the blessings you are receiving and to send gratitude to the angelic healers. Set up a special signal with your director to show you when you need to give yourself a well-deserved break through play, beautiful music, exercise, or sleep.

14. Rest in the awareness that your inner healer and your circulatory director are steadily converting Solar light into energy to heal and evolve all the cells in this system.

15. Make notes on ideas that come to you over the next few days. Be alert to what you can do to continue the healing that the angels have begun. You may be drawn to read a certain book or article or to attend a lecture on healthy hearts, healthy diets, or healthy exercise. Watch for intuitive ideas about higher love and opening your heart to your soul's healing light.

You have now begun the work of clearing all obstructions around your heart center and evolving the director of your circulatory system so that your body can heal itself with the angels of divine love. Let this love circulate into the world around you through the harmonious rhythm of your healing heart.

Chapter 14

Revitalizing Your Mind and Nervous System

The more developed and sensitive your brain and nervous system, the more acutely you can feel pain—and the more exquisitely you can experience joy and bliss. Your nervous system is your body's information-gathering, storage, and control system. Its overall function is to gather information about the outside environment and your body's internal state, to analyze this information, and to initiate appropriate responses. Basic survival responses, such as shivering to generate warmth and withdrawing from something hot, are automatic functions of the nervous system. Your desires create its more complex processes—the desire for happiness, pleasure, and learning, or the desire to avoid pain, anxiety, and frustration. Your nervous system responds automatically to many built-in programs; however, it can evolve dramatically by learning new processes.

Your entire nervous system is organized like a computer system that controls a highly complex machine. Think of the central processing computer as the central nervous system. This includes your brain and spinal cord with billions of interconnecting neurons or nerve cells. Motor instructions go to the skeletal muscles, to the muscles controlling speech, internal organs, and glands, and to the sweat glands in your skin. The cables that carry this information are the nerves that extend from the central nervous system throughout your entire body. All nervous activity is based on the transmission of impulses through these intricate networks of neurons. Underlying these networks are tiny threads of light in your etheric body that carry the impulses of your soul and the angelic healers along with your thoughts and feelings. These etheric nerves are your connecting link to your future and the radiance it holds for you.

Evolving Your Nervous System

The director of your nervous system works from your brow and crown centers and also from your solar plexus center. This is your most complex and evolved director. This director is so sophisticated that its complex functions can't be duplicated or even traced with the most advanced computer programs. As this system evolves, it invents new pathways for brain cells that bring the wisdom of your higher mind and soul to your conscious mind. You become more intelligent, capable, and creative each time the golden light of your Solar angel and soul flows into your crown and brow centers.

As you evolve this system, you can reach your Solar angel and soul more easily, think with greater clarity and focus, see your higher purpose, and develop higher intuition. You can receive from the great intelligence of your soul. Your nervous system director begins working closely with the higher will of your soul and brings this will to your awareness. Your mind becomes brighter, more organized, and focused. With an evolved and balanced nervous system, you are no longer vulnerable to other people's emotions or thoughts. Your refined and lighted mind can direct your emotional life and free you from overattachment to people, things, and controlling situations. You can stand free to know who you are and why you are here. Your will is no longer held down or suppressed by others' plans for your life.

Problems of the Nervous System

Some of the problems of this system include hearing loss, vision problems, headaches, nervousness, oversensitivity to physical and emotional pain, memory loss, fuzzy thinking, difficulty concentrating, sleep problems, neuralgia, sweaty palms, overheating, worry, anxiety, and repetitious thoughts. This director is also in charge of your pituitary and pineal glands. More serious problems are nerve damage, multiple sclerosis, brain seizures, or tumors.

Think about your nervous system and sense the intelligence of its director. Do you feel that this system needs rest and restoration, or do you feel it needs more stimulation? An overstimulated nervous system feels jangled, as if the circuitry is overloaded with pressures and tensions and thoughts. Repeated thoughts and a churning mind filled with worry create mental exhaustion and signal an overstimulated nervous system. Environmental noises, too much intellectual focus, or too much talking can keep your mind repeating thoughts when you want it to turn off. When your nervous system director is overworked, you could feel irritable over events that don't make any real difference in your life, or be oversensitive to criticism and thin-skinned. This is the time to call on the angelic healers and sit quietly with them. As you bring this system into balance, the nervous system director and the angels can help you create a funnel that becomes a magnetic center to your soul's wisdom and intelligence.

Follow Your Inner Knowing

Another challenge of the nervous system may come when your heart or soul is pulling you in one direction and your mind pulling you in another direction. If this is true for you ask yourself if this conflict is due to some decision you made long ago before you were in touch with your higher intuition. Look over your life, and see if you have let other people's beliefs or desires dominate your life rather than putting your own life plan as your first priority. The penalty for ignoring the guidance from your soul and inner healer gets higher as you evolve. Following your inner knowing eliminates the ongoing sense of conflict that goes on in the mind when it is trying to follow two masters—the desires of your personality and the higher awareness from the soul plane. Imagine how your life might be different if you followed your higher intuition about your life. Stay with the director until you know what that decision was. You can work with your inner healer to help to free you from any decision that does not honor your inner knowing, and then follow through on a wiser choice.

Decisions That Limit Your Enlightened Mind

Some people discovered from their director that decisions they made in junior high school were holding them back. They deliberately changed these decisions, such as "I am not as smart as these kids; I won't even try to learn much," and installed

155

a new decision, such as "I *will* excel in my field. I can learn anything that I really focus on." They began freeing the creative energy that had been suppressed by their earlier decisions.

One man realized that when he was fourteen he had decided to live a mediocre life by placing himself in the middle of the curve in his classes. He felt safer that way than if he had reached to his highest level. He changed this decision and told everyone of his new decision. Now the director of his nervous system is matching his decision and revealing to him just how intelligent and bright and creative he is. You can change any belief that puts an artificial ceiling on your creative mind. You were the one that installed it, and your inner healer and your nervous system director are the ones who can show you how to put a new program of intelligence into this system.

If you have unconsciously decided that you may be sick or weakened or in pain for a long time, if you have decided that your mind is slowing down or that your memory is failing, if you have been afraid of some genetic mental illness, or of losing your bright mind as you grow older, you can make a new decision. Once you consciously choose another path, you can build this path into your blueprint. When your director responds, it will be from a much broader vision of how much is possible. In connecting with this director, you get a sense of the ease with which your mind brings to life *whatever* it focuses on.

Opening the Path to an Excellent Mind

There are several clues to healing and rebalancing your nervous system. Ask how you can transform sporadic efforts to a steady and persistent focus. Ask how you can build a higher vibration from which to live. Your questions open the path for your spiritual energy stream to reach your nervous system. They enable you to release unnecessary mental activity and regain a good balance in your nervous system. This balance gives your director the opportunity (perhaps long awaited) to heal and regenerate your nervous system.

If you feel your brain needs more nutrients and is becoming forgetful, narrow, or rigid, you can find out why. One student was surprised to learn from the director of his nervous system that his mind was sluggish because his digestive system was overworked. The headaches he was having were not from too much thinking; they were from the overheating caused by too much fuel in his stomach and large intestines. His inner healer suggested that he eat less of everything and that he focus on salads and cooked vegetables. He eliminated a surplus of carbohydrates and sugar and added light broths and juices. Since then, he has not had headaches, he can think more clearly, and his temperament has become calm and cheerful.

Regenerating Your Nervous System Through Play

When you communicate with the director of your nervous system, you may find that play and relaxation are the only "medicine" it needs. Play is healing; it creates balance and brings all the nerves up and down your spine into balance. Relaxing through play may be the single most valuable therapy for your nervous system, including every pill on the market. This system needs the rhythm of work and play and rest to handle the light flowing into it. Play gives your brain time to integrate the new pathways that the director of your nervous system is having built. Play dissolves the cobwebs in your nervous system and clears your thinking. You may realize the best ideas you ever had came through play. You can create a wonderful atmosphere for revitalizing your mind by relaxing through play. Your sense of what is work and what is play may shift. The way you relate to others, especially the people you know best, is very likely to improve automatically. These changes will have a positive impact on the directors of your digestive, circulatory, respiratory, and muscular systems. They can serve you better as you bring lightness and humor to your life.

Creating New Images for Your Rejuvenated Mind

Your imagination is a great ally to invent different healing modes for your nervous system. Imagine how you might express the creative artist in yourself—through sculpting, painting, drawing, drama, music, writing, or poetry. Add brilliance to the pictures you make in your mind. Make them sparkle with light and color. Add the sounds of your voice as well as music. Create an image of yourself playing, singing, or making music just for the delight of it, and paint this image on an enormous billboard. Imagine placing the billboard where everyone who knows you will see it. Imagine those you know that you would rather not have see this picture of you so happy and at play, and call on the angels to help you resolve anything that inhibits your innate ability to sing and play in a joyful spirit.

158

Creating Small Pleasures to Release Mental Stress

A woman who was suffering from nervousness and irregular sleep patterns imagined a billboard of herself at play and in perfect balance and realized that of all the people she knew, it was her mother she didn't want to see her this way. She realized she was trying to make her life fit her mother's image for her. She was loyally living out her mother's images ("Idle hands make idle minds") rather than following her higher intuition. The pressured pace she kept was her mother's pace, even though they lived three thousand miles from each other. It was such an unhealthy pace that her own mother had almost died from a heart attack when she was exactly the age of her daughter. Yet, somewhere in the back of the daughter's mind, the picture still existed that made her push herself to exhaustion every day. As soon as she recognized this compulsion to overwork her mind and body, she began planning relaxing excursions, such as simple picnics and long walks with friends. She and her friends would go to a lake, a mountain, a park, or anywhere they could be in nature. These excursions brought back childhood memories of play and helped her release the inner compulsion to be someone she wasn't.

This woman made a list of more than thirty small pleasures that she enjoyed, and whenever she began to feel a strong inner pressure to do more and to do it faster, she pulled out her list and selected one relaxing and rebalancing activity to put into action that day. This simple practice is working so well that her voice has become soft and lovely. In your healing journal, begin a list of the small pleasures that give you delight. Visualize yourself with the awareness to shift into one of these when you are tense and tight–or to simply sit and do nothing at all!

These are suggestions to release tension and stress in your nervous system. Select one or two that you like and experiment this week with them.

- Flex your spine gently to offer more space for the millions of tiny nerves in this system. Stretching opens space for your nervous system to breathe and expand. If you can do so comfortably, walk with both feet and hands on the floor for one minute each day to help rebalance your nervous system.
- Follow a simple stretching routine, or walk, swim, jog, bike, row, paddle, or climb stairs until you can feel energy nourishing your brain.
- Go outside the human experience. Connect with a life outside of human evolution–a bird, an animal, the sun, a tree, a flower, a mountain, or a river. All contact with such natural beauty is healing to your nervous system.
- Play with sound. Sit beside a brook or river and listen to the water. Learn to become a part of water sounds and of other healing and regenerating sounds in nature.
- Play chimes, and find the notes that are most healing to you. Play an instrument or listen to the music that feels most relaxing.
- Choose active movement play that has no winner or loser–something you play just for the fun of it.
- Play with colors–watercolors, poster paints, acrylics, pastels, or fabric colors. Focus on the colors that calm and regenerate your mind.

160

- Place a cool, wet cloth over your eyes, and imagine that you are beside the waterfall on the Island of Regeneration.
- Send any excess mental energy out to some group or country by visualizing light streaming into the minds and hearts of all the people.
- When you feel especially energized, offer a grateful mother an afternoon of rest while you take her child out to play with you (and your own children if you have any). You can pretend to be teaching the children, but in reality the children are teaching you how to play—to relax, to smile, to laugh with spontaneous delight, to build castles in the sand, and to dig tunnels to carry water. You know who the real teachers are, the onlookers know, the child knows—everyone knows! But pretend you are the teacher just the same. Together you can crawl, hop, march, leap, and laugh your way into the joy and humor of life at its best.

Regenerating Your Nervous System

1. Take a shower of light, and let the drops of color permeate your entire energy field, cleansing and refreshing it.

2. From your Temple of Healing, create your triangle with your Solar angel and soul and let the golden light flow on the director of your nervous system.

3. Bring this light to the cells in your nervous system—to all parts of your brain and to your sympathetic and parasympathetic nervous systems that run on either side of your spinal cord. Sweep the light from the top of your head to the area just outside your spinal cord, and bring it all the way down your back to your base center. Let your nerve cells bathe in

161

this wisdom and absorb the golden light of your soul. Imagine a mist of gold forming around your nerves and thinking cells. Now sweep the golden light back up your nervous system and into your head. Visualize the director being enlightened by billions of particles of golden light.

4. Imagine what it would be like if your mind and memory were absolutely clear, creative, focused, and organized. Think about the times when you felt a perfect rhythm as you worked. See your nervous system coming into balance—alternating periods of relaxation with periods of holding a creative and productive point of tension.

5. Create a picture of what you want in the future. Imagine how you would sit, breathe, talk, and move if you had a poised and perfectly balanced nervous system. What if your brain were perfectly synchronized with your soul? What if your mind began spontaneously creating dynamic thoughts and pictures of your body vitalized and regenerated? What if your nervous system director became so receptive to the light from your triangle with your Solar angel and soul that this light entered the core of your brain cells and enlightened you? What if your nervous system director began transmitting your soul's higher image of you (your healing hologram) to all the cells in your nervous system? Imagine what these shifts would mean in your life.

6. Now it is time for the healing angels to come, to begin spinning out cells that cannot handle the higher light and are creating obstructions and to bring in new subatomic building blocks for new thinking cells. The angels of divine love on the rose hue are here first to build a bridge between the director of your nervous system and the director of your circulatory system. Imagine this line of light taking form now that connects these three centers—your crown and brow centers with your heart center. Imagine the healing angels surrounding you with a

mist of silvery rose as an ongoing nutrient for your nervous system to bring you a sense of peace, serenity, and inner stillness.

7. The angels who work with your brain are on the yellow and gold rays of Solar light. They are very highly evolved. They are clearing the carbon that fatigues your brain so your brain cells can receive more oxygen. The colors they are using are helping to reorganize the patterns so they can resonate with your soul. The angels are adding color where it is needed and brightening colors that are dim. The violet, rose, and green angelic healers may also come to heal the symptom you are working with.

If your nervous system is overstimulated by the environment, the angelic healers will use a beautiful hue of green or blue to bring it into balance. If your creativity has been obstructed by some belief, they will touch your mind and inner eye with a silvery yellow gold so that you can see as your soul sees and hold the vision that carries the light of your soul. This can also improve your physical eyesight.

8. Now these angels are using sound frequencies to clear out old beliefs, thought patterns, and memories—whatever holds you back. You can assist this healing by releasing the sounds that have not been fully expressed. Sigh, moan, chant, or sing any sounds that want to come out. These may begin with a sad or angry tone, or with a whining tone. But as these denser frequencies are spun away through sound, the sounds will come from a finer frequency and become increasingly beautiful. They will become so pure that they echo the sounds that the angelic healers make as they work with the director of your nervous system.

9. Imagine your inner ear being stimulated so that you can hear the messages of your soul. Feel the angelic healing sounds moving into your brain from the left side to the right side of your brain and back again. Feel them moving from the top to the bottom of your brain to reach the network of tiny

strands of light that underlie each nerve plexus. Repeat this process two or three times. Tune to the purest sounds in the universe now, and listen for a beautiful note that comes to you from your soul.

10. Imagine the billions of nerve cells that lie on each side of your spinal column lighting up as if receiving a gentle charge of energy. From the base of your spine to the top of your head, feel the healing angels working. Send this healing energy through your brain, down your neck and shoulders, and down your spinal cord to the last vertebra of your spine. Bring the energy down your legs to your feet and into the Earth.

11. Ask your director to begin evolving your nervous system to match the rhythm of your soul. Let your director help align your brain with the vibration of your soul. Imagine moving as the soul, thinking as the soul, speaking as the soul. Imagine this director being illuminated with light pouring in from your Solar angel and soul now. Imagine this director able to keep you in communication with your soul and Solar angel.

12. Make a picture in your etheric body above your head of a lotus that has one thousand petals. Visualize the golden light of your Solar angel and soul vibrating these petals as they work with your director to help it evolve. Imagine just how much difference it would make if your nervous system were in perfect balance, your brain acting as a clear receptor for your soul and for the wisdom of the universe. Imagine what you could do with an illumined mind that combined knowledge in a creative way and helped many, many people. How much would your life change if the future stood revealed before you? Imagine how these changes would add meaning and purpose to your life.

13. Now bring the director of your nervous system to meet with your inner healer to bring your soul's vision for your evolved mind to you. Hold your pictures of an evolved nervous

system in your mind so they can give you ideas and suggestions of your part in creating these changes.

- Ask what changes in your lifestyle will help create a better memory, clearer focus, and closer connection with your soul.
- Ask where you are presently misusing energy. The right use of energy day after day will give your director the greatest possible support in healing, balancing, and evolving your nervous system.
- Ask what foods will nourish your brain and whether you need special supplements to adequately nourish your brain, especially if you are forty-five or older.
- Ask what kinds of activities will be most restorative to your brain and mind. Include the amount of exercise, sunlight, and sleep.
- Ask to recognize any decisions you are making that limit your director from rejuvenating your nervous system.
- Ask your inner healer and your nervous system director to show you your next step in aligning your brain with your higher mind and soul.

14. Open to a deep sense of gratitude for the light being held on you to stimulate your mind and bring it to the next level.

15. Set up a signal with your director to show you when you are overbalanced with mental activity. Ask for a reminder if you get overly serious and forget to laugh, or if you are missing the beauty around you of sparkling sunbeams dancing across the Earth. Keep in mind how you will rebalance your schedule when you get this signal. Whether you decide to relax your mind by listening to angelic music, a guided meditation, or simply sitting beside a fountain and listening to the water flowing and splashing, be sure that you honor your commitment to take some action.

Chapter 15
Healing Your Respiratory System

Your respiratory system provides your lifeline to exuberant health and vitality. It sends fresh oxygen into your blood every second. The oxygen passes through the tiny membranes of your lungs to your circulatory system and then travels into every tissue and cell through your bloodstream. Your cells breathe the oxygen and release carbon dioxide as they take another breath, just as you do. You can expand the capacity of your lungs to absorb more oxygen to keep your body youthful and vitalized all through your life. Oxygen energizes your body, clears obstructions, retards collagen breakdown, and prevents premature aging. With sufficient oxygen charged with life energy from your soul, your body is purified and wastes are efficiently eliminated. Germs, viruses, parasites, fungi, yeasts, and plaque in your arteries are destroyed. Oxygen can improve or heal sluggishness, candida, edema, heart disease, tumors, and autoimmune diseases. A good respiratory system can carry the oxygen to lift depression and bring vitality to the mind and body. It eliminates the chronic oxygen starvation of tissues and cells from which many people suffer.

When you evolve your respiratory system by adding light to its director and cells, you can tap into an inner core of energy, and find the confidence to speak truthfully, express yourself powerfully, and become poised and at peace with your world. You can become highly creative and speak from love and an inner strength in ways that heal yourself and others. You can develop new artistic skills in painting, drawing, making music, or writing.

When Your Respiratory Director Needs Help

Problems in this system include upper respiratory tract infections and nose, throat, sinus, and larynx dysfunctions. The most common infections are the common cold, tonsillitis, laryngitis, and coughs or croup. Lower respiratory tract infections affect the trachea, bronchial tubes, and lungs. These can cause pneumonia, bronchitis, and asthma. Other respiratory problems include shallow breathing, fast breathing, or anxious breathing. If you have sore throats, a hoarse voice, difficulty swallowing, goiter, bronchitis, coughs, asthma, allergies, or frequent colds, your respiratory director needs help. Toothaches, gum problems, flu, a stiff neck, and an overactive or underactive thyroid are other signs that the director of your respiratory system is overworked.

To heal problems in this system, the angels will help you claim the courage to act on your higher intuition and to express your deep feelings so that they are heard. This courage gives you the freedom to take conscious breaths of joy and love that can loosen congestion in your lungs and bronchial tubes. Breathe several deep and slow breaths right now, think about your will to be as healthy as you can imagine, and you can feel your energy level start to surge.

The Breath of Healing

To communicate with the director of your respiratory system, you will use the note of your soul. You can breathe so that this celestial note is broadcast by your Solar angel and reverberates through your lungs and entire respiratory system. As you read, imagine that the note of your soul is permeating the room where you are sitting now and calling in the angelic healers.

Two circumstances help heal your respiratory system. First, your body needs good air, as clean as you can find. Chronic coughs, sore throats, and asthma may clear up when you are breathing air that is not contaminated with pollutants. The ideal health-giving air is uncontaminated by chemicals from industry and automobiles and free of toxins from people's fears and anxieties. The next major vitalizing agent for your respiratory system is creating a finer essence quality to the air. This allows each breath to energize and regenerate you more fully.

Finding Healthy Air

A fifty-year-old NASA scientist thought he must be getting too old to run, but when he moved out of a metropolitan area and into a quiet, rural region where the air was very pure, he found that he could run as well as ever. The toxic air in the metropolitan area was part of the problem, not his lungs' capacity to get oxygen to his body and brain. The toxic psychic atmosphere of mass fears and worries was the other part. Think about the air you are breathing, about how fresh and pure it is or isn't from physical and emotional debris.

Imagine what you can do to raise the quality of the atmosphere you live in. If you are living or working in a highly polluted area, begin visualizing living where the air is purer. These images will open a path for you to live where the air is better. Hold an image of people and industries reducing the pollution on a global basis, so we can all breathe cleaner air.

Spend as much time outdoors as you can. The Earth has a magnetic field that is quite healing and revitalizing. A weekend or even an hour in nature can stimulate many levels of healing. Being in nature is especially energizing if you tend to be fatigued or have headaches. You can lie on the ground to absorb the Earth's energy. Being in nature purifies your respiratory system. All healthy plants, trees, and flowers also produce subtle healing energies. The air is continually cleansed and recharged by the plants and trees. Wrap your arms around a stately tree, and bring its energy into your body. If you can't get into nature on the physical plane, or if you are living in a polluted area, consider using an air purifier in your home.

Raising Air Quality

The second aspect of healing your respiratory system comes from your love for your soul and for all the people who are evolving themselves with light and love and service— your extended family of spiritual brothers and sisters. A great inpouring strength comes into you through this love. This sets up an essence quality as you breathe that strengthens your respiratory system and extends your active and healthy life. This love enables you to draw from the air the sound frequencies of the angels of divine love and of your Solar angel. Your breathing deepens and comes in all by itself, at its most healing depth and pace.

An artist experienced years of coughing problems until she worked with the director of her respiratory system. She learned to slow down and look at her life. She saw that her pressured lifestyle had closed parts of her lungs off to avoid seeing what she didn't want to see in her life. She was afraid to listen to her inner healer for fear it would tell her to make changes she wasn't ready to make. When she realized that serious respiratory illness could result if she continued this lifestyle, she saw how deeply she loved her soul and her life, and she took action. She went to a homeopathist for assistance and also worked with a therapist to dissolve the fears that were short-circuiting her life energy. She exercised by walking at least half an hour each day. She began to create time for solitude to be with her soul and to link with her spiritual brothers and sisters (her soul group) on the inner plane. Her annoying cough cleared up, and she is still receiving even greater rewards – including greater productivity with less effort, the ability to speak up and honor her own intuition, and the capacity to be with those who can see and honor her as a soul.

Regenerating Your Respiratory System

1. Go into the most restful, restorative wooded area that you can imagine on the Island of Regeneration. Wade in the mountain stream, and fill your lungs with fragrances of lilacs blooming nearby. Smell the fragrance of the pines and wild orange blossoms. Feel the texture of the trunk of a special tree, and absorb energy and strength from it. Sense how deep and

secure its roots are, nourished by the nutrients of the earth. Watch the tree synthesizing the sun's vitality to feed itself with light.

2. Connect with your Solar angel and soul to form your triangle of light. Let this sparkling light flow into your heart center and throat center to the director of your respiratory system. See these rays of golden light illuminating this director, who is in charge of your higher creativity and closely connected with your circulatory and nervous system directors.

3. The angels of divine love are coming in through your triangle now to heal and help evolve your director. All the lighted love this director receives will be sent to your thyroid gland, larynx, sinuses, throat, and lungs to regenerate and add light to their cells. Feel these angels around your throat and heart centers as they work with the director of your respiratory system.

4. Other angelic healers are coming now to add iridescent colors to your respiratory system and thyroid gland. Let these colors move into your throat. They may be golden, blue, green, yellow, or violet—each hue iridescent and slightly silvery. Breathe these colors into your sinuses and lungs. If you don't have a sense of special colors, imagine a white light that has all the colors within it.

5. The healing angels work with sound and vibration next. Imagine that you can sense them singing in beautiful celestial tones and melodies as only angels can. Imagine this music moving into your lungs as you breathe and circulating healing vibrations into your bloodstream and to every organ, tissue, and cell in your body.

6. Imagine how creative you can be in regenerating your life energy and using this energy to bring a form to something that you value deeply. Imagine how what you create will sparkle and become a beam of light. Visualize angels clearing your sinuses and your throat of congested energy, bringing oxygen

to your cells. See this oxygen revitalizing and rejuvenating your whole body. See yourself speaking with confidence from the life energy this oxygen brings, expressing your knowledge and wisdom clearly.

7. See yourself consciously loving your soul as it comes closer to you and teaches you. See yourself able to love others with wisdom and compassion. See your life centered around the work that has true meaning to you. These pictures create the blueprint that is part of your healing hologram. They empower the angelic healers and your soul to transform your respiratory system and your throat center to hold more light. Project these pictures to your director and your inner healer.

8. Now bring your inner healer and director together to answer your questions and show you what is needed from you to heal and evolve this system. Ask everything you need to know. Think of the problem you are working with in this system. It might involve your thyroid gland, larynx, sinuses, throat, or lungs. The angels will help heal this problem first.

- Ask for your breathing to be free and natural, unhindered by fearful emotions that have restricted it in the past. Ask that memories be erased to free you from the past and bring you in close touch with your highest purpose for this year.
- Ask to see the location of any obstructions that block the flow of oxygen in your body.
- Ask your director to show you how to breathe to fill your cells with life energy and how to breathe to inhale the joy of the angelic healers.
- Ask how you can help vitalize your respiratory system and what foods will be healing to it. Find out if any foods are causing allergic reactions.
- Ask about what kind of exercise will open your lungs to receive more oxygen.

- Ask in what ways the director of your respiratory system is handicapped by your holding back what needs to be said or by your talking too much.
- Ask about solitude and how much time with your soul and Solar angel will best evolve this director.
- Ask to see areas where you can speak with words that are healing to you or to others.
- Ask to see any inner conflict that prevents your lungs from receiving enough oxygen. Ask if you need an outside healer to assist in this healing.
- Ask which quality will help the angelic healers to revitalize your respiratory system, considering qualities such as vitality, cheerfulness, joy, love, energy, harmony, or beauty. Mix this quality into the air around you to bring it into your lungs. You may sense a light and happy feeling with long-lasting effects.

When you work with the angelic healers to rebalance and evolve this system, you may notice feelings coming to the surface that had been hidden from you. If you let these feelings emerge and flow, your breath will also begin to flow through your whole body as it did when you were an infant. (Breathing tends to get constricted as one grows older in an effort to suppress what one does not want to know or feel.) Observe how much stronger and more courageous you feel when you sit quietly and breathe deeply for ten minutes and let feelings that are suppressed come into the open. Observe how quickly these feelings can flow through you like leaves fluttering from a tree on a winter day to make room for the new buds of spring. ("Ah, there's a yellow one, there's an orange one, there's a green and yellow one.") There is no need to examine these leaves closely; simply observe them, and then focus on the new buds forming. In the same way, take the position of an observer, and allow all feelings to flutter out of your mind and body ("Ah, there's a feeling of anger, there's a feeling of superiority, there's a bunch of feelings—jealousy, envy, fear, selfishness, and so forth"). Then focus on the new budding feelings that now have a place to sprout. Now experience the light-filled oxygen filling your lungs. Do not be surprised if you notice an immediate sense of new vitality and optimism about your life. You have cleaned house through your breathing and opened to a closer contact with the pure joy of the angelic healers.

Chapter 16

Strengthening Your Immune System

The director of your immune system works through all your energy centers to protect your body from potentially harmful microscopic life forms, such as bacteria, viruses, and fungi. If these manage to penetrate the outer layer of your skin, your white blood cells attempt to destroy them. If this line of defense is unsuccessful, a second line of immune defense, called your adaptive immune system, adjusts its response specifically to stop the invading organisms. It stores the memory of this invader so that defenses can be rallied instantly in the future. The system director plans a strategy to dispose of the invaders, orders extra immune cells, and goes to work. If the microorganisms return, these scouts move quickly to surround and digest the cells that are out of tune with your body. Your T-cells cause the molecules of the virus to collapse. The action ends almost as suddenly as it began. The strategy of your T-cells is quick, clean, and focused.

Your immune system director is in true service to you, always alert to form a cushion of protection from invading organisms. When your immune system is in top form, your health is so well protected that you are not even aware of a potential invader, and you experience no symptoms, no fever, no aches or pain. Your director handles the situation so smoothly and rapidly that your heart never skips a beat. Immune system scouts and workers are produced in the right balance with ample reserves for any possible emergency. The rapport between the director and its teams is very clear. The director activates its memory bank to find the antibodies and enzymes needed to digest the new invading bacteria.

When your immune system is filled with the light of your soul and Solar angel, it becomes even stronger so that it can keep your body so clear that your body does not go through normal stress patterns of fighting off a potential disease. It thus remains relatively unaffected by normal aging processes.

When Your Immune System Director Needs Help

There may be occasions when your director needs help from you and the angelic healers. For example, your immune system scouts may be putting out too many fires at once to catch a foreign invader before it gets established. These scouts may be handicapped by too many antibiotics, heavy metals, radioactive materials, or accumulated doses of medicine. Symptoms of immune system stress include diseases, illnesses, viruses, fungus and parasite infection, premature aging, depression, fatigue, irritability, and other negative emotions. A disease or an infection can only take hold when your immune system is unable to protect you against it. In some cases, the immune cells begin attacking the body's own proteins by mistakenly identifying them as "foreign." This can create an autoimmune disorder, such as arthritis, allergies, lupus, or multiple sclerosis. If you are sick or about to get sick, bring the healing angels to your immune system first.

Finding the Emotions That Damage Your Immune System

Any emotion that blocks your happiness can weaken your immune system. Underlying unhappiness and negative feelings work against a state of health. An underlying sense of cheerfulness fosters the natural state of health. Both kinds of emotions, lighted ones and dense ones, begin on the emotional level and then move into the physical level. They either strengthen your immune system or weaken it. Irritation is an emotion that creates toxins that can weaken the immune system. A bad temper, when one reacts with fury when things do not go as desired, can create headaches and spew poisons into the atmosphere. These subtle toxins weaken the immune responses of others as well as one's own immune response. Bad temper can come from learned roles as a child from a parent, and it can also come from eating the wrong food, living the wrong lifestyle, and setting up the wrong sleeping patterns for your soul's purpose.

Feelings of being mistreated and misunderstood can create toxins in your bloodstream. Pent-up energy from having to be silent or feelings of powerlessness can also weaken the immune system. Self-pity can overwhelm your natural immune protection. Intestinal problems, indigestion, and head colds may result. Feelings of being trapped or exploited can cause chronic bronchial infections, stomach ulcers, and teeth or ear problems. Constant introspection can cause liver problems and indigestion. Most of these emotional reactions are subtle. They may be hiding in your cells rather than expressed. Either way, they can seriously weaken the immune system.

Expressing Deep Feelings

Your inner healer can help you find a way to express your deepest emotions and free yourself from an enforced silence. When you release pent-up emotions and establish the habit of independent action, you open a space for the healing angels to heal your body. Many times, correcting this kind of stress is the single most important action you can take for the director of your immune system. These patterns of reacting to situations in ways that compromise your immune system nearly always can be healed much more quickly and thoroughly with the help of a good therapist rather than by blaming someone else and insisting that he or she change. With good therapeutic assistance, you can eliminate negative patterns of reacting and build in new, positive, health-giving patterns. Then if the same situation comes into your life again, you can respond to it from a clear and calm awareness of your soul's higher destiny for your life. The chances are that the illness will not reappear, because the fuel or energy that once inflamed those emotions within you is now being directed to your triangle of light and transmuted into a finer energy.

Vitalizing Your Immune System With Positive Emotions

If you want new ways to respond to challenging situations, ask the angelic healers to work with your emotional body to strengthen your immune system. Calm emotions, backed by the desire to be harmless, plus the will to help and heal the world, bring the inner harmony that strengthens your immune system. Jovial, confident, optimistic, and en-

178

couraging emotions heal disease; they rejuvenate your whole body. Illness, even common illnesses such as colds and sore throats, are unlikely to take hold when you feel cheerful and content. Cheerfulness gives you a light spirit, a healthy sense of humor, and a sense of positive expectation. You gain the confidence to accept whatever may come.

Even when you have steady and smooth emotions, it is still important to your immune system that you have the high moments that completely release tension through delight and play. Build delight, laughter, and joy into each day. Begin with making a clear picture of what these light moments would be like. Call someone who recognizes and honors the sun within your heart. Do one thing this week that you have never done before. Reach past the boundaries of your daily routine to recognize the sun shining from within.

Vitalizing Your Immune System With the Correct Diet

Besides creating a cheerful emotional base, you can help the director of your immune system by eating the right foods for you. No diet is right for everyone. Even your own best diet shifts at different stages of your life. After you decide on the correct diet for yourself now, find the best quality of that food available. Get organic vegetables if possible. Find out when they are delivered and pick them up that day. The food that still carries the vibration of the Earth and sun in it has specific healing energies. The angels can transform this energy for your body to use. Processed foods have only minute amounts of life energy left, and they cannot help your immune system to evolve. A thirty-five-year-old realtor was bringing the angelic healers through her triangle of light every day, yet she was still having difficulty healing injuries, bronchial infections, and gum disease. When she communicated with her director, she could see that toxic chemicals in her cells from medically prescribed drugs were creating ongoing stress in her immune system. If they were released too quickly, her inner healer showed her that her immune system would be overstressed and the DNA of the cells would be affected. The DNA is the genetic code for health in the center of each cell. It is like an inner computer program that determines the work to be done by each cell. This woman realized the angelic healers needed better materials to work with, that she had to change her diet to the foods and supplements that would bind with the chemicals in her body and gradually cleanse them from her system. Over the next several months, she rebuilt her immune system. First, she studied how foods heal, and then she selected a balanced macrobiotic diet of mostly grains and vegetables. Her infections all healed, and she feels like a new person.

Vitalizing Your Immune System With Sunlight

Your director needs the angelic substance that comes from the sun to be fully vitalized. Each wavelength of the sun's rays has unseen nutrients that exist beyond the physical light of the sun. The sunlight vitalizes your etheric body, which in turn vitalizes your physical body. It keeps your hormone rhythms synchronized, stimulates your pineal gland, and vitalizes your metabolic and hormonal balance. Sunlight penetrates into your tissues to irradiate the blood in your capillaries, which are near the surface. It helps stimulate the production of red blood cells, influences liver metabolism, and vastly increases your ability to eliminate toxic chemicals. Sunlight also helps your levels of calcium and potassium to stay in balance. It helps protect your teeth and balance your insulin. Sunlight can lower cholesterol levels, lower blood pressure, and help prevent osteoporosis. Depression responds immediately to sunlight, as do other interfering emotions. Sunlight also stimulates your pineal gland to secrete its hormones of melatonin so that deep sleep can take place. A single exposure to sunlight can boost your immune system; however, frequent showers of sunlight are best.

Whenever you can, go out in the morning sunlight and bathe in it. If the sun feels good to your body, get into the sun each morning. Since your body can store sunlight nutrients, twice a week of sunlight may be enough to keep your immune system supplied with its beneficial rays. If the sun is too strong, go into open shade under a tree.

Vitalizing Your Etheric Body With Sunlight

You have three receptive points where the angelic substance in the sun's rays vitalizes your etheric body – between your shoulder blades, above your solar plexus, and above your diaphragm. These receptive points may be shrunk from years of being covered with clothes; however, they can become receptive again by gradual exposure to the sun. To receive its vitality, let the direct rays of the sun reach these points. These points are more receptive when your spinal column is in alignment. This is an area you can correct through exercises such as yoga or with the help of a chiropractor or other professional healer.

With the increasing intensity of the sun, carefully select the time of day and the length of exposure to the sun. Begin with very brief periods of sunlight early in the day, and add a few minutes more as your body is receptive. Fifteen minutes of sunlight is a true tonic. Avoid middle of the day high-intensity sunlight so that you do not get sunburned. Too much sun can weaken your etheric body and cause it to lose resilience or to vibrate too rapidly for the physical body. Too much sun causes your etheric web to become too thick for your Solar angel and soul to reach your physical body.

If you are working in an office or other indoor environment, install full-spectrum lighting at work and at home. Regardless of how bright fluorescent lights may be, they do not contain the essential nutrients that your body needs. Certain colors are missing, which can throw your systems out of balance.

Vitalizing Your Immune System With Sleep

Good restful sleep is another essential agent for a healthy immune system. Set up a quiet and dark sleeping room. Your pineal gland needs total darkness to secrete the hormones that produce deep and restful sleep. Sleep outdoors whenever possible and comfortable. The Earth's magnetic field of energy is particularly healing to your body. Sleeping close to the ground is especially revitalizing because the Earth's vibration is weaker indoors. One man who had very low energy learned from his immune system director and inner healer that his sleep wasn't deep enough to restore his body. His mind was too full of too many thoughts; he needed sessions of solitude, long walks alone, or a quiet room to find himself before he went to bed. This man found these changes so energizing that he went on a solitary retreat for four days, sleeping outdoors on a nearby mountain and hiking during the day. When he came back, he began sleeping better than ever before. He felt completely restored. Now he goes on a retreat every few months to store the pure energy of trees, mountain streams, wildflowers, and sunshine in his body again. You don't have to go into the mountains to restore your immune system, but if you find an opportunity to be in nature even for half an hour or so, you may find that you can sense the angelic healers more easily in this kind of solitude and beauty.

Sleep is easier when your mind and body have a regular time to turn off at night. Before you go to sleep, fill the room with your golden triangle and ask your Solar angel to be with you as you sleep. If you have trouble going to sleep or if you wake up during the night, spend that time with the healing angels. Nightly repairs to your liver, gallbladder, pineal gland, and other glands take place in the early hours of the night while you sleep. If you go to sleep at 10:00 P.M. each night, you are available for healing from the higher teachers and the angelic healers. They begin around 11:00 P.M. and work while you are in the deep sleep beyond the dream state.

Vitalizing Your Immune System Through Oxygen

Oxygen purifies your cells and destroys germs, viruses, parasites, yeasts, and plaque in your arteries. It energizes your body and clears obstructions. People who are overweight or who have candida, arthritis, chronic fatigue, multiple sclerosis, or AIDS may need more oxygen in their cells. A lack of sufficient oxygen in the cells can create a sense of depression and heaviness. Through regular exercise and visualizing a greater supply of oxygen to reach your bloodstream and cells, you are preparing a healing path for your angels to fortify your immune system. Through this action, you are saying to these angelic healers, "Come now with your healing colors and sound into the center of my cells." When you are exercising, especially when you are doing aerobic exercise, by thinking of the angelic healers, you call them to you and the extra oxygen you are processing gives them an excellent medium with which to offer healing to you.

Vitalizing Your Immune System by Doing What Brings Meaning to Your Life

Besides food, sunshine, exercise, and sleep, your immune system becomes stronger almost immediately when you are doing what brings meaning to your life. You learned about finding those things that give meaning to your life when you worked with your will to be well in Chapter 2. Review this chapter to get new clarity about the goal of what you want to do as you gain more energy. A man in his early fifties asked his director to show him how to strengthen his immune system. He swam and worked out in a gym several times a week, yet he was catching every new virus strain that went around in his community. He imagined his immune system as a rosebush. When he visualized the rosebush, he was surprised to sense that it had no roses in bloom. His inner healer and the director of his immune system suggested that he greet the sun each morning as the first rays of the sun appeared. He did this and discovered an extraordinary new connection with his Solar angel. He could sense this angel coming to him through the first rays of the sun. Then he took quiet walks in solitude before going to work. Four weeks later, when he visualized his immune system rosebush, he could see rose-buds forming all over it. Three large red roses were fully open. His immune system had responded fully to the power of his greeting the sun as it appeared each morning. He needed more than the exercises to keep fit; he needed the energy of the rising sun and the joyous solitude of walking in the early morning. Not only did his bouts with viruses end, his spirit lightened. A small change, yes, but through honoring the simple advice that came to him, this man created a strong immune system and a happier life.

Raising Immune Systems for Groups

An executive accountant began creating a mist of joy and love around her staff of six in the office. Each morning she set up an atmosphere that was filled with beautiful colors. She selected the colors that were calming or energizing, depending on the group needs. Any employee who was ir-ritable would receive rose as the woman brought in the an-gels of divine love. The irritation would dissolve. She called this process "fluffing up their auras." Sick leave soon went down dramatically. The staff began to love coming to work. It soon became evident that the colors brought in through her golden triangle had strengthened their immune systems. The presence of the angels gave everyone protection that winter from the colds and viruses that were rampant in other offices. Try this simple procedure for any group to build in group protection from harmful bacteria and from harmful emotions.

Healing and Evolving Your Immune System

1. Stand under the sun in the courtyard of your Temple of Healing, and take a shower of light.

2. Create a triangle of light with your soul and Solar angel and bring its illumination into you. Visualize this spiritual stream of energy flowing from your triangle to vitalize the director of your immune system. Imagine this director absorbing and integrating this light and becoming stronger and wiser in creating immune cells that can handle any invading bacteria.

3. Imagine what it would be like if your immune system could stop all unfriendly bacteria from multiplying in your body. What if this director had the resources to purify your bloodstream, your liver, your glands, and your kidneys effortlessly so they did not deteriorate or age? Imagine what you could do with your life if you were in excellent health year after year.

4. The angels of divine love are coming first to work with the director of your immune system. Visualize these angels surrounding the director, touching each of your energy centers, and upgrading your immune cells to show a higher path to perfect health.

5. Many angels are bringing translucent colors now to cleanse and purify your immune system. Imagine a golden orange hue flowing over this director and all the immune cells. Visualize the angels using a beautiful blue-violet color as an antiseptic to any infection, virus, or parasite in your body to heal it.

6. Angelic sounds are reaching the director now to strengthen your immune system. Sing or chant the sacred word AUM in a strong voice to help this director loosen any parasites that do not belong in your body. Sound AUM again, and visualize your immune cells cleaning up toxins in your body. Pronounce AUM a third time very softly to assist the angels in bringing to your

director the substance to create more intelligent and efficient immune cells. Visualize the healing angels evolving your immune system so that it offers complete protection to you.

7. The angelic workers take their cue from the blueprint you project to them. Focus on how your body will be when it is functioning perfectly. Think of what it would be like to have the endurance to do all that is truly important to you. Visualize your body healthy and clear of any infections at age ninety and ninety-five. See it strong and vital, alert and graceful, supporting your work and your life. Imagine this system being rejuvenated year after year, working in perfect harmony with your other systems.

8. Now bring your inner healer to the director of your immune system so that they can decide how you can best assist in strengthening and evolving this system to fit the blueprint you are visualizing.

- Ask for specific suggestions of foods that will strengthen your immunity to disease, such as fresh garlic and onions, foods with zinc, and so forth.
- Ask about the appropriate sleep patterns to build a finer immune system. Again, be specific about how many hours and which hours are important.
- Ask about getting more oxygen in your cells. If they need more oxygen, ask about a regular exercise program for this.
- Ask how you can best receive the vitality and immunity that direct sunlight offers to you.
- Ask to be shown emotional reactions that handicap the director of your immune system.
- Describe the goal that gives your life meaning to your inner healer and the director of your immune system. Ask for refinements in this goal to make it a more powerful healing agent.

187

9. Let the director and your inner healer communicate to you as you make notes. Resolve to do all you can to provide the materials this director needs for your immune system. Be alert for more ideas over the next week.

10. See your whole body with an aura of health and vitality. The changes you are visualizing are being received as you send them to the director. They will continue to unfold over a long period of time.

Chapter 17

Regenerating Your Endocrine System

In this chapter, you will be working with the angels as they heal and regenerate your endocrine system. The seven glands of this system are the key transmitters of spiritual light from your etheric body to your physical body. These include the pancreas, the gonads, and the pineal, pituitary, thyroid, thymus, and adrenal glands. They set the tone for your life experiences. No one has a perfectly evolved endocrine system at this point in human evolution, but you can do much to help the director to strengthen this system. As your endocrine glands become more evolved and in balance with one another, you can experience excellent health as well as an underlying sense of serenity, enthusiasm, joy, and love. You will have a calm and composed emotional body, displaying courage and the desire to serve.

How Your Endocrine System Evolves

The stream of spiritual energy from your soul and Solar angel helps evolve this system. These glands are the tuning keys, the driving forces of your body. When they are healthy and balanced, they secrete the frequencies of your soul through their hormones. They secrete these hormones directly into your bloodstream to enrich your blood with a living energy. It is not necessary to focus directly on your glands to heal them. The angelic healers do this. The best way to heal and evolve these glands is to connect with the endocrine director and let the angelic healers use colors, sounds, and light to do the healing. Your director and inner healer will show you what you can do to have an endocrine system that has the sparkling light of your healing hologram. They might tell you to connect with the angels of divine love frequently through bringing a certain color or beautiful music into your environment. They might suggest that you create affirmations as part of your role in helping to balance these glands. Or you might see that you need to be fully honest about who you are and why you are here. You cannot fool the endocrines. You must be completely honest with yourself and with everyone else to keep them healthy.

The Role of Your Endocrine Glands

Pineal Gland

The pineal gland is a very small cone-shaped gland located deep within the brain, just above eye level. An active pineal gland brings you illumination. It also brings greater immunity to disease, promotes youthfulness, and improves your sleep. You have been gently stimulating this gland through the triangle with your Solar angel and soul. As the golden light of your triangle flows through your crown center, your endocrine director stimulates this gland to become more active. Sunlight also stimulates your pineal gland. When it is stimulated by inner or outer light, the pineal gland produces melatonin, which helps strengthen your immune system and purify your bloodstream. Problems caused by an inactive pineal gland are insomnia and a lack of higher intuition and spiritual connections. If you believe this gland needs to be more active, sound the A-El-I-O for love, and repeat the second syllable, "El," several times. This helps build a direct link to your highest source of light. Thus, it activates your pineal gland on very subtle levels.

Pituitary Gland

The pituitary gland is a tiny structure that lies just below the optic nerves in a cavity of the skull. It is called the master gland because it controls the activities of other endocrine glands. Your pituitary gland secretes hormones that stimulate your adrenal glands, thyroid, and reproductive organs. Through this master gland, your pituitary acts as the director of your whole personality—body, mind, and emotions. It works with your inner healer from your brow center. If you have problems with the adrenal glands, thyroid, reproductive glands, or kidneys, the pituitary gland may need strengthening and healing first. If it is not functioning well, ask your endocrine director for assistance in this chapter's guided meditation. Sound the third syllable of A-El-I-O to stimulate this gland. Sound the "I" (pronounced "ee") from your brow center. The director of the endocrine system receives this vibration and transmits it to the pituitary gland, which produces hormones and places them directly in your bloodstream.

Thyroid Gland

The thyroid gland is located in the front of the neck, just below your voice box. Its two sides look like two wings of a butterfly. It handles your heat production, bone growth, calcium balance, and metabolism. It also affects the menstrual cycle and the amount of fluids in the body. If you are experiencing low energy, if you are tired, have dry skin, hair loss, weight gain, or oversensitivity to cold, this gland may be understimulated. If your life feels too intense, your thyroid gland may be overstimulated. An overactive thyroid can cause anxiety, panic attacks, palpitations, sweating, weight loss, and diarrhea.

The director of your endocrine system works with your thyroid gland from your throat center. Visualize this gland handling your heat production, bone growth, and metabolism with ease. Imagine it being so perfectly balanced that your metabolism is in your soul's rhythm, bringing you the energy you need and enhancing your longevity. Imagine its hormones going into your bloodstream and generating an internal heat in the center of your cells that gives you greater immunity. Visualize your bloodstream being permeated with the high frequency that these hormones bring. It thrives on a calm and poised emotional state, on words and thoughts that carry light. See your thyroid gland sharpening your memory and thinking processes. If your thyroid gland is out of balance, focus on it as you meet with your endocrine system director in the guided meditation in this chapter. When the angels work with this problem, they will help distribute the energy more evenly between the director of your endocrine system and all the other directors. Bring the angelic healers to this part of your endocrine system. They will bring new energy to it through colors and sounds. Focus on the last syllable of A-El-I-O, sounding the "O" several times to help the angels stimulate this gland.

Thymus Gland

The thymus gland strengthens your immune system. It has two lobes and is located in the upper part of your chest, behind your breastbone. It produces the hormones that play an important part in your body's defense against infections. As your spiritual stream of energy increases, this gland is activated. It evolves through the higher love that flows through your heart center. If this gland is underactive, focus on it as you meet your director. Bring the angels of divine love into your heart center. Chant or sing A-El-I-O as if your soul were sounding it through your voice. Focus on sounding the first syllable from your heart, "A" (pronounced "ah"), to stimulate the petals of your heart center to open and energize or regenerate your thymus gland.

The Pancreas

The pancreas lies behind your stomach and secretes digestive enzymes to break down carbohydrates, fat, proteins, and nucleic acids. It produces insulin to regulate the level of glucose in your blood. Sugar, alcohol, and drugs can damage its ability to function. Your endocrine director works with your digestive system director to heal and evolve your pancreas. If you have problems with digestion or low or high blood sugar, focus on this gland in the following guided meditation. Bring the angelic healers to your solar plexus center, and visualize these two directors repairing and regenerating your pancreas, keeping your digestion, glucose, and blood sugar levels totally balanced and healthy. To help regenerate your pancreas as the angelic healers work with it, sound the A-El-I-O of divine love and repeat the syllable "A" several times. This helps it to link with the divine love of your Solar angel in your heart center. This vibratory sound soothes and calms your pancreas and brings it a new vitality.

Gonads

The reproductive glands—the testes in males and the ovaries in females—are regulated by the hormones released by the pituitary gland. The director of your endocrine system works from your sacral center to regenerate this gland. If this gland is not receiving energy or is overstimulated, focus on it in the guided meditation. Ask your endocrine director and your inner healer what you can do to assist in vitalizing or rebalancing this gland. Whether you are trying to conceive and cannot, or you are having menstrual, menopause, or prostate problems, work with the angelic healers by repeating the "O" several times after your soul sounds A-El-I-O to link your two creative centers (throat and sacral) and help distribute the energy between these two glands (thyroid and reproductive) in perfect harmony.

Adrenal Glands

The adrenal glands are located on top of the kidneys on the right side of your body. They provide energy, maintain

194

blood pressure, and balance the salt in your body. If your life has been stressful for a period of time, your adrenal glands may be exhausted. To heal and restore these glands, bring the angelic healers to the director of your endocrine system in your solar plexus and base center. If you want to increase the light in these glands, ask the angels to help you raise some of the energy in your base center to your crown center. Build a connection between the director of your nervous system and the director of your endocrine system. They can work with your adrenal glands to regenerate and purify them. To assist in their regeneration, sound the word of healing love, A-El-I-O, and focus on the "El" by repeating it several times as you work with the angels of healing to bring this gland into harmony with your crown center.

Healing and Evolving Your Endocrine System

1. Begin by going to the Island of Regeneration and to the Temple of Healing and taking a shower of light and colors.

2. Create a golden triangle with your soul and Solar angel. Bring this golden light from above your head to the back of your head and down your spinal cord to touch each energy center lying an inch or so behind your back. Your endocrine director uses your seven major energy centers to evolve the seven major glands.

3. As you direct the golden light to these centers, visualize the director of your endocrine system receiving it and transmitting sparkling light to your pancreas, your reproductive organs, and your pineal, pituitary, thyroid, thymus, and adrenal glands. See these glands producing hormones in perfect timing and sequence. Visualize the hormones carrying the signature

of your soul—its color and note. See your soul's life force keeping you young and naturally healthy.

4. Briefly recall any glandular problem you have, and then imagine new energy and health flowing into you to balance this gland with your other glands. Visualize this gland or glands actively supporting your other systems. If all glands seem healthy, imagine them evolving into a higher vibration of energy and light.

5. The angelic healers are coming through the light in your triangle now to assist your director to vitalize and rebalance these seven glands. The angels of divine love appear as you attract them with the sounds of spiritual love, A-El-I-O. Bring these sounds through the love in your own heart, and speak them aloud softly seven times, focusing on one gland each time. This helps the angelic healers to charge these glands with spiritual love.

6. Angelic color treatments for your endocrine system director and glands are next. As the angelic healers begin, they use a golden orange to clear out any obstructions in these centers so the pure colors can reach them. Some glands are now receiving stimulating colors to bring more energy to evolve them. Other glands are now receiving cooling colors to bring them into balance and allow some of their energy to be used by a center that needs it. Imagine each gland immersed in the perfect hue and tone—radiant blues and greens for overstimulated glands, and rose, yellow-gold, or orange for understimulated glands. If a gland is seriously out of balance, the healing angels may use violet or yellow. Give permission for these colors to cleanse, heal, and evolve your glands.

7. Healing frequencies and sounds are now being brought to each gland. Sound the note of your soul to bring your mind and body into a more receptive state for this angelic healing. Use the sacred word AUM silently or aloud as you visualize this healing vibration permeating every gland that needs healing.

8. Imagine what it would be like if your endocrine system were so evolved and balanced that your moods, emotions, and energy levels were in perfect alignment with the spiritual frequencies flowing into you. Imagine having the energy and calm spirit to do what is important to you, with a balance between the knowledge from your intellect and the love from your heart. Imagine what you could do with your life if your pineal gland were fully activated and transmitting the light of your Solar angel into your bloodstream, and if your pituitary gland were sending the light of your soul into your bloodstream. Visualize what your life could be like if your thyroid gland were consistently elevating your moods, your thymus gland bringing spiritual love to your heart and circulatory system, and your pancreas receiving love from your heart center and transmitting this love through its hormones to nourish your body. Imagine what your life would be like if your two creative centers were linked. Imagine the director of your endocrine system linking the reproductive organs in your sacral center with the thyroid gland in your throat center, your higher creative center. Imagine how much more powerful and productive your creativity could be with both glands in perfect balance. Imagine the energy you would save if your adrenal glands were completely vitalized and healthy, illumined by the light of your Solar angel and soul. Visualize them able to protect you in an emergency, yet in such perfect balance that you would not be distracted by fears that overstimulate your adrenal glands. Instead, you would respond to all challenges with wisdom and a calm poise.

9. See your whole endocrine system illuminated. See each gland related to the others as in a close and loving family. Hold this part of your healing hologram of a perfect endocrine system up to your endocrine system director. Bring your inner healer and this director together. Let them show you the part

197

that is your responsibility in this process of regenerating and evolving your endocrine glands.

- Ask about the best diet and supplements to heal any gland of your endocrine system. If you are working with a specific gland, ask about that one.
- Ask about your thoughts and about how to live in your daily life what you believe to be true.
- Ask about creating the atmosphere that is naturally regenerating to these glands—in lifestyle and in goals and life purpose.
- Ask if there are special needs you have overlooked.
- If a gland is not functioning well, get information about its needs on the physical level. It takes both spiritual healing and physical action to heal and regenerate any system in your body.

10. Imagine every gland being cleansed, cleared, and rejuvenated. Focus on your endocrine system working in perfect harmony with your soul's purpose.

11. Review the action that you learn would assist your endocrine glands to be energized and healthy. Be alert for other ideas that may come to you over the next week.

12. Offer sincere gratitude for the work of the angelic healers. The changes will continue to happen over a long period of time.

Chapter 18

Healing and Rejuvenating Your Other Systems

You now are familiar with the steps to regenerate and evolve the directors of your key systems and connect them with the angelic healers. You now know how to begin getting the information you need to support all the healing and the purification that the angels are stimulating. You can use these same steps to meet with your other systems' directors, going through each of the seven rooms of the temple and bringing the spiritual processes of healing to each director. You can meet with and learn from the directors of your digestive, muscular, skeletal, urogenital, and elimination system. You can also bring the angelic healers to more specific areas, such as your eyes, your ears, or your skin, to learn what you can do to help regenerate that area.

Your Digestive System

Your digestive system includes your liver and pancreas, as well as your digestive organs. If you are having any difficulty in this system, you can help by connecting with the director and calling on the healing angels. The director of the digestive system may be overwhelmed, as it tries to work around the dull colors that worry, anxiety, and stress bring in.

Any stress can feel like hunger even when the body doesn't need food. The hunger may be for the gentle healing light of your Solar angel rather than for food. If there is any chance you are eating more than your body actually needs, ask the director of the digestive system to remind you before you have consumed too much food for it to handle well. Ask for assistance in discriminating between true hunger for the body and hunger from the heart for spiritual light and spiritual love. By connecting with your triangle before you eat, your sense of hunger may lessen. You may also realize that the craving for some foods has been an attempt to find a substitute for experiencing a deep and profound love of your soul. As you increase the soul's flow into your whole mind and body, you may be surprised at how moderate your appetite will become. As you eat less, you will want to choose the foods you do eat by how much life energy they contain.

Honoring Your Director's Guidance

When you consult with your director, you can learn which foods have life force and nourish your digestive system. A musician was shown by his digestive system director that he was eating too much chocolate, too many raisins, and too much sugar. His inner healer suggested leafy green vegetables and rice for a gradual release of the toxins from antibiotics for previous infections and from meat that contained antiobiotics, which he ate for many years. After a few false starts, this man has now shifted his diet to one without sugar, chocolate, or raisins and has eliminated his earlier digestive problems altogether.

Allergic reactions to food may affect your moods more

than your body. By working with your digestive system director and your inner healer, you can find the foods that help heal this system. Observe, listen, and honor the information that you receive. Your healing hologram contains a blueprint for a perfect digestive system.

Digestive problems are frequently a symptom of too much energy congesting the solar plexus center. If you have digestive problems, you can help your digestive system director by raising the energy from your solar plexus to your heart center. This helps you to feel calm and centered and find your inner strength and power to develop your real purpose. If you want to evolve your digestive system, make a connection with its higher corresponding center. To do this, link your solar plexus energy with your heart center as you pronounce the word AUM.

Transferring Energy From Your Solar Plexus to Your Heart Center

1. Pronounce AUM as you inhale, and imagine bringing the energy from your solar plexus to your heart center. Your heart center has the higher frequency of love which is the most beneficial to your solar plexus center.

2. As you exhale pronounce AUM a second time, and dedicate this energy to serving evolution through the vibration of divine love.

3. Repeat this a second time. Do not look for immediate results. If you do this every day for nine to twelve months, you can bring about changes in your emotional states and reduce the stress in your life. You will be able to live with greater poise and serenity, and thus heal and rejuvenate your digestive system as a side effect.

Your Reproductive System

Your reproductive organs, the ovaries in women and the testes in men, are fed by the energy in your sacral center. This is the center where your reproductive system director is energized. Problems in this center might center around your ability to conceive if you desire to or around problems in the ovaries or testes. Sometimes energy builds up in this system and causes congestion. If you want to relieve this director from an overstimulation of energy or to raise the light in this system, you can lift the surplus energy to your throat center. When you meet with the director of this system and with the angelic healers, use the sacred word AUM, and dedicate the energy you are bringing to the higher corresponding center. It is not necessary to know which form this creative energy will take.

Your Muscular System

Your muscular system not only gives you mobility, dexterity, and expression, it holds your bones in place. This director needs to get oxygen into your muscle fibers. This means that your bloodstream needs to be charged with oxygen at all times. Problems in this system may stem from muscles that do not get enough oxygen or are not used enough to keep them supple and strong. When you communicate with your muscular system director, ask how much weight-bearing exercise you need to keep this system healthy. If you have muscular problems or weak muscles, work with your inner healer. Emphasize your muscles in your hologram, and show it to this director. Ask for the angels of the violet hues to help you

202

heal and strengthen your muscular system. If there is any infection or disease in your muscles, bring all the angelic healers in through your triangle of light so they can begin healing and regenerating your muscular system to complement any outside healing you are receiving.

Your Skeletal System

The director of your skeletal system provides a strong, stable, and mobile framework for your body and muscles. Your skeletal system supports and protects vital organs, such as your brain and spinal cord and your heart and lungs. It produces blood cells in the bone marrow and acts as a reservoir for essential minerals. Problems in this system might be bone cancer or osteoporosis (loss of bone density), bone fractures, or aching bones. Humans tend to develop osteoporosis if they live long enough unless they take measures to prevent it. In this denser level of your body, you must supply the materials needed for good bones – minerals, calcium, and daily weight-bearing exercise. The angelic healers can only help you when you are doing your part. Learn now how to keep your bones strong, throughout your life. As you reach one hundred years old you can still go on hikes and be active. Read and find out how much walking (or other weight-bearing exercise) is necessary each week to keep your bones dense enough to support your body fully. Find out the diet and amount of the minerals and the calcium needed to prevent osteoporosis. Start now. If osteoporosis runs in your family, your action is very important. Visualize yourself at age ninety-five with a beautiful posture. Meet with the director of your skeletal system, and hold up an image of your body with very strong bones all of your life. Ask your inner healer and your director to show you what to eat and how to exercise to maintain strong bones. Loss of bone density rarely leaves warning signals until a fracture happens. Watch for new studies on bone density, and put the best ideas into practice.

With the guidance of her inner healer, an eighty-year-old woman who had serious bone loss was able to increase her bone density every year through walking and using natural progesterone and vitamin and calcium supplements. Several years later, she had achieved the bone density of a forty-year-old. Another woman began walking fifty minutes a day every day because her director showed her it would save her bones from becoming porous. Her bone density increased dramatically by the end of a year. Another woman changed her work habits when the director of her skeletal system told her to get out of her office and find something to push against. "Your bones are strengthened by pushing against gravity – walking or doing push-ups or sit-ups. At least every few hours, push against something." Once this student began communicating with her skeletal director, she stopped worrying and took the action her director recommended. She began stretching exercises and walking every afternoon for forty-five minutes regardless of how busy she was.

Your Urinary System

Your kidneys lie underneath your liver and spleen. Their function is to regulate the blood and eliminate waste products. They also control the balance of acid and alkaline, produce the hormones that regulate the production and release of red blood cells from bone marrow, convert vitamin D into an active hormone, help regulate blood pressure, and promote the reabsorption of salt and the excretion of potassium in your body. If you have problems with your kidneys or bladder, work with the director of your kidney system. If you have a kidney infection, ask your director to help you find the best healer to assist in clearing this problem when you go through the steps of healing and regenerating this system. Your director may help you determine what kind of healer to use—such as a doctor of medicine, a doctor of acupuncture, a doctor of homeopathy. Bring the angelic healers to add healing colors and sounds for your kidneys. Confer with your inner healer and director on what you can do to help heal this system. Ask about water—how much to drink, how pure it needs to be, and which periods of the day it will serve you best. Ask about purifying your kidneys with food, supplements, and other nutrients. If you want your kidneys to work perfectly for your entire life, ask about diet, especially about the right amount of sugar and salt to eat. Get current information on both conventional and alternative treatments for your kidneys.

You have now finished working with the directors of your systems. To create your own guided journey for the systems in this chapter, follow the sequence of steps in the circulatory or other system journeys. You are ready to learn how to rejuvenate your whole body, to become younger, more energetic, serene, and poised so that you can focus on what you love doing most.

Part Four
Becoming Younger

About Part Four

Now that you have begun healing the systems that need healing, you are ready to bring your whole body to a higher frequency of sound and color, to rejuvenate your body now and in the future—ten, twenty, or more years from now.

You will be learning in these chapters to perceive your body as quantum physicists see it—as tiny particles of substance that are moving at lightning speed, appearing and disappearing, changing form from moment to moment. Physicists would see your body as a river that is always moving and changing; the body you had when you began this book would appear very different from the body you have now. The tiny particles (or molecules) that make up your body have already disappeared, and new ones have taken their place.

Becoming younger not only means that you *look* younger to your friends, it means that you *are* younger from within. You will plan a personal program of rejuvenation with your inner healer. This program can change your body at the cellular level and transform your cells to hold more light. You will learn what it takes to create a long life in which your body stays healthy, flexible, and fit. You will think about how to transform your emotions and your mind to clear, focused, and creative instruments that serve your true purpose throughout your life. You will also learn how to reverse damage from an accident, an illness, or a chronic problem.

Chapter 19
Choices That Keep You Young

Practicing external techniques does not produce rejuvenation. However, when good nutrition, exercise, and vitamins are added as the effect of inspiration and a higher vision of how much is possible in your life, they can play a major part in your rejuvenation. Choices about taking care of your body are much easier when they come from the revelations of your soul. These revelations increase your will to take control and change whatever your soul and inner healer show you is blocking your life-renewing stream of energy.

Your next step in rejuvenating yourself will never be a mystery. It will be brought up right in front of you by your soul. Whatever conflict you are facing right now—in a relationship, work, family, or health and vitality—is the next step in becoming younger. Begin with any friction that comes up, and create harmony out of that conflict. The process to do this begins with seeing new choices and choosing the path of light above all else.

Think of one or two major choices you have made in your life that turned out very well. Take a few minutes to notice how you made these choices. Did you take a long time to decide? How did you know when you had come to the wisest decision? Did you try out other ways and then decide on that choice as the best way? Did you get other opinions and then set those aside to make your own decision? Did the results of this choice make a big difference in your life? Did you get energized as you began carrying out this choice? Inspired? Creative? Did you experience a greater sense of being in control of your own life?

The choices that inspire you are the choices your soul stands behind as the sponsor. Your soul brings you the energy to do whatever it takes to carry them out. It gives you intuitive ideas and guidelines and offers you the boldness you need. If you get distracted, your soul inspires you and keeps reminding you to stay with it. Carrying out this choice might involve many years, such as the choice to have a child, start a business, or educate yourself for a new career. With your soul as sponsor, you have the perseverance and courage to continue acting on this new choice. The choice may also be one you can carry out in a month or so. As long as you make a choice freely and know it to be your own decision, the result of your choice can bring waves of rejuvenation to you, in spirit, body, and mind. Your wise and conscious choices provide the dynamic energy that rejuvenates you.

Major choices have enabled you to take important steps on your life path. You probably considered such choices in your mind for some time before you made a decision. You probably imagined what the outcome would be and perhaps shifted the choices around until you could imagine getting the success you wanted. You have every right to choose to wait before you make important choices. One woman waited eight months before she chose a healer to treat her rheumatoid arthritis after conventional medications did not help. She chose well. This doctor was instrumental in assisting her in a complete recovery.

Inspired Choices From Higher Dimensions

Now that you have built the connections to your Solar angel and soul, and to your inner healer, you don't have to wait so long to get to the point of choosing wisely. You can make the choices that your soul is sponsoring and energizing without long periods of searching for the best decision. You can become aware of its inner guidance opening up a new future for you. While you may need a period of time as you take all the steps in this decision, your overall direction will be clear and compelling.

A woman in her late fifties made such a change. She was meeting with her Solar angel and soul every morning in meditation and then going about her work as usual. One day while she was preparing lunch, she was surprised by a completely unexpected inner message that her metabolism was slowing down. Next, a clear picture flashed into her mind showing a woman growing old in mind and body, becoming less and less active. She made a choice right then to take this inner message seriously. She read about metabolism and learned about ways to improve it. When she realized that metabolism meant how efficiently oxygen was converted into energy for the body, she decided to work through exercise to raise her metabolism. She joined a local health club. For eighteen months, she went three times a week to boost her aerobic and endurance levels and raise her metabolism. She hired a coach to teach her which machines she could most benefit from and how to use these safely. Now, five years later, she continues to be more energetic than before, and thus she retains her youthful energy and clear mind.

At a key transition point, you may suddenly recognize

211

that you can do much more than you thought to rejuvenate and evolve your body, to slow or reverse aging, and to enjoy life to the very last moment that you have a physical body. You may become aware that you are "writing" the age of your body with the choices that you are making each day. As you recognize that you are choosing moment to moment what you are doing with your time and how you are living, you are free to make new and wiser choices.

You have the power and the light to make all decisions that affect your body. Instead of saying to yourself, "I don't want to do this, but I don't have any choice; I have to do it," you can say with honesty, "Doing this is absolutely my best choice for now—considering all the circumstances—my expectations, my experiences, my hopes, and my fears. As these change, I can make a new choice." When you can say this, you have just opened the door to new choices.

Taking Action on Insights

A forty-year-old teacher from England wanted to rejuvenate herself, but she hadn't been able to get her body healthy enough to focus on getting it younger. She had been in a healing crisis for years, with a series of chronic complaints. She couldn't understand why she couldn't get herself well—until she was clearly shown what the underlying problem was. She describes her startled reaction: "How could I have ignored all these symptoms for so long! The headaches, earaches, teeth problems, general fatigue, digestive problems—they were there all along. My soul had to show me that I am not helpless, that this is not the inevitable result of getting older. It was as if I woke up from a deep fog. It was as if some-

212

body lifted a veil, leaned over, and showed me the slowly degenerating state of my body and what to do about it. I saw for the first time how my cells look even though I am eating an excellent diet of vegetarian food and working with Solar light every day. The only thing is that I love sugar, and I consume a lot of it."

Her inner guidance showed her two paths. One was a path of slowly disintegrating health, and the second was a path leading to the body of a twenty-five-year-old, if she did everything she knew to rejuvenate her body for the next eighteen months. She was then shown three stages of her healing path. The first was to regulate her blood sugar; the second, to clear out toxins and purify her bloodstream; and the third, to build in higher quality cells, using food, vitamin and amino acid supplements, and herbs.

After seeing these two paths, she made the clear and committed choice to take the path of rejuvenation, a path that had been there all along, but which she hadn't been ready to see. She read every book she could find on these subjects and realized that her immune system had been stressed for years from small infections. She consulted frequently with her inner healer on the practical details and started energizing her soul's vision for her in her hologram several times a day. She chose to get outside help to clear the infections, using acupuncture for the first six months and later homeopathy. Eleven months later, her chronic problems were healed, and her immune system is now working well. As a side benefit of letting go of all sugar, she has lost eight pounds, her skin is clear and youthful, and she is well on her way to the twenty-five-year-old body that was shown to her

The Importance of Common Sense

Sometimes you do not consciously recognize the choices that are coming to you from your soul. Instead, you wake up one morning, and you simply know that you need to make a new choice. It may seem like simple common sense as the silent voice of your soul awakens you to make a new choice about your life and your body that you haven't seen before. Your soul can show you how very important that choice is and how it will affect the rest of your life. The rest is up to you. If you become aware of needing to make a particular change, you can either ignore it or study the possible outcome of this choice. It is up to you to learn the possible consequences of not making this change and the rewards of making it. Next, learn the different paths of creating this change in your body. Study conventional medical interventions and alternative ways if you need an outside healer. You have free will to choose the way of health and rejuvenation or a path of gradual degeneration in mind and body. It is wise to act quickly when a choice is presented to you. Becoming younger isn't always something that you can put off. The sooner you begin, the easier you can make the great shifts.

For chronic problems, study the illness you have and educate yourself on all healing possibilities. Then ask your inner healer. This gives your inner healer more options to offer you. Once you have investigated every good choice for healing and connected with your inner healer, if you are still not sure, see how much time you have to decide without undue risks. Listen and receive each day. Then use your common sense to make a final decision. Your common sense will be infused with your soul's guidance. Then look for the

214

best doctor who is an expert in the therapy you have chosen.

Many cities have a support group for a number of illnesses. If there is one in your area, attend and meet others who are also studying the latest research on healing the illness you have. They may have information you have not found. They will certainly understand what you are going through and can reach out with encouragement and give you a loving hug.

A twenty-three-year-old woman made a spontaneous choice to stop smoking when she realized she couldn't ski down the mountain without stopping to catch her breath even though she was a good skier and in excellent physical shape. She was a chain smoker, and although chain smoking can be a very challenging habit to break, she stopped cold once she faced the damage that was being done to her body. In truth she had known about the damage of smoking for years. What happened was that she was suddenly face to face with the truth. She experienced the crisis so clearly of choosing between further degeneration or recovering her youthful lungs that she stopped denying that smoking would age her body prematurely. Standing on the side of that snow-covered mountain, she acknowledged what smoking was doing to her, whereas before she had ignored it. She then made the clear and committed choice to quit smoking and regain her vitality. She never smoked another cigarette. Since she was so young and athletic, she was able to regain her full vitality back in less than a year.

When Your Future Stands Revealed

The chance to see a potential problem or a slowly degenerating path may only come once. It is as if the veils are parted and you can see your future for one second. You are shown a picture of something you want to understand and are willing to act on. Once you begin thinking about rejuvenating yourself, watch for new insights and choices to appear. Many choices are far more subtle than quitting smoking or overcoming a sugar addiction. Some choices involve your state of mind as you eat or before you go to sleep. They involve the kinds of pictures you see all day—both pictures outside of yourself, for example, on television and at the movies, and the pictures you make on the screen of your mind. You are the only one who has the authority to make the choices between filling your mind with pictures that rebalance, heal, and inspire you and those that cause fear and anxiety to age your body. These choices can be as important to your rejuvenation process as replacing a habit of irritation with the habit of acceptance and appreciation.

If you feel pressured by others to look or act younger, any change can seem like too much trouble. When you see two paths in front of yourself, one of rapid aging and the other of becoming younger, change becomes an adventure, initiated by your own decision.

Your choice must be made with a sense of commitment behind it, not casually or automatically. Automatic choices are easily forgotten. Casual choices are dropped when a distraction arises. Once you make a very clear choice to take the path of rejuvenation, you begin finding the specialized information you need. Energy starts being released that was trapped in your muscles, nerve cells, joints, and arteries. As this energy bursts forth, you may wonder where it came from. You may still be living exactly as before, yet instead of having to push yourself to get going, something within you keeps taking you to the next step.

216

Getting Cooperation From the
Part of Yourself That Resists Change

Once you have made a choice that feels like your wisest path, you are ready to get the cooperation of your inner critic. Your soul does not criticize you. If it seems to do so, you are actually in contact with your inner critic, not your soul. If it should interrupt your soul contact, treat it as you would a child demanding your attention – with compassionate understanding and also with firmness. Your inner critic has many skills; put it to work where it is useful – for example, asking it to discriminate whether vegetables at the store are truly fresh or to gently remind you to slow down when you get in a rush. If any other sides of your personality are resisting your rejuvenation, win their cooperation. Once you have full cooperation from all sides of yourself, constricted blood vessels can open, sinus blockage can release, and nervous headaches can disappear. In Book I of this series, *Bridge of Light,* you can learn more about the parts of your personality that can sabotage your best efforts to change. You can understand your subpersonalities more fully and learn ways to gain their full cooperation.

Your Body Ten or Twenty Years From Now

Now you are ready to choose the age that feels "old" to you and make the choice to rejuvenate that part of your life. Think about your future, and select the age when you think that you will need to slow down or you picture yourself as an "old" person. This age may be ten, twenty, thirty, or forty years in the future. If you are thirty now and forty feels old, use ten years. If you are forty and sixty sounds old, use twenty years as you imagine your body in the future. Wherever your unconscious pictures decide you are old, you will be–in spirit, in mind, and finally in your body–until you change these pictures to reflect the vitality and radiance of your soul.

A forty-year-old psychologist playfully imagined what her body ten years in the future would be like and was shocked to sense her body slouched, flabby, and much older. Her chest was sunken and her shoulders rolled forward. This was not the body she wanted. She realized that she had been struggling too hard, working too hard, trying too hard, and that she didn't have to do this. She decided to be more fit in ten years than she had ever been. But when she checked in several months later, her future body had changed very little. She realized that she would have to make larger changes. After several months of a better diet, exercise, and relaxation time, she could still only see a slight change when she looked at her body in ten years.

Then she went to the Room of Images until her soul's radiant images of her came alive and she could look in the sparkling eyes of herself in the future and feel the energy of this self coming back to her. Getting younger at age fifty meant that she would leave behind the cells that couldn't evolve into greater light. As this happened in her soul's hologram, she realized that her body in the future had also shed several pounds and had become quite fit. She saw how simple her lifestyle could be for her happiest and healthiest life. She saw herself in ten years with abundant time to do the work she loved doing, writing and assisting others. She brought her future self close to her many times for a moment during the day. The hologram became brighter, more colorful, and richer in detail. She could sense its energy coming into her whenever she thought of it. She then made the changes she had not been able to make herself do before. She began eating well, establishing a good sleep schedule and exercising regularly. Now when she imagines her body ten years in the future, she sees a healthy, vitalized body that is graceful and strong.

In the guided meditation that follows, you will look at your body in ten or twenty years. The body that you sense then will help you to experience the two paths that are open to you. This experience provides the opportunity to make a committed choice to take this step beyond healing and actually begin rejuvenating your body now.

Choosing to Rejuvenate Yourself

1. Touch your forehead to take yourself to the Island of Regeneration and to your Temple of Healing. Take a shower of colors to clear your etheric body.

2. Create a golden triangle with your soul and Solar angel, and let this light flow into your mind and brain so that you can see your body in the future.

3. In the Room of Images, place a screen on the other side of the room. Put the date at the top of the screen when you think you will be "old." This may be ten years, twenty years, or forty years from now. Use any date you like.

4. Ask your inner healer to show you your body on that date. This will be your most probable body condition if you continue living as you are now. Bring this future body into a clear focus and enlarge it. Note its condition and energy, its posture, agility, spinal flexibility, skin, and eyes. Even if you don't actually "see" anything, your inner healer sees your body in that year and can impart it to you as you relax and open to receive. Is this body the body you want?

219

5. Describe what you sense about your body in the future, even if you think you are making it up. On a fresh sheet of your healing journal, write or draw the characteristics of this body.

6. Now ask to see the body you can have if you rejuvenate yourself now. Describe this body in your journal. Note its posture, grace, strength, and alertness.

7. Look at both descriptions of your possible body in the future, and make a clear decision of your choice. If you are choosing rejuvenation, ask for assistance from the angelic healers and your inner healer. Ask for a greater flow of light from your soul and Solar angel. Ask only if you are ready to follow the guidance that you receive from these higher dimensions of light. If you have more healing to do before you begin rejuvenating yourself, you can choose to wait until this healing is done.

Two or three times a year, look again at how your body will be in ten years or twenty years. This gives you plenty of time to take the action needed. You may only need to change one habit, or to replace an overcrowded schedule with a new schedule that is more balanced. Whatever you see as your first step, the angelic healers will come and assist you in making any changes that your soul energizes.

Chapter 20

Rejuvenating Your Body

Rejuvenation starts with opening the flow of spiritual energy. When spiritual energy flows in to your mind, you become inspired with ideas. You begin to interpret events differently. You have more insight into causes rather than only the effects. Spiritual energy sweeps out crystallized habits of thinking. When spiritual energy flows into your emotions, you have a sense of calm, with an underlying sense of cheerfulness and optimism. It drives out the negative feelings of self-pity and oversensitivity that cause hurt feelings. You develop a sense of beauty, delight, and gratitude. When spiritual energy flows into your physical body, your cells are able to hold more light. This is what rejuvenation is all about—solar light flowing into the whole personality. When you bring the light of your soul and Solar angel into your golden triangle, energizing changes inevitably happen.

A rejuvenated body needs very little attention. It frees you to put your attention on what you love most. As you rejuvenate yourself, you are purifying your body to handle the next level of light. You are bringing the light into your cells, which not only helps reverse symptoms of aging and gives you greater energy, but also lights up your life. You will be the first to notice when you have more energy, and you will be the first to benefit from having a body that is vibrant and younger than before. However, you will probably not be the first to recognize that you *look* younger and that your eyes sparkle and your face has a subtle glow. Nor will you be the first to know that your posture has become aligned and beautiful, or that your walk is more graceful. Your friends will notice first, especially those you haven't seen lately.

The year you were born has little significance to your true age. Scientists now measure your true age by your body's internal functions and the condition of your cells. This age can vary as much as twenty years or thirty years from your birth age. When your body and mind are rejuvenated with the light, love, colors, sounds, and wisdom of your soul day after day, your body is gradually transformed. You not only look younger, you are younger! Your mind becomes brighter and younger and sharper. Your emotions are more positive and caring. Your body is healthier, and you can live longer and more fully. You develop a magnetic center of energy that nothing else can give to you. You may feel the tingling sense of enthusiasm and the desire to learn new things, explore new areas of life – to actually become the person you always wanted to be.

Periods of Adjustment to Greater Light

Every time you move up to the next level of light, your body needs another level of refinement to stay in harmony with you. Think about the past ten years, and you may realize that after you adjusted to one set of changes and became somewhat comfortable again in your life, another set of changes moved in and you were challenged to make adjustments to these. Adjustment is what rejuvenation is all about – repeatedly adjusting your life and your body to a finer frequency of light.

Change is a sign that your soul is reaching and influencing you, urging you to move forward as quickly as you can adjust to the last expansion of light and love and prepare for the next expansion. Adjusting to changes means that you are responding to your soul, which is far ahead of your personality on the path of illumination and beckoning to you to follow. Each step forward into more light requires you to purify your body and emotions further. You want to bring your whole family of selves along with you—your physical body, your emotional body, and your mental body. Nothing is left behind.

True and permanent rejuvenation begins on deep levels and gradually works its way outward. Many times an automatic pattern is preventing your inner healer from adjusting your body to more light. The first step is to break up that pattern so that it will no longer override the soul's song as its energy flows into your mind and body. As resistance to the soul's higher note dissolves, dense cells are spun out, others are brought up to a higher center, and still others are lifted to a higher energy center to their next level of evolution. If a physical challenge comes, it may only be because you have succeeded in bringing in more light than your body was prepared to handle.

Recognizing and Assisting Periods of Adjustments

When the light flowing into you purifies whatever is in its path, your physical body has to make adjustments at a cellular level to accept this light. Adjustments are your body's way of purifying itself to be able to receive more light. You may find that you will make major adjustments to greater light more than once in this life, and many minor adjustments along the way. As you make each adjustment, the door of opportunity opens again, and more spiritual wisdom and love are possible. With each adjustment, you learn how to set up a finer harmony with the note of your soul. This harmony rejuvenates your body.

When an adjustment to greater light is made through your physical body, it can be completed fairly rapidly and cellular harmony restored again. If the adjustment does not reach your physical body, you make the adjustment through your emotional body. This adjustment can take more time; it requires you to develop an outgoing love that reaches across all boundaries created in the past. In both cases, the healing angels will work with you and accelerate this purification to bring your body and emotions into harmony with the higher light of your soul and Solar angel.

If one day you feel discouraged or too fatigued to think clearly, these may be signs that your body is going through an adjustment to higher frequencies of light. After this period of adjustment, an old symptom such as joint pain or indigestion has now left for good. As the rejuvenation process reaches deeper tissue levels, it may be clearing out an illness pattern that was suppressed with antibiotics rather than cleared out of your energy field. When the disease that has been pushed down meets your now-strong immune system, your immune system easily mobilizes to digest the unfriendly bacteria and clear your etheric body of its patterns. This time, if a symptom from your past emerges, it can run through its cycle quickly and leave. The symptoms may last only a short time.

Making the Right Decisions

The power of the angelic forces combined with your soul can drive out degenerating forces. During *all* adjustments to the greater light in your physical or emotional body, create your powerful triangle of transformation with your Solar angel and soul. They will bring in the angelic healers, who will use colors, light, and sound frequencies to upgrade your body. They will also inspire you to make the right decisions about how to assist. For example, sometimes you will realize you need to ignore all symptoms and get on with your work. Other times you will get a distinct feeling that you need to clear the congestion of light by sending it out to others. You will know that too much light has reached your mind and body without being circulated outward to the world. Occasionally you may decide that outside assistance is necessary and find the best medical or other professional intervention. During these periods of adjustments, you will also get tremendous support from your inner healer. Talk with your inner healer and ask for assistance in bringing your whole personality into harmony with your soul's note.

Lightening Your Burdens and Playing

Honoring adjustments is part of moving into your soul's rhythm. During a period of physical adjustment, *lighten your responsibilities and play* a little each day to fully absorb the higher light of your soul. These adjustment periods are shorter—often only a few hours or less as you learn not to stress your body when it is assimilating the higher light flowing in.

When rest has achieved its purpose and your body has

adjusted to the higher level of light, another, wiser part of yourself will begin reaching toward the next step. Use every opportunity to take this step—with angelic light in your heart and mind. If you are tempted to envy those who seem only to play through life, remember that they may need a long period of adjustment to integrate some major shifts they have already made. It is also possible that their play is a meditation. What looks like play to others may be their soul as a creative artist in action!

Expanding Your Sense of Humor

If you find yourself resisting the efforts of your soul to flow into your body or your life, you may see what is happening and yet not be able to stop it immediately. The push-pull between the wiser way and the familiar way can be either frustrating or amusing, depending on your sense of humor at the time. By allowing yourself to see the humor in these situations, you can move through them much more easily. The sense of fighting against another part of yourself actually energizes that part of you. Befriend the part that resists and create an alliance with it. Humor can establish cooperation when nothing else will. As you replace one habit of resistance with a wiser habit, the next one is much easier to uproot and replace with a wiser one. Gradually, your will to create a truly fit instrument for your soul becomes stronger than the desire for things that age your body and dull your mind.

If you find yourself in a push-pull between an old habit and the new way, go to your inner healer and talk. Get out two chairs, one for you as the questioner and one for you as the inner healer as you did in the Room of Wisdom.

Together you can create a plan that brings your mind and emotions and body into greater harmony. Make sure it is a plan that is practical and workable for you. But first, you may want to review the principles that create rejuvenation so that you can include these in your plan.

Principles of Rejuvenation With Light

1. *Harmony Within Your Body.* Rejuvenation is the result of eliminating friction between your cells, your emotions, and your thoughts. You become younger as you create harmony with your soul. Build into your plan of rejuvenation the ability to discriminate and the will to choose what creates harmony with your soul.

2. *Love That is Focused Upward, Outward, and Inward.* The simple act of loving your soul focuses love upward and rejuvenates you as much as any technique. It creates a beautiful pattern of light between your heart and soul. Your emotions begin resonating to your soul's light, its color, and its note. This is a joyful vibration, a note of courage that moves in to give you enthusiasm, love, and a larger focus in your life.

Love focused outward means that you care about others and that you hold them in light when you think of them. Love focused inward means that you are listening to your soul and the angels of divine love. You are looking into the future and sensing through your intuition how you can use your life energy to give something to others. All love is a powerful force of rejuvenation. The more people you include, the greater the force.

3. *Gratitude and Heartfelt Thanks.* When you are feeling genuinely grateful for your soul's presence and its guidance to illumine you, you are serving the plan of evolution—and as a side effect, you are rejuvenating yourself in body, mind, and

227

spirit! Remember to give thanks to the angelic healers. They have come many times when you did not know of their healing work with you. Let waves of gratitude flow over you to all the people in your life. Gratitude is a powerful rejuvenating force. It adds sparkle to your eyes and to your cells.

4. *Living in Your Soul's Rhythm.* You have already begun to live in your soul's rhythm with your golden triangle of light and as you have worked with the angelic beings. You may not realize how steadily you are already shifting your old rhythm of thinking and living to your soul's rhythm. This does not mean you will be giving up your job or your friends. It means your work and your friendships will become richer and more fulfilling.

Your soul has the perfect rhythm to continually rejuvenate your body year after year. Learn how to breathe and move and walk in your soul's rhythm. Imagine you are giving your soul complete authority over your body, and notice how much more graceful, balanced, and energized you feel. You can do this now as you read by imagining your triangle with its golden photons of light flowing into you. Read even more slowly—with your breath and your pulse slowing. Join your crown and heart centers with a line of light to your spiritual stream of energy. Pause for a moment and notice the expanded state of awareness that comes into your mind. You can let this state deepen as you read further. Bring this golden light into your mind, your eyes, and your throat. Feel these golden particles flow into your heart center. Imagine that you will know the best place to put your attention for the rest of the day and will continue allowing your soul's rhythm in your body even when you are focused on something else.

Gradually, you can expand these periods of experiencing the love of your soul flowing into you with your eyes wide open. Think back several years, and you may realize that you have been preparing for this shift for a long time. Your rhythm of living is probably different from even a year ago, and quite different from ten years ago. Imagine how imaginatively you can live in ten more years as you move closer to your soul's rhythm.

5. *Developing an Open Mind.* Can you imagine yourself even brighter, clearer, and more creative then than you are now? When your mind is connecting with your soul, your creativity is stimulated. Only the light of your soul has the power to transform your future. Solar light flows in and illumines your mind. Your thoughts have a different quality; they become steadier and more positive. You are more focused than before. This is also a state of rejuvenation, for you are building a harmony into your mind that reduces conflict and stress—two major stressors in aging.

Experiment with extending your healing hologram farther into the future. See yourself in this hologram during the last decade of your life, dynamic and healthy and high spirited as your soul intends you to be. Build into your hologram the face of a wise and loving person and the body of an active, healthy person. Imagine yourself having a conversation with this hologram of yourself. After you speak to it, let it respond and tell you something about how it achieved this state of rejuvenation.

As you build the skills to use your illumined mind to carry out your soul's pictures, you can ignore any other pictures of your possible future. Engrave your soul's hologram of you on the screen of your mind. You are exchanging a picture that had some of humanity's common fears in it for a much more beautiful picture that has the light of your soul illuminating it.

Train your mind to hold the future you want. One man had several layers of fears about aging. He thought he was getting old (he was forty-two) and soon would not have enough energy to really enjoy life. He felt the best of his life was coming to an end. One night he had a dream in which he was shown how rapidly this thought was aging him. It had seemed like a harmless belief, but its energy was reaching into his future and setting up limitations on how long he would have a youthful and energetic body in spite of how well he cared for that body. When he realized this thought alone was aging his body, he changed what he was saying to himself. He talked with people twenty and thirty years older than he who were healthier, more energetic, and more focused than they ever had been. Soon he developed a new image of himself at fifty, sixty, seventy, and even eighty—enjoying life with all the energy he needed to do what was truly valuable to him. If you catch yourself misusing your imagination, stop and acknowledge what this is doing to your body. Remember how loyal your body is to what you think and the words you speak! Play with creating the opposite image to any negative pictures in your mind.

6. *Sunshine, a Good Diet, Exercise, and Sleep.* Be outdoors as often as you can. Exercise not because you have to, but for pleasure. Every year you can have a new and improved body. Ninety-eight to one hundred percent of the atoms in your body will not be there next year. They are replaced by new atoms. The cells inside your mouth are completely new every two weeks. Your liver cells are replaced every six weeks. Your skin cells are replaced every month. Your bone cells are replaced every three months; your stomach lining, every five days; and your brain cells, every year. All of this happens automatically as part of the built-in program in your cells so long as nothing interferes with it.

Now you have the six steps to build into your plan of rejuvenation with your inner healer and soul. You are ready to draft this plan. Later, your inner healer will refine it even more. You may see more ideas and ways to get more information if needed.

Building Your Plan of Rejuvenation With Your Inner Healer

1. Bring in your Solar angel and soul through the triangle of light.

2. Open to the angels of divine love. Feel your heart center being vibrated and opening to release your innate healing power through divine love.

3. Open to the angels of rejuvenation as they use radiant transparent colors to create three concentric circles in your energy field. One color feeds and rejuvenates your physical body. The second color rejuvenates your emotions and gives you a tremendous sense of gratitude for all that is being done for you, for all that you are learning, and for your soul's redeeming power. The third color rejuvenates your mental body and removes veils that stand between you and your soul. This color vibrates your pineal and pituitary glands, stimulating and invigorating them to produce their hormones of youthfulness and vital health. Give thanks to these angels for upgrading your mind, your emotions, and your body.

4. The angelic healers are now surrounding you with three sound frequencies, one to bring your body into your soul's rhythm, one to bring your emotions into your soul's rhythm, and one to bring your mind into your soul's rhythm. These frequencies are all in harmony with the note of your soul. They are celestial sounds of exactly the tones and qualities that will bring harmony among these three parts of your personality and your soul. Listen with your inner ear, and imagine the purity of these sounds. They may sound like a delicate bell, a chime, or a flute. They are bringing your body in tune and eliminating

231

discordant notes that cause friction and aging. Experience this inner harmony building within you now.

5. Call your inner healer to illumine your mind with bright, clear pictures of yourself evolving into a more confident, poised, and creative person. Ask how frequently to focus on this guided meditation to energize your rejuvenation.

6. You are now vibrating in tune with your soul. The colors in your energy field are the colors of rejuvenation. Build in the physical rejuvenating agents now. See yourself getting the ideal food for your body type, and the ideal levels of sunshine, sleep, and exercise. See yourself building the light spirit that allows you to smile and laugh frequently, to be close to friends, to dance within to beautiful music, and to enjoy the delicate beauty of nature—the trees, the raindrops, the snowflakes, and the flowers.

7. Build the steps of rejuvenation into your hologram. See yourself living in harmony, your heart opening to love and to forgiving all mistakes, yours and others'. See yourself expressing heartfelt gratitude, living in your soul's rhythm, illuminating your mind with your inner healer, and providing the physical agents of vitality for your body. Take these one at a time and create a specific scene that embraces each one.

8. Imagine yourself right now surrounded by many good friends as you celebrate your one hundredth birthday. Notice what you look like and what you are doing at this party.

Now look at the pictures you automatically made of yourself at one hundred years of age. Were you sitting down? Then stand yourself up. Did you look weak or feeble? Then put some vitality into yourself at age one hundred. See yourself making a birthday speech with wisdom, wit, humor, and love. If this is too great a stretch in years, lower your projected age to seventy or eighty. You can rejuvenate yourself to match these pictures so long as you keep learning more from your soul or teaching others how to live more fully and joyfully. A 102-year-old physician, who still practices medicine, has rejuvenated herself to match her pictures. Another doctor, a pediatrician of ninety-two, sees his young patients each day. However, it isn't just your age that proves you have rejuvenated yourself. The quality of your life, your joy of living, and your fullness of spirit and of discovery are what count.

9. You can also anchor special experiences in your future—even your near future. You do it by playfully imagining them. Set up a pleasant surprise for three days from now. Imagine yourself as you awaken receiving energy and rejuvenating colors from the angelic healers. Visualize clear, translucent colors flowing into your body, going into the pores of your skin and into your tissues, organs, and muscles as you awaken three days from now. See these colors clearing your eyes, softening your skin, strengthening your voice. Mark the date on your calendar, and when that day comes, notice if you feel better than usual, even more energized, joyful, and balanced than you do now.

10. If you find yourself alternating between a positive and negative picture of your body in the future, explore these alternating pictures. Bring the negative picture in, look at it, fade it out, and then bring the positive picture in. Look at it, fade it out, and then bring the negative picture in again. Do this several times, giving no more than one or two seconds to each picture. Next, make the positive picture brighter and the colors quite vivid. Enlarge it to double the size. Add sound to the positive picture of your future and let it come alive. As the negative picture comes in, make it fuzzy, out of focus, and in black-and-white. Keep alternating the pictures until when the negative picture comes up, there is no image left on it—only a blank white card. Now merge your positive picture of yourself rejuvenated with your hologram and look at it until its light and colors are clearly imprinted in your mind.

Chapter 21
Raising Cellular Light

You are the ruler of a very large kingdom, and there are more inhabitants in it than the population of the entire planet—more than sixty trillion. All the cells in your body are your subjects. Their world is your body; you are their god. They evolve as you evolve. If they are not evolving with you, you are prevented from going farther; the inner conflict becomes too strong, and they cannot support you. Even though the consciousness of your cells is limited, they are serving and evolving to more specialized work as they move up. Your cells listen to and obey your thoughts and your words. These are their commands, their laws. They live according to the laws that you make!

Whatever you think about is broadcast to your cells immediately, and they loyally assume the same posture. When you speak negatively about yourself or your body, they respond. When you speak positively about yourself, they respond. The cells under every director are loyal, dedicated servants, working ceaselessly to match the commands you send to them, just as your directors are working ceaselessly to match the commands you send to them. So long as these cells live in your kingdom, they are entirely dependent on you for their life and their evolution, just as you are dependent on them to have a physical life on this planet.

Cellular Resonance With the Soul

Raising cellular light enables your body to handle more light than before. Your cells begin absorbing Solar light; they begin to have a bright center point of light. On the physical plane, raising cellular light reverses aging more than any one change you can make. You began to raise your cellular light when you first stepped onto the Island of Regeneration. The light you are bringing into yourself as you work with the angelic healers and your soul is already affecting your cells. The work you are doing with your triangle of light, the communication you are building with the directors of your systems— all of your new connections are systematically building new channels that raise your cellular light. Even as you read this chapter, you are building light-responsive cells and spinning out cells of lesser light. This is an ongoing process that will continue as long as you continue meeting with your soul and your Solar angel.

You can reach much higher in the spiritual planes when you raise your cellular light. As a larger percentage of your cells is able to hold more light, your systems and organs and glands begin resonating to the vibratory note of your soul. A harmonic resonance is set up that heightens their efficiency. Your whole personality can then resonate to your soul's clear note of love. This means that not only can you reach higher when you are meditating, you can also hold these flashes of illumination that come to you for longer periods of time.

Raising cellular light goes hand in hand with spiritual advancement. You can move to the next step on your path as larger percentages of the atoms, molecules, and cells in your energy field carry more light. Each time you form your triangle of light with your soul and Solar angel and work with the angelic healers, a higher voltage of energy circulates through your etheric body and through your energy centers. From there, this energy goes to your endocrine glands and blood-stream to bring Solar light to each cell in your body.

Building Solar-Lighted Cells

When you are bringing your soul's light into your life, cells that were adequate before you brought in so much light may become too slow and dense to handle the higher frequencies of light. They don't have receptors for Solar light and thus become inadequate for the greater energy flowing in. They can't create a youthful, vibrant body and mind. They have a limited span of reproducing with precision. The DNA in these cells, your genetic codes, begins to misspell the proper codes. These cells vibrate too slowly to be in harmony with your soul's vibratory note, but most of these cells can be transmuted into cells with Solar light as you work with the angelic healers. Cells that cannot be upgraded to fit into your new body are spun out to make room for the new cells that can. The process of raising cellular light is complex. Fortunately, you need not direct each step of this process. You only need to take the steps that make these changes possible.

Solar-lighted cells use new building blocks of subatomic matter. These cells sparkle like tiny suns. Their molecules and atoms vibrate with Solar light. These cells are resistant to disease because they are resonating to higher frequencies. Being in harmony with your soul, they do not wear out so quickly as Earth-lighted cells. These cells are more efficient; they have a longer period of dividing with precision than cells of a lower frequency. They build an entirely new type of body. When you have a certain proportion of Solar-lighted cells in your body, the vibration of your whole body is heightened. Your brain is more receptive to the soul planes, your heart is stronger, and your endocrine system becomes more active and balanced. Your arteries and veins tend to regain lost elasticity. Your oxygen intake improves, your memory clears, and your emotions become smoother and more positive.

Nourishing Solar-Lighted Cells

Solar-lighted cells are very discriminating cells and require a finer quality of food, sunlight, and oxygen. They cannot live on inferior nutrition, and they cannot thrive in dark places. They flourish with exercise that has a gentle, smooth rhythm, exercise that you find enjoyable. More than anything else, however, they must have the nutrients that only your soul and Solar angel can provide, the constant flow of spiritual light from the directors of all your systems and from your inner healer.

You are the agent to provide this channel of life force for your transmuted cells. You act as the agent by sitting quietly and creating your triangle of golden light with your soul and Solar angel. You do this when you recognize that the light you are bringing into the world is going to make a difference. You are motivated to work with your soul in response to its call to you—the call to embrace even greater wisdom and joy in your life and to pass that on to others in the best way you know how. Solar cells are created by those who are on a path of light—a path of service through light, love, and wisdom.

Emotions: Your Secret Agents of Cellular Rejuvenation

Your emotions color the energy that comes from your soul to your cells. When the emotions you experience are calm, clear, and light-filled, your cells are receiving soul light free of any obstructions. If your emotions are continually filled with regret of the past or worry about the future, their colors block out a good deal of the soul's light.

Your emotions are transferred to your cells by a chain of command that is virtually instantaneous. Your cells are so closely linked with your emotions that when you experience even a whiff of joy, your cells also experience joy. They are constantly responding to the tone of your feelings about yourself and your life. If you are in a state of lightness and good humor, your cells follow this pattern—they also become light and in good humor. They are calm when you are calm, happy when you are happy. When you are meditating, they are nurtured and in a state of peace. When you are acting with love, their aura expands.

Broadcasting to Your Cells

Whatever feelings of a positive nature you experience—hope, cheerfulness, optimism, or enthusiasm—are infinitely rejuvenating to your cells. These become the energizers of your cells. Each positive emotion carries a message to your cells. Laughter, for example, creates powerful immune cells, lung cells, heart cells, and kidney cells. Quite coincidentally, you are sending a command to your cells to become healthy and strong. When you feel love, the cells in your bloodstream receive a rejuvenating treatment. When you experience beauty, your skin cells are rejuvenated. Even if you only remember times when you experienced these emotions, your cells are rejuvenated. They are rejuvenated when you vividly imagine what it would be like to feel loving and grateful, to laugh, and to see beauty. Your cells do not distinguish between the past, the present, and the future. They are nourished by all such messages of delight and love.

When you fully realize this is true, you have a great motivation to build the emotions that are so transforming to your cells. You can create the feelings you enjoy most just by thinking of a time in the past when you had these feelings by imagining yourself with them in the future. Doing this begins bringing these experiences into your present. At the same time, you create a pattern that draws to you the most loving and joyful sides of others. You can restructure your emotional life and substitute light-filled emotions for darker emotions in any situation once you make the choice to do so. Even as this process is taking place, you start feeling more optimistic about yourself and your life. Your cells immediately pass the word around. You broadcast a new law for them that builds exactly what you want in your body.

A Journey to Evolve Your Cells

1. Go to the courtyard of your Temple of Healing, and take a shower of light and color. Take a deep breath, and pause as you make a triangle of light with your Solar angel and soul.

2. Let the angels of divine love bring deep shades of rose to touch each of your emotions. Sit with these angelic healers for several minutes.

3. Now visualize the angels sending green, blue, and lilac hues to lighten your emotions and add a sparkling quality to them.

4. The angelic healers are using sound frequencies now. Let these pulsing messages create a dance of love within the DNA of your cells. Imagine these sounds attracting the molecules that produce tranquillity, the molecules that give you energy, and the molecules that create a sense of joy. Pretend that you can sense these finer molecules giving your cells longevity, strength, and immunity to disease. Imagine them emitting the signals that transmute your cells in exactly the right sequence into Solar-lighted cells.

5. Let your inner healer show you how to support the work of the angelic healers. As these colors and frequencies of Solar light flow into your emotions and cells, they naturally create superior cells. See these cells multiplying and emitting a soft halo of light around your head and shoulders, around your chest, and down your arms.

6. Add this experience of your emotions and cells being transmuted through light, love, color, and sound to your hologram of rejuvenation. See your cells sparkling with light, radiating with a new longevity and vitality that will last your whole life.

Chapter 22

Reversing Chronic Illness and Accidental Injuries

If you have chronic problems, such as heart disease, arthritis, joint stiffness, or bronchial or glandular problems, you may believe these are permanent and irreversible conditions. This is only a belief. You can reverse much cellular degeneration, regardless of how serious this damage appears to be. You can also reverse damage from an accident. In this chapter, you will see how others have reversed conditions you may have always believed were irreversible, and you will learn how to do this for yourself. As you will see, this process is not mind over matter; it is a process of using spiritual streams of energy over mind and matter. Reversing damage is about freeing your cells from ancient patterns of reacting to shock and trauma.

Setting New Boundaries

Several years ago, a woman who was rapidly losing the ability to work, even to walk, from stiffness and swelling in her joints decided she would have to reverse the damage to her body through her own creative efforts—or else end up in a wheelchair in a few months. Her condition was worsening rapidly, and medical procedures were not working. Studying everything she could find, she put her whole self into reversing the damage to her joints that others said was impossible to repair. She did not know that she would succeed, but she had nowhere else to turn. She began by asking her soul and the healing angels for assistance. She started a practice of chanting and singing and meditating with her soul several times each day. Next, she began taking care of her body's physical needs by eating differently. Then she began clearing her emotions by standing up for herself and establishing boundaries in her life. She cleared her mind by deciding just how much responsibility she could handle and sticking to her limit, and by changing the negative comments she was making to herself about herself to conscious and positive statements about herself. She became receptive to her soul's guidance and took each step that came to her. She searched for six months to find a healer who could help her reverse this damage before she actually found the right healer. At first nothing changed. Then gradually her symptoms lessened, and at year's end her joints were almost free of pain, and she could walk better. The reversal of her symptoms continued until she was totally well again.

This happened eleven years ago, and today she is not only symptom free, but she is functioning above the level where she was before the arthritis began destroying her body. She is vibrantly healthy, youthful, and enthusiastic. This woman is running a very successful publishing company, keeping a balance between work and play. She only publishes the books she believes are both healing and transformative. She swims every day, eats a healthy diet, and meditates each morning and evening.

Clearing Emotional Toxins

Another woman took the healing with light course and reversed the damage to her body that had begun limiting her ability to function in the world. She had developed such severe arthritis in her hands that she could no longer open a door and had such stiffness in her knees that she could only walk with extreme pain. When her doctor couldn't find anything that worked for her, she began to ask for help from her soul. She was shown that her body was filled with a toxic substance that was created by an inner conflict. On the outside she had hidden the conflict, but it was so strong that her body had stored this conflict in her joints. From the moment she asked for help from the angelic healers, she was guided every day toward the next step in her healing process. Books came into her hands that showed her gentle water exercises for her hands and knees. She found guided meditation tapes on healing with light and listened day and night. Her body felt as if it was shedding heavy burdens. The swelling went down and the pain went away. She soon regained the full use of her hands and legs and is now free of all symptoms.

You can reverse the damage in your body as these women did by getting assistance in clearing out anything that blocks the healing light of the angelic healers from reaching your cells. If you have any disharmony in your body, consider it an invitation to work with the angelic healers every day—not just once in the mornings, but several times a day for a few minutes, and especially as you go to sleep. Use everything that gives you the support and encouragement to continue until your symptoms are completely reversed, such as meeting with a friend or a group with similar interests, reading spiritual books, or listening to meditation tapes.

Reversing Damage From Accidents

This next account of damage reversal is extraordinary. If you accidentally hit your head or leg or toe, turn your ankle, cut your finger, or stumble and fall down, you can reverse or dramatically lessen your body's natural response to the accident. The quicker you work, the more completely you can reverse the injury or wound and stop the pain. The process is simple and yet very powerful. Even though you may not need it now, keep this technique in the back of your mind so that you can use it if you should have an accident.

The first step to remember if you have an accident—major or minor—is that damage *can* be reversed when you take immediate action. Next, you will go back over the steps that immediately preceded the accident and change these steps to create an alternate reality in which the accident does not happen. This works best if you physically retrace your steps or body movements rather than simply imagining the new reality. You will work with the angelic healers to change the damage signals being sent through your nervous system and with your inner healer to imprint the new reality that reverses the damage.

One woman used this method after she sprained her ankle while hiking in the woods alone. At first the pain was so intense that she rocked back and forth holding her ankle. She knew she had to get out of the woods quickly while she could still walk, but she was in too much pain to stand. She created a triangle of light with her Solar angel and soul and was able to retrace her steps, carefully stepping around the hole where she had twisted her ankle. She gave her inner healer a new picture in which no accident happened. She felt skeptical, believing that once something happens, it's done and can't be changed. In spite of her doubts, she persisted, walking back several times to replay the new scene and create the new reality. When she finished, the pain was almost gone. She went home and waited for the pain and swelling in her ankle, but they never came. It was as if the accident had never happened. Her inner healer had accepted the new reality and repaired the damage in her etheric body before it actually damaged her physical cells. She realized the healing angels had a major role in this reversal, but they could not have been so effective without her willing cooperation to create and insert a new reality for her inner healer.

In another case, a man almost lost consciousness when he hit his head on the sharp end of a table. He remembered the technique of replaying the action and took his body several times through the correct way to bend down and miss the table. The pain quickly disappeared, and the big bump he expected never came. Another man cut his finger in the kitchen and immediately repeated the steps leading up to the cut to show his inner healer a new reality. The wound, which normally would have taken a few days to heal, immediately closed and healed so rapidly that the line where the skin had grown back together was barely visible the next day.

Some physicians have learned to speak with patients and convince their unconscious mind that the damage to their body after a serious burn or explosion accident is minimal and already healing when in fact it is very serious and would ordinarily take months or a year to heal. These physicians direct the patients' inner healers to begin reversing the damage and shrink the normal healing period. This has been done by physicians who specialize in reversing damage by changing what actually happened to a much more positive picture. Serious burns have healed rapidly that might otherwise have required skin grafting over a long period of time. Instead of third-degree burns, the damage can shift to first- and second-degree burns, which then heal quite rapidly. The physician may not consciously realize he is calling upon the angelic healers to work with the patient's inner healer, yet the angelic healers produce this extraordinary reversal of damage just the same. As the physician or healer brings the positive suggestion to the patient's mind that the healing will be rapid and that it is already happening, the inner healer of the patient works from these new images, just as you have been working with your hologram. With the help of the healing angels, the inner healer responds to these pictures as the truth.

You can learn how to reverse or to minimize damage from an accident in the following exercise. The process is simple and, like all healing with light, does not depend on faith or the belief that it works—only on your will to create a new reality and your connection with the angelic healers.

Reversing Accidental Damage

1. As soon as an accident occurs, apologize aloud to the part of your body that was injured. Apologize to the director of this system, to your cells, and to your inner healer. Tell them that you will correct the mistake. Do not blame the accident on the weather, the road, the path, or someone else. Take full responsibility. As you apologize to your inner healer, impress

246

upon it that you are taking immediate action to correct the potential damage. Take 30 seconds for this step.

2. Create your triangle of light with your Solar angel and soul. Take around 60 seconds for this step.

3. Replay the scene of what happened. Recall the first step that led to the accident, and begin replaying the accident scene two or three steps before the movement that caused the accident. Reenact the scene, this time playing it out where each step, each movement, is perfectly executed. Your balance is perfect, your aim is perfect, you step carefully so that there is no accident. Continue through this scene, adding a few more steps that fit in this new reality. Point the kitchen knife differently to slice the tomato if you have cut your finger. Or walk around the object that you tripped on. Place your foot square on the walk where you turned your ankle, and continue walking without turning your ankle. You are demonstrating that you understand now how and why the accident happened and that you now know how to do this task right, without an accident.

4. Go back to the beginning of the scene, and go through the new motions a second time with your movements perfectly timed and in balance. Act this scene out several times until the new reality seems almost as real as the one that actually happened. You are substituting this new scene as the reality for your body to respond to. Ask the angelic healers to use their knowledge of vibrating sounds, colors, and light to insert this reality into your nervous system as they erase the memory of the original accident.

5. Imagine the healers restoring your cells to normal to match the pictures of this new reality. See your cells responding to the accelerated restoration of the angelic healers.

6. Visualize the new reality as the blueprint for your inner healer and for the director of that part of your body to

copy. Imagine the original damage erased altogether or greatly
lessened.

While you may not fully understand how all of this takes
place, experience will show you that it does work again and
again. As you are playing out the new scene, there may be
a part of you that does not believe you can erase what has
happened. Ignore this part of your mind, and continue your
"play." Your rational mind will at least believe that your play
is a harmless fantasy. The most profound reversals come when
you can get into the spirit of play to see what will happen.
Once you see how much effect you can have by replaying
your actions, you will not have to experience a sense of help-
lessness after an accident. (If you believe you have fractured
a hip or other bone, or are seriously injured in any way, use
common sense and lie still until professional help arrives. In
this case, you can imagine the new reality several times without moving and still be able to prevent much of the swelling
and pain.)

Reversing an Oncoming Illness

You can also use this reversal technique with an illness
the first minute you feel it moving into your body. Frequently,
when an illness starts to take over, you have unconsciously
given permission for this to happen. At the time you gave
this permission, a brief illness seemed like a good idea–
perhaps to get you out of something you dreaded doing. The
type and severity of the illness will fit these needs perfectly.
A small need, such as a day to rest, may bring on a simple
one-day illness. A big need, such as the need to rethink your

finances, may call forth an illness of greater duration, perhaps a week or more. It is the resistance to doing these things when you are well that opens the door for an illness to happen.

A Journey to Reverse an Oncoming Illness

1. If you should feel yourself getting sick, instead of criticizing yourself for missing sleep or meals, letting your emotions disturb your body chemistry, or blaming someone for "giving" this cold or virus to you, make a new decision about being willing to be sick, and decide to reverse the oncoming illness.

2. Apologize to the director of your immune system for the confusion that you have caused by unconsciously agreeing to be sick and now changing your mind.

3. Look for the moment when you realized that you should be taking better care of yourself or when you became very angry or depressed about something—and didn't do anything about it. That was the moment you unconsciously gave permission to create an opportunity to work out a better way to handle something—while you were sick.

4. Make a deliberate choice to remain well. This means that you are willing to handle whatever you have been ignoring while you are well rather than having to be sick to learn it. If so, state your choice clearly and loudly or write it on paper. Explain that you are ready right now to spend the time and the attention needed to fill the needs of your body and emotions without having to be sick.

5. Acknowledge to the director of your immune system that you sent the wrong pictures and you want it to gather all of its forces to bring your body back into harmony.

6. Create your golden triangle, and open to the angelic healers of love, colors, and sound.

7. Ask your inner healer what you can do to boost its power. You may realize that you need to rest, get outdoors close to the Earth, or go on a day's retreat to read or do absolutely nothing.

8. As soon as you get a good idea of what is needed, shower and change clothes to get the "sickness" frequencies out of your energy field. Next, use your shower of colors to purify your energy field. Your body will get what it most needs one way or another, and it is more fun to take a day off to let your body and mind have a well-deserved break than it is to have to be sick to take a day off. If you are at work, and you don't think that you can go home unless you are really sick, tell your boss that you feel the beginnings of an illness that may be contagious and that you think you can reverse it if you leave for the day.

9. Create a hologram of yourself feeling well, vitally strong, and healthy later today.

10. Plan something very simple that you would truly enjoy in the next few days. The spirit of anticipation allows your inner healer to work with the director of your immune system to bring these pictures into your physical life.

Reversing Chronic Disease

In the case of chronic illness, some weakness has been building for years. This, too, can be transmuted and corrected. Recent medical research has provided substantial evidence that heart disease can be reversed when the patient follows a full program of meditation, group support, diet, and exercise for one year or less. Experimental groups reversed serious heart disease that had built up over many years, and they also reversed damage to their lives that had built up from not knowing how to connect with a higher power through meditation.

Poor eyesight is a handicap that can also be reversed. Many people have unconsciously accepted the prevailing belief that their eyesight will get worse. A woman who wore thick glasses decided she wanted to see clearly. She asked her soul and Solar angel for guidance, created a hologram of herself with perfect eyesight, and was led to books that gave her eye techniques to practice. Every night she would meet with her soul and ask for help in seeing clearly. She fell asleep imagining that she could see perfectly, and at times she felt as if the angels were working on her eyes. Gradually, she realized that her glasses were creating a blur and that she could see to do some things without her glasses. As her eyes got stronger, she could read and do everything but drive. Within a few months she had an eye test for driving and passed it without her glasses. Today, five years later, she still has good eyesight. Even though she is fifty, when most people expect their eyesight to get worse, her eyesight is holding strong.

When you are reversing any chronic problem, changes can happen very rapidly or very slowly. By comparing the state of the problem before and after you began to reverse it, you can monitor your success. Even with a chronic problem, you may look back after several months and realize that the problem you only hoped to relieve has gone away and there is no sign of it left in your body.

Boosting Reversal Time

The angels can continue reversing cellular damage from an illness or from aging while you sleep if you set this in motion. They work especially well through sounds. Before you go to sleep each night, see yourself synchronized with the note of your soul. Practice using your imagination to create beautiful sounds in your Temple of Healing—flutes, harps, bells, chimes, angelic voices, and birds singing. Place yourself in these scenes, and imagine yourself merging with the light of your soul. Allow yourself to become a part of these celestial sounds as you drift off to sleep.

The angelic healers can also work through the day if you set this in motion. As you awaken, go to the Island of Regeneration and walk to the great waterfall. You can hear it all over the island. Listen to the water roaring with its clear call to cleanse and refresh the air as the water cascades over the falls, dancing and sparkling in the first rays of the sunlight. Look up at the beautiful rainbow just forming in the mist as the sunlight reaches it, and count the colors in the rainbow. At first you may sense only one or two. As more come into your field of imaginary vision, you can see more colors. When you can see all seven colors, stand under the rainbow and visualize its protective rays over you all day.

Additional Years of Vitality

You now have the processes to reverse cellular aging or other damage through the help of your Solar angel and the angelic healers. Play with these processes and be willing to be surprised by how successful they can be. Too strong a desire to reverse a problem and to avoid pain or illness actually gets in the way of your success. Consider any improvement an extra reward or an unexpected dividend as you experiment with these processes to enrich your life energy and use them to supplement other healing methods.

As you feel healthier and younger, use your new vitality to bring light to others, beginning with those closest to you and with your own community. When you combine your learned and innate talents with your greater vitality, you can be very effective with a minimum amount of time or energy. No matter how small or how large a project, let whatever you do with your finer health and vitality be infused with the sparkling light and love of your soul and the angelic healers. Thus, it will make a vital difference in someone's life, probably in many lives, and that difference will give you additional years of vitality and service. You may discover that your best years are just ahead of you—filled with many unexpected dividends of pure delight, wisdom, and joy.

Chapter 23
The Highest Healing Possible

Absolute perfection on the physical plane at this time is an ideal, a worthy image to hold for your inner healer, but absolute perfection is not a manifested reality for the human body. Any path in life has challenging points or it is not a path, merely a resting place. Don't be discouraged if you have a particularly stubborn illness or other problem. Consider any changes that you are creating with the angelic healers a triumph, even the smallest shifts. Each improvement that you fully acknowledge and experience gratitude for helps to build the next shift. Remember that you have the support of the angelic healers to heal any illness or damage from the past, and that their support is a tremendous force.

Consider the possibility that any illness you experience may be lingering because some part of your energy field is not yet woven quite closely enough to resist it. The vibration of this illness may come from a belief or emotion that has caused an obstruction to your soul's healing light. Or you could have inherited this pattern from a parent along with other genetic traits that are very useful to you. You can use any opportunity—an illness, an accident, or a chronic problem—to spin out any vibrational patterns that are not in harmony with your soul and your Solar angel. The angelic healers are reweaving your golden web of light as you do this, spinning its protecting and energizing lines of light in beautiful patterns around you.

Tracing the Origin of a Stubborn Illness

You may be able to trace the origin of a pattern to some decision that you once made which is no longer a wise decision for you. For example, you may recognize that a part of yourself doesn't want to be here on Earth. You may resent the limitations of having a physical body or feel that you are not contributing anything of value here. You may have unconsciously decided to prove to someone how deeply you have been hurt or mistreated and believed you could get this person's attention by being sick. You may have felt that your burdens were so heavy that an illness was the only way to get relief. Even if one of these decisions plays only a small role in permitting the physical problem to linger, changing that decision can make the difference in reversing this problem and regaining your good health.

If you want to discover beliefs that are blocking or slowing your recovery, bring in the sparkling light of your soul and ask about them. Allow yourself to listen and to write these in your healing journal, and you may be surprised at how quickly they come into your mind. Some unforgiveness, some kind of bargain you made with your unconscious mind, some ultimatum that you gave entirely without thinking—any of these could be holding your illness in place until you change that decision.

The more evolved your soul, the more rapidly new ways of thinking and relating to others may need to be made. You may awaken to realize that you need to upgrade the structure of a relationship, your work, or even your whole lifestyle. Some of your best traits may be keeping the chemistry of your body off balance by causing you to be too serious, too tense, or too tired to live a balanced life. They may keep you from getting outdoors and walking, listening to great music, or enjoying the companionship of friends.

If you have a chronic condition and are not getting results after three or four months of working with the angelic healers and the directors of your systems, check to see if you have been too busy to honor the ideas that are coming to you from your soul and inner healer. Solar light is stimulating and can cause you to scatter your energy in too many directions, keeping yourself pressured and rushed. If someone claims your time and energy as his or her own, you may want to set new priorities. Examine every "yes" response to see if it is part of your joint work together. Your soul responds with powerful healing energy when you are cooperating to fulfill its highest destiny. You already have this freedom. It only waits for you to use it.

Listening to Your Words

One woman realized that she was so determined to make her marriage work that she said to herself, "I will make this marriage work if it is the last thing I ever do!" Five years later, she realized just in time that it was almost the last thing she would ever do. She had developed the beginning stages of cancer. Because she had refused to acknowledge a lack of mutual purpose together and had tried to force a relationship that was no longer a natural outcome of shared purpose, her soul was beginning to withdraw its vital life energy. She awoke just in time, and she and her husband decided to live separate lives. Now, twenty years later, both of them are healthy, energetic, and at peace with their lives.

A wealthy businessman realized that he had said to himself many times about his wife, "This woman has got me by the throat." He began having frequent sore throats. All of these cleared up only after he worked out the conflicts in his relationship with the help of a good therapist.

Repeating to himself the statement, "I can't stand this any longer," resulted in a young engineer's legs becoming very painful when he walked until he cleared up a disagreement that was giving this message to his body. If you have a physical challenge that is lingering, think about the kinds of things that you have told yourself for the past few months or years. You might find several clues to the cause and to ways that you can reverse this illness or disease.

The Inner and Outer Causes of Illness

Disease, illness, chronic fatigue, and other chronic problems are the result of two causes—an outer cause and an inner cause. The inner cause of disease is the conflict between the higher frequencies of your soul and the lower frequencies of your body, mind, and emotions. Before foreign bacteria can create a disease in your body, there must be some fear or other toxic feeling or belief that weakens your immune system. Illness can develop only from an ongoing conflict between the soul and personality. It reflects something that is out of harmony with your soul, some part of your life, a belief, or an emotion that is too slow in vibration and is causing friction. Frequently, you already know what this conflict is—such as an underlying fearful, critical, guilt-ridden, blaming, or selfish attitude that won't go away.

If all the parts of one's personality have an equally low

vibration, and there is no soul connection or higher love developed, then everything has the same vibration and there is no illness. You may have heard about people who seem to get by with abusing their body without getting sick—people with a violent temper who shout with rage over insignificant matters, who are incredibly self-seeking and harmful to others, yet have a totally healthy body.

Developing Harmony With Your Soul

An evolved soul cannot get by with these attitudes and behaviors. As greater light flows in, even a lifestyle that worked last year may no longer be healthy. The more evolved the soul, the more rapidly new ways of thinking and relating need to occur if one is to be healed and stay healthy. Your soul shines Solar light into your body to enable you to follow your true destiny. The light also stirs up toxins and reveals where inner conflicts have settled in your body. That's where sore muscles, a stiff neck, angina, or other physical problems can temporarily appear.

The more evolved soul and personality may step into many snares that weaken the body's natural immunity to disease. A family member or close friend claims one's time and energy to fill his or her own insecurities, desires, or wishes. If this happens to you, you may realize that some part of you knows that you are ignoring the wisdom of your soul to make the other person happy. Deep within, you know that something is out of balance. Another snare that can set up an illness is voluntarily giving too much of yourself away, literally scattering your energy in all directions until you can hardly sense your own soul's direction. You can know when you

258

are doing this by the feeling that you are always "getting ready" to *live* your life, but you are too busy right now to do it. The disharmonious vibration of rushing through each day can build up in your energy field and draw a toxic substance into it. This substance can travel into your heart, arteries, lungs, nerves, and intestines and weaken these systems. It makes a nesting place for any stray bacteria floating in the atmosphere, the perfect environment for a disease to develop. It is your unexamined "yes" responses that can set up an illness. Saying yes to all requests is the easiest way to avoid potential outer conflict, but your soul is frustrated by these trespasses that delay its destiny. It wants and needs your conscious collaboration to keep you on your path of health, vitality, and higher purpose.

Honoring the Wisdom of Your Soul

If you are not healing even though you are doing all that you know to do, see where in your life you have been afraid or too busy or too sick to honor the wisdom of your soul. This is more important than anything else. Your healing is dependent on courageously obeying your inner wisdom regardless of others who would like to control your life. This is the work of the healing angels—to help you build a body of vitality that gives you the energy to be courageous, wise, and focused. The angels are working to make you free and independent to be close to your soul. They come in response to your willingness to claim your freedom as a soul and to act on what your soul reveals. The change may be to listen to your soul's voice and obey that voice—and only that voice. Don't wait for others to hand your freedom to you. You will know if you forget to live in the illumination of your soul—you would find yourself trying to please all the people you know at the expense of meeting your own destiny.

Examining Your Best Traits

The traits that slow or prevent health and vitality are never hidden too deeply. They are right in front of you. If you can't think of any, recall a trait of your own that you feel pleased with, such as being generous, understanding, patient, or kind. State this clearly to yourself, and then write it down in your healing journal. After you have written it, imagine that, in some subtle way, this very characteristic might be setting up a particular weakness in your immune, nervous, circulatory, endocrine, or respiratory system. Look for how this might be so. The attribute you feel most confident about could be carried to extremes and prevent a good balance in your life. It may keep you too serious, too tense, or too tired to be truly healthy, creative, and joyful. It may keep you so critical of yourself that you are imprisoned by the desire for absolute perfection. It could prevent you taking the time to go for long walks or other forms of exercise to keep your body healthy. As you begin freeing yourself from being overly influenced by others or from any imprisoning trait that is less radiant than your soul, you can become the director of your own life.

As the director of your whole personality, you will also recognize how important it is to allow others their freedom and expect nothing from them, yet to lend a helping hand to lift them upward in a time of need or difficulty. You begin recognizing everyone who comes into your life as a fellow traveler, a younger or older soul, yet all members of a common family, making the same journey toward the light.

The Transition Stage

Don't think of yourself as off your path if you are unable to reverse a physical problem. Rather, you are in a transition stage. The denser molecules in your cells are coming into conflict with the newer and lighter molecules that are flowing into you. Recognize that you are in the midst of replacing dense emotions with lighted emotions and of replacing dense thoughts with lighted thoughts.

During any transition stage from the old to the new, focus on the part of yourself that is healthy and offer it to your soul for its purpose. Great shifts can come from offering all that you have and are right now to the divine Self within you.

Rather than depending only on traditional authorities if you have problems, such as back trouble, joint problems, a stomach ulcer, or kidney stones, also check alternative ways to heal these problems. Trust your intuition. It is working only for you. Find the lifestyle, food, and supplements that are proven to be effective for the problem you are experiencing. Read all you can about your illness. New research from all over the world is being published each year. If your body can't supply enough of a specific enzyme or hormone, find the supplements that are effective. Angelic healers also work with nutritionists to improve the quality of the human body. Keep your mind and your eyes open. Many new discoveries are coming.

The idea in healing yourself with light is to complement whatever treatment you choose with the spiritual power of

your soul and the angelic healers. As you practice these techniques, you also develop your awareness of the healing method
that is best for you, of who to hire as your doctor or healer,
and increase your ability to place yourself in the vibration
or beam of the healing angels so they can help you.

Educating Yourself About Outside Means

If you are getting conflicting advice from different doctors and healers and you are feeling confused, take as long
as possible in solitude to be with your soul and inner healer.
Give yourself time to consciously receive the knowledge that
your inner healer and soul are sending to you. Make a thor-
ough study of the illness you have, and educate yourself on
the sound choices that have healed this problem for others.
This gives your inner healer more options to choose from.
Once you have investigated every good choice for healing and
connected with your soul and inner healer, if you are still
not sure, see how much time you have to decide without undue risks. Relax for an hour or so each day just to listen and
receive. When you have all the information possible from
outer resources and from inner resources, use your common
sense to make a final decision. The chances are that your common sense is now infused with your soul's guidance, and even
if it feels like something you knew all along, this choice will
be your best choice on choosing further healing treatment.

Many cities have a support group for a number of illnesses. If there is one in your area, attend and meet others
who intend to take the wisest course of action for the illness
that they each have. They may have much information that
you have not found. They will certainly understand what you

are going through if your illness is serious, and they can give you a loving hug or hand of encouragement.

Positive Predictions of Your Healing

Whatever method of healing you choose, you can also call on the angelic healers. If you go to a hospital, bring the healing angels in the room to be with you, your doctor and all the staff who are assisting. Ask several friends to visualize your highest outcome and to join their soul with yours. Take an angel music or meditation tape with you to listen to with headphones so that you can maintain your focus. Make sure that your professional healer believes that you *can* get well. The directors of your systems hear everything, even unspoken words, and they need positive pictures to produce your best healing. Your immune system is immediately strengthened and energized by positive predictions about your rapid recovery. Encourage everyone to make these pictures and describe them in detail to you.

If You Have a Life-Threatening Disease

If you have a disease that does not respond to your efforts to reverse it, such as AIDS or cancer, and you have done all that you know to do, continue to create your golden triangle of light and to receive from the angels of healing every day. Do this as often during the day as you think of it. Use everything your inner healer shows you will assist your body to create cellular harmony and greater vitality. Your participation is equally important. Even though you may not perceive that healing is taking place, healing may be working its way through your other bodies first. Eliminating an obstruction in your mental or emotional body may be the natural order of healing for you. Your physical body can be the last to show healing when a serious illness is involved. As healing takes place in your thoughts and your emotions, it clears a path for your cells to respond. You may be letting go of an old hurt or fear, or unforgiveness toward someone that is opening the way for a stronger spiritual stream of energy to reach your etheric body and flow into your cells.

It is also possible that your soul is withdrawing its energy from your physical body to accept a new opportunity on a higher plane. Your soul knows that your present body is a temporary vehicle for its expansion. It knows that when it helps you to release your physical body, you will move through increasing dimensions of light until you meet and merge with it. Your body and emotions and mind are instruments for your soul to bring light into the physical world, and it is through your Earth experiences that your soul expands to create a higher destiny.

Knowing Yourself as Transcendent Light

Through the eyes of your soul, you realize that you cannot die but will simply be freed from the limitations of an Earth body to travel with your soul to its true home. This transition from your Earth body to your light body can be the highest point of your entire life. Your Solar angel will meet you. The angels of divine love will be with you. Other angelic beings will sound celestial notes of ascension around you. You can clearly see their bodies of light and hear their songs of joy. Your own spiritual teacher will greet you. You can continue to absorb angelic light and to add light wherever you are. For the first time, you can know yourself as you really are—as a soul of transcendent light and infinite beauty, a point of light within a greater light. You can know yourself in the great pulsing heartbeat of the one creative being—a stream of loving energy within the stream of divine love.

As for all of humanity, the physical body eventually wears out when it cannot hold enough light for the soul's expanding light and purpose. When you do finally journey with your soul to its next mission, decide to be conscious on the inner level as you release your physical body. The next body to serve and evolve your soul will reflect its shining light and love more clearly than ever before.

Clearing Your Past

However, unless you feel very strongly that your soul is withdrawing, even if you are in your eighties or nineties, assume that you can reverse the disease. In a serious illness, great opportunity is given to develop very quickly what would take ten or twenty years of ordinary living to develop. Make a list of all misunderstandings or wrong action in your life, and clear these up by calling or writing the people involved. Ask for forgiveness and offer forgiveness for everything that comes to your mind as unloving or uncaring. Meet with your Solar angel in the Room of Inner Stillness and join with your soul in the Room of Light. Let them surround you with the angelic healers in the Room of Love, the Room of Colors, and the Room of Sound. Think about and plan what you will do when you feel more energetic. Ask for help in developing the soul quality that this illness is providing the opportunity for you to develop.

No one can guarantee you a complete cure. This is between you and your soul. Your soul is looking at your highest destiny. If this destiny includes extra service for the soul through your present body, your soul will show you the route to better health and take you there as fast as possible. Some kind of evolution and healing will always take place even when the results are not immediately visible. Meet with your inner healer, and let your healer assist you in empowering your healing hologram until it is vibrating with energy. Use everything you have learned from your directors—including diet, rest, sunlight, sleep, lifestyle, and supplements. If you haven't found your best healer or healing method, continue to research all possibilities. Tell your friends how to hold a focus of light for you and to bring the pictures of your future into focus that you are energizing. Set up a small pleasure that you can enjoy each day—a phone call, a note to someone, a fresh flower an herbal bath, or a favorite movie or video.

Miracles: Where Spirit and Matter Meet

Miracles can and do happen. They happen at the point where spirit and matter meet. You touch the point where spirit and matter meet each time you merge with the golden light of your soul and your Solar angel. As you reach these higher dimensions of light, begin to think of yourself as a soul with a body rather than a body with a soul. This is the essence of you that never dies. It cannot die—only expand and expand into greater light.

Regardless of any physical challenge, healing will always

come where it will make the greatest difference—in the spirit within. The most powerful healing of all is to unite with your soul, to heal the separation between your soul and you. As you link with your soul again and again, the barriers to its ability to charge your body with its love and vitality begin dissolving. Illness, pain, or suffering of any kind simply accelerates this process until you actually merge into the infinite love and beauty of your soul. It is this connection with your soul that you take with you as your greatest achievement when you complete this lifetime journey.

A Word of Encouragement

The transition from your old body to your new body is now well underway. It began as soon as you stepped on the boat to go to the Island of Regeneration and reached up to meet your Solar angel in the Room of Inner Stillness. It will continue so long as you continue to draw the golden light of your Solar angel and soul into your life and your body. As you begin living in the healing rhythm of your soul and seeing how every part of your life affects your body, you are creating a life of vitality as well as a body of vitality.

Inventing and Experimenting

The mark of an awakened soul is the ability to learn from each experience and then to let go of the box it came in. Ask to learn everything possible that a physical problem or illness is pointing out to you. Then give yourself permission to really enjoy the journey of healing, regenerating, and rejuvenating your body. Experiment with the colors that are healing to your body. Experiment with the music that strikes healing chords within your cells. Invent ways to bring your personal healing hologram to life. Ask your soul to keep energizing and refining it for you.

Allow yourself to use every experience—of illness or health, of sadness or happiness, of sorrow or joy—to add to

269

the light that you can bring into your life and the lives of those around you. You cannot possibly fail to succeed in what you are learning when you meet with your soul and your Solar angel every day. Look for more than a digestive system that begins working well again or a heart pain that goes away. Look for the powerful spirit of love that is evolving within your heart center. Watch for the spirit of compassion that resonates from the vibration of the healing angels to grow stronger. Let these flow into you to heal your body and rejuvenate your life.

Don't feel you are a failure if you can't meet the high standards every day that you have set up. No one reaches the ideal every day. Rather, use one or two of these healing methods at a time, instead of criticizing yourself for what you have not done. If you could do all of them at once, you would already be a master of life, and there would be no more Earth experiences for you to learn from. When you make notations in your healing journal, describe what you *are* doing, rather than what you aren't doing.

Simultaneous Healings

Do not be overly concerned if you have moments of discouragement. If a physical change you want is slow to come, it doesn't mean that nothing is happening. Deep and lasting changes happen first in your etheric body, which then sends the new patterns to your energy centers and the directors of your systems. The directors send it to your endocrine glands, which then deposit the substance of healing directly into your bloodstream. Every cell receives new energy to evolve into more light. There is no way to be aware of all the changes taking place. Many happen at the same time. They not only happen in your cells, they happen in your heart, sometimes creating waves of compassion and love for all people.

Remember, healing is not linear. You may have days of feeling that you have gone all the way downhill, particularly when your body is releasing toxins. Even if you have a temporary setback on the physical level, do not consider this a reason to give up. Go back to the guided meditations that stimulate your soul and Solar angel connection, and focus on these as you work with the angelic healers. Notice that the things you most dread in the future rarely ever happen as you imagined. Observe that the things you most regret have given you an exceedingly profound understanding of what has true value in the world. Tune your creative mind to the note and the color of your soul and immerse yourself in its transformative power.

Recognizing the Healing You Are Creating

If you have been the least bit critical of yourself, feeling that you are not able to make as strong a connection with your soul and Solar angel as you want to make, let go of any expectation about what this connection should be like. When you have no expectations, you can observe with a clear eye just how powerful your connection is becoming. You can see how your inner knowing is expanding. You may not know where this knowing came from; you just know it is true. Soon, you may realize that many of the things you are doing now to vitalize your body are things that you could never get yourself to do in the past. Your will to take charge of healing and rejuvenating your body has become dynamic and strong. You are beginning to trust your inner healer, to take showers of light every morning, to form your golden triangle, to link with the angelic healers, and to send your heartfelt gratitude to them again and again. These changes happen even when you have secretly feared that you didn't really have a connection!

Be aware that communication from your soul and Solar angel is not as loud and persistent as the voice of well-meaning friends and authorities, or the voice of your own personality. Listen to all advice, but stay in charge of your life and your body. Use your intuition, your knowledge, your experience, and your own common sense to make all decisions regarding your body—as well as your life.

The Continuing Transformation of Your Cells

Read and reread Part One and Part Two to strengthen your soul connection and your work with the angelic healers. Each moment that you are reading or practicing the exercises, you are in your soul's presence, surrounded by its light, lifted up in its light. A deeper understanding and healing will come. It is only through much repetition that your mind can release ancient thoughts and fears inherited from an earlier culture. By your conscious and frequent connection with angelic and soul light, your cells will gradually be transformed into cells of Solar light.

The future is yours to create—yours to add light to, yours to add love to. As you bring greater light into your cells, you become a channel for light—a true healing agent for others. With this kind of healing, you need not think of yourself as healing another. Healing happens naturally because you have purified your etheric body and evolved your cells with the angels. This energy is dynamic, and it is powerful. Use it wisely from a center of love.

All the energy you receive in the Temple of Healing on the Island of Regeneration is moving energy. It flows into your mind, into your emotions, and into your body. Once your cells are saturated with this lighted energy, you will need a worthy place to use it so that congestion does not build up in your body. Look around and see who you know who might be ready to connect with the angelic healers. Your own experience can make a world of difference for them. As you share these angelic healing processes with friends, you may also discover a greater depth of power and understanding. More than that, you will be giving something of true value. Teach one or two others, and discover for yourself how much difference it can make!

May your healing and rejuvenation journey be a joyful adventure of discovery—a treasure hunt that yields gems of wisdom, humor, and love. Long after the angels of healing have completed their work with you, your Solar angel—the shining one who will always be with you—will continue to illumine your life. May every blessing be yours.

The Chart of Angelic Healing

The Chart of Angelic Healing gives you ideas on where to begin the healing process. Use it when you need extra insight. As your connection with your soul and the angelic healers becomes richer, you may rarely need this chart. *Always put your higher intuition above any suggestions in this chart.* There is no set rule for healing any symptom. The angelic healers use many colors and sounds to transmute your cells into cells of greater light and vitality. Listen to and trust your own inner guidance.

When you use this chart to treat a particular symptom (listed in the first column), first imagine yourself in the Temple of Healing on the Island of Regeneration. Say the AUM or A-El-I-O as you take a shower of colors to clear your energy field for healing. Say it as many times as you need to move into the healing space of the angels. Then form your golden triangle to receive the gift of your soul and Solar angel.

The second column of the chart lists the divine gift that your triangle brings into your energy field especially for this problem.

The third column lists the gift of the angels of divine love for this problem.

The fourth column suggests colors the healing angels frequently use for this problem.

The fifth column suggests a question for your inner healer to show you your part in accelerating your healing.

The sixth column suggests a visual picture that opens your mind and heart to the angelic healers.

Feel free to add to the condensed questions and to your visual pictures for your healing hologram. For more information, refer to Part Three of this book to check the system and energy center this symptom is related to. Also, you may want to review Part Two about the angels who worked with you in each room of the Temple of Healing.

If the problem you are healing is not listed in the chart, check other problems affecting that system and the system itself. If a gift from the healing angels for another problem lifts your spirit and seems healing to you, use this gift, too. All gifts are available to you through your soul and Solar angel.

Do not try to heal a problem with this chart alone. Use it as a supplement for the journeys in the book. Get a diagnosis from a doctor for any serious problem. When outside healers are needed, use this chart to complement any therapeutic remedies you are receiving.

If you wish to help friends heal themselves with this chart, be sure to give them the whole book. The Chart of Angelic Healing is only a condensed reminder of what you have learned as you reach each chapter. Your familiarity with each process will allow the chart to work effectively for you.

THE CHART OF ANGELIC HEALING

Area to Heal	Solar Angel and Soul Bring	Angels of Divine Love Bring
Accidents	Heightened awareness of your creativity with light	Inner strength and courage
Adrenal glands	Greater wisdom to live with less attachment to outcomes	Serenity and freedom from controlling or being controlled
Aging	Wisdom and compassion	Freedom from past worries; freedom to express wisdom and love
AIDS	Revelation of your shining essence Self	Deep and abiding angelic companionship
Alcohol	Spiritual courage and a new sense of purpose	Healing, transformative angelic love
Allergies	Spiritual power	Strong link with infinite healing love of A-El-I-O
Alzheimer's	Spiritual light	Self-awareness
Anemia	Spiritual courage	Abundant life force energy
Angina	Divine harmony	Expanded love

Healing Colors	Question for Inner Healer	Healing Image
Violet and gold	Apologize to injured parts, and ask how to create a new reality.	See the angels reversing any injuries and restoring your body to normal.
Restoring colors— sapphire blue, green, orange	Ask for help in creating a calm, peaceful rhythm of living.	See the healing angels restoring your adrenal glands with Solar light.
Rose and gold	Ask for information on rejuvenating each system.	See the angelic healers bringing new life energy to your mind and body.
Golden orange to clear toxins and vitalize; rose for an optimistic spirit	Ask how to regenerate your immune system through food, exercise, sunlight, and joy.	Listen for the angels as they use sound frequencies and colors to heal you.
Rose for discouragement; orange for vitality	Ask how to fully nourish your brain and body.	Visualize golden angelic healers touching your mind and emotions all day.
Golden orange	Ask for ways to strengthen your natural immunity.	See the angels building a sparkling blue mist of protection around you.
Rose, yellow, and gold	Ask for ways to stimulate new neural links.	Visualize golden light from the angels around your head to revitalize your neural pathways.
Red-orange	Ask how to build and enrich your blood with food, exercise, and joy.	See the healing angels bringing transfusions of sparkling light.
Alternating rose and green	Ask for assistance in healing life's heartaches.	Visualize the angels healing your heart with sounds of joy.

277

THE CHART OF ANGELIC HEALING

Area to Heal	Solar Angel and Soul Bring	Angels of Divine Love Bring
Anorexia	Divine acceptance	Ability to give and receive love
Anxiety	Divine serenity	Peace that transcends all understanding
Arrhythmia (irregular or rapid heartbeat)	Divine rhythm of the soul	Serene acceptance of life and all events as teachers of love
Arteries (atherosclerosis)	Spiritual purification	Inflowing and out-flowing of deep compassion
Arthritis	Divine peace of mind	Total forgiveness for self and all others
Asthma	Divine freedom to express all hopes and fears	Courage to take control of your life in a new way
Autoimmune diseases	Divine insight into the higher meaning and purpose of your life	Strong foundation of love
Back/spine	Spiritual freedom of choice	Lightening and transformation of burdens

Healing Colors	Question for Inner Healer	Healing Image
Golden orange and rose	Ask how to release all pressure for others to be different or for yourself to be different.	See yourself absorbing the angels' healing frequencies all around your body.
Turquoise, rose, and lavender	Ask how to transform this energy into a creative work.	See the angels lifting you into the vibration of serenity and divine love.
Clear, deep rose	Ask how to establish the authority over your heart to regulate its beat.	See the angels using sounds of joy to restore your heartbeat to its perfect rhythm.
Orange flame and golden amber	Ask for help in building new beliefs.	See the healing angels clearing your arteries to hold greater light.
Sapphire blue and rose	Ask for help in reversing all damage.	Visualize angelic healers placing sheaths of warm liquid light around your joints.
Green to open breathing; pale rose and magenta for optimism	Ask how to express your power in new areas of your life.	See angelic healers clearing and strengthening your lungs with showers of light.
Rose, violet, and green	Ask how to bring in energy to serve your higher purpose.	Visualize the angels surrounding you with songs of joy and love.
White up and down spinal cord; green to relieve pain; yellow for other back problems	Ask for a new posture and balance in your body and in your life.	See the angelic healers placing circles of Solar light up and down your back.

Area to Heal	Solar Angel and Soul Bring	Angels of Divine Love Bring
Bladder	Elimination of non-essentials in life	Release of the past to embrace the new
Blood pressure	Divine recognition of your own power and control	A new awakening to wisdom in love; release of feeling pressured or controlled
Bones and skeletal system	Spiritual strength to move forward on your path	Deeper link with the Earth; rootedness in family and community
Brain	An experience of being in touch with your soul's vast intelligence	Understanding through love and compassion
Breast tumors (non-malignant)	Divine freedom and independence	Merging of love with wisdom, giving you wise love
Bulimia	Divine gratitude	Your true value and identity as a divine being
Burns	Divine serenity and detachment	Forgiveness to transform pain and burn damage

Healing Colors	Question for Inner Healer	Healing Image
Yellow to purify; sapphire blue to clear infections	Ask for exercise, diet, sunlight, and supplements to rejuvenate bladder.	Visualize the angels purifying your bladder with their light.
Green and rose	Ask for inspiration to see new avenues of purpose and joy.	See angelic healers bringing the soul's perfect rhythm into your body.
Deep clear violet and indigo	Ask for diet, supplements, and exercise to create strong bones.	See angelic workers adding flexibility, strength, and density to your bones with cosmic sound frequencies.
Yellow and gold	Ask about inner and outer nourishment— for your mind and your brain.	See your Solar angel weaving a bridge of many colors around your head to stimulate and heal your mind.
Sapphire and teal blue	Ask for ways to release congestion in your heart center and to purify your bloodstream.	Visualize angelic workers raising excess energy into your higher centers with light and sound.
All hues of rose to embrace higher will	Ask for one or two things you can do today that bring great joy to your heart.	Imagine the healing angels surrounding you with joy and love.
Green and rose, both deep hues and lighter hues	Ask for assistance to replay scene immediately to reverse damage.	See the angels placing a soothing, healing substance on your skin to heal it.

THE CHART OF ANGELIC HEALING

Area to Heal	Solar Angel and Soul Bring	Angels of Divine Love Bring
Cancer	Divine power; stimulation of your higher will to live and to be healed	Unconditional love and forgiveness
Candida	Divine freedom and autonomy	Divine love into every cell
Chronic fatigue	Divine freedom to control your own life	Rose light of divine love to clear discouragement and bring cheerfulness
Circulatory system	Divine autonomy	Deeper penetration of divine love into your bloodstream
Colds	Higher vision of your soul's rhythm	Ability to see beyond false obligations and to choose freely
Coughs and bronchitis	Divine self-expression	Opening of the heart center to loving understanding
Cysts	Divine distribution of energy	Peace of mind

282

Healing Colors	Question for Inner Healer	Healing Image
Sapphire blue to energy center nearest cancer; white to the higher energy center	Ask how to let go of the past and make a plan for the future to do what you love doing.	Sense the Solar angels healing and nurturing your life and your body with sound and colors.
Orange to purify; gold and white to bring Solar light into cells	Ask for suggestions on food, exercise, and sleep.	Visualize angelic healers sending a purifying light through your cells.
Orange for clearing toxins and vitality; green for rest periods	Ask for help in creating a new lifestyle that energizes you.	Visualize angelic energy evolving cells of lesser light into cells of greater light.
Red-orange to vitalize bloodstream; orange to raise cellular vibration	Ask for guidance on an exercise program and on receiving soul love.	Imagine the Solar angels sending a sparkling light through your bloodstream.
Medium yellow to clear head and sinuses	Ask how to control your life and work without undue fatigue.	See the angelic healers restoring your cells with love and joyous sounds.
Green to relax coughing; orange to clear congestion of energy	Ask how to strengthen respiratory and immune systems through diet, sleep, and sunlight.	Visualize the angelic healers creating a healing vibration to heal you.
Yellow-green and sapphire blue	Ask for assistance in bringing more balance to your life.	Visualize the angelic healers surrounding you with a sense of balance and peace.

Area to Heal	Solar Angel and Soul Bring	Angels of Divine Love Bring
Death (preparation for)	Divine light of vision	Forgiveness for all mistakes—yours and others
Depression	Illumined sense of power over your life	Shaking off of heaviness and fears to reveal deep joy within
Digestive system	Profound trust in your soul	Magnetic pull of energy from solar plexus to heart center
Dyslexia	A higher, clearer vision	Serenity and clarity within and without
Ears	Divine awareness	Whisperings of the soul's love and protection
Endocrine system (see also individual glands)	Divine balance	Ability to see a higher truth within and to express it
Epilepsy	Divine power, courage, and harmony	Healing experience of the soul's gentle rhythm

284

Healing Colors	Question for Inner Healer	Healing Image
Gold and white	Ask for ways to be conscious throughout the process of moving into your higher body.	Visualize the angels beside you as constant companions.
Translucent rose hues for optimism; bright orange to irradiate highest truth	Ask for help in expressing deepest feelings (the worst and the best) through moaning, toning, and humming.	See the angels lifting you through layers of clouds and into the bright sun.
Green—the shade that feels most healing, from pale green to forest green	Ask for creative ways to find and hold a calm, inner peace.	Imagine the healing angels blessing the food you eat with you and rebuilding your digestive system with light.
Rose and gold	Ask how to link nervous system director with inner healer.	See angelic beings clearing your inner and outer vision with sounds and colors.
Gold and white	Ask how to hear more clearly with the inner ear.	See the angels healing your hearing and ears with a beautiful note that resonates with your soul.
(See individual glands.)	Ask for ways to develop perfect balance of light in all seven endocrine glands.	See angelic healers sending a sparkling silver light to your glands to heal and balance them.
Rose and green	Ask how to live independently, free of being controlled or controlling others.	See the healing angels rerouting electromagnetic energies, helping to balance the energy flowing into your brain.

285

Area to Heal	Solar Angel and Soul Bring	Angels of Divine Love Bring
Epstein-Barr	Divine inspiration	Compassion and understanding with forgiveness of all debts
Eyes	Divine vision and insight to see your true path	Soft, gentle eyes that carry the energy of divine love
Fatigue	Vitality and balance of work and play	Deep relaxation and an optimistic spirit
Feet	Divine freedom to walk your own path of light	A sense of humor and laughter
Fever	Divine power to drive out all infection and purify your body	Inner peace and serenity
Flu (Influenza)	Divine power to drive out the invading virus	Inspired will to enjoy life
Food poisoning	Divine power to cleanse your stomach of the poison	Trust in the natural wisdom of your body

286

Healing Colors	Question for Inner Healer	Healing Image
Rose, indigo, and magenta	Ask how to strengthen your immune system director and find the ideal diet.	See a glowing light around your body as the healing angels heal you.
Gold; white for vision; sapphire blue for infection	For left eye, ask how to clear fear of seeing perfectly; for right eye, ask for assistance in clearing spiritual vision.	See angelic beings giving your eyes healing treatments with sparkling colors.
Orange to energize and wash away toxins	Ask for three revitalizing steps to fluff out your aura this week.	Visualize a healing angel on each side of you adding light to your energy field.
Blue violet for athlete's foot or other infections; rose and/or green for aching feet	Ask about a new posture and balance for your body and your life.	Imagine the angels bathing your feet in liquid colors.
Rose and green hues; blue mist around your body	Ask for old beliefs and fears to be burned out of your energy field with the fever.	Visualize angelic healers around your head and body, building new cells with joyous sounds and colors.
Orange for aching; green for fever; sapphire blue for coughs or infections	Ask how to build a stronger immune system through sleep, rest, and visual pictures.	Picture angelic healers relieving all aches and pain with soft, translucent colors.
Orange to clear toxins; deep blue to heal stomach	Ask how to free your body (and your mind) from all toxins.	Become aware of the healing angels placing sparkling colors around you.

THE CHART OF ANGELIC HEALING

Area to Heal	Solar Angel and Soul Bring	Angels of Divine Love Bring
Gums/teeth	Divine light to drive out any infection	Inner peace and stillness
Headaches	Divine wisdom to see a better response to tension and stress	Calm, peace, and relaxation
Heart	Divine trust in the goodness of the universe	Inclusive love that leaves others free and lightens burdens
Immune system	Divine balance	Release of tension and anxiety to strengthen immunity to disease
Indigestion	Divine harmony	Powerful digestive juices of A-El-I-O— the spiritual food of love
Infections	Divine vitality	Cellular purification through divine love for deep healing to happen
Insomnia	Divine trust in the protection of your Solar angel	A deep state of peace and inner stillness

THE CHART OF ANGELIC HEALING

Healing Colors	Question for Inner Healer	Healing Image
Gold to strengthen; sapphire blue to heal infection	Ask about supplements, food, acid-alkaline balance, and the appropriate amount of sunshine.	Visualize angels placing light and sound in your gums to heal them.
Sapphire and teal blue for tension; orange to neutralize polluted air	Ask for ways to send energy into your hands and feet until they are very warm. Ask about food, lifestyle, and exercise.	See the angelic healers gently lifting inner and outer pressures.
Gold	Ask how to share your feelings and lighten the load you are carrying.	Visualize the angels of divine love rejuvenating your heart with joy.
Golden orange to purify; blue-violet to strengthen	Ask for ways to upgrade food, sleep, oxygen, sun, and your life purpose.	See healing angels purifying your blood cells and strengthening this system with orange.
Green or yellow	Ask how to create inner harmony and serenity each day.	Visualize the angels infusing your stomach with healing colors.
Sapphire blue as a disinfectant; rose to upgrade messages going to your cells	Ask how to strengthen your immune system through sunlight, food, exercise, and rest.	See the angels bringing Solar light to your cells to create resistance to all disease.
Rose to be closer to the angels of divine love; gold to be closer to your soul	Ask for ways to create balance of exercise and inner stillness for restful sleep.	See the angels of divine love surrounding and lifting you into higher dimensions all night.

Area to Heal	Solar Angel and Soul Bring	Angels of Divine Love Bring
Joints (arthritis, elbow, knee, fingers, shoulders)	Divine freedom	Pure joy in being alive and free to merge with your innate divinity
Kidney/urinary system	Divine liberation and courage	Ability to release the past and embrace your future with love
Lungs	Divine vision of your highest future	The breath of love and rejuvenation
Menstrual/PMS/ menopause	Divine insight	A new identity for your feminine beauty and power
MS (multiple sclerosis)	Spiritual strength	A healing love that eliminates self-criticism
Muscular system	Divine power	Greater flexibility in muscles and mind
Neck	Divine understanding	Expanded heart vision for the future, past, and present moment

Healing Colors	Question for Inner Healer	Healing Image
Deep, clear hues of rose and blue or green	Ask how to find new flexibility to play.	Visualize angelic healers massaging your joints with a balm of translucent colors.
Clear burgundy to strengthen; sapphire blue for infections	Ask how to strengthen this system with exercise, food, and liquids.	Visualize the angels using purifying, cleansing light rays to heal this system.
Violet or indigo mixed with silver	Ask how to prepare for angelic healing through visualizations and the will to be fully healed.	Visualize angelic light flowing into your lungs to purify them to hold more light.
Cool colors—deep blue and green to relieve pain or tension; amethyst or orange to purify	Ask about foods, supplements, and exercise.	Imagine angelic healers releasing all tension and rejuvenating you with joyous sounds.
Golden amber and medium yellow	Ask how to eat and exercise, and how to expand the reach of your life purpose.	See the angels rebuilding nerve sheaths and bringing perfect muscular coordination.
Orange to purify toxins; blue to relax and heal	Ask how much weight-bearing exercise is needed to release emotional and physical toxins.	Picture the angels and the director of this system building flexibility and power into your muscles.
Golden hues; indigo	Ask about origin of neck tension and how to lighten burdens.	Feel the angelic healers around you lifting the weight from your neck and shoulders.

Area to Heal	Solar Angel and Soul Bring	Angels of Divine Love Bring
Nervous system	Serene inner stillness	Finer connection between crown center and heart center
Osteoporosis	Divine vitality	Renewed vigor to step forward in your life
Ovaries	Divine gratitude	Thankfulness for femininity and its unique opportunities for enlightenment
Pain	Divine nonattachment	Revelation of the beauty and love all around you
Pancreas	Divine serenity and security	Inner strength of confidence in the universe
Parasites	Divine detachment	Spinning out of parasites through divine love
Prostate	Divine wholeness	All-embracing acceptance and love for the world

Healing Colors	Question for Inner Healer	Healing Image
Silvery rose, violet, silvery green, yellow, or gold	Ask about releasing nervous tension with sounds and song. Ask about mind stimulation exercises.	Visualize Solar angels upgrading your mind and nervous system with gold around your head.
Red-orange or burgundy to build density	Ask to find new research on raising bone density with exercise, diet, and supplements.	See the angelic healers strengthening your bones and soothing aches and pains.
Silver with rose for tumor; silver with amber and violet for revitalization	Ask how to balance energy between both creative centers— sacral and throat.	Visualize angelic workers healing and evolving these cells.
Rose, green, and sapphire blue	Ask for new ways to handle pain through play, love, joy, and music.	See healing angels placing a blue mist over area to eliminate pain and to heal you.
Orange to stimulate; sapphire blue to heal	Ask how to energize this gland through lifestyle changes, diet, sleep, and emotions.	Visualize angels healing your pancreas with sound frequencies.
Orange as a flame of purification; blue-violet to resist parasites	Ask how to be connected but not dependent on others—loving, yet independent.	Visualize healing angels radiating light into your cells and clearing out parasites.
Sapphire blue or silvery blue and rose	Ask how to fully trust your creative power in all levels of life.	Visualize healing angels balancing the energy in your two creative centers— throat and sacral.

THE CHART OF ANGELIC HEALING

Area to Heal	Solar Angel and Soul Bring	Angels of Divine Love Bring
Rash	Divine cleansing	A sheath of protective energy around your skin
Reproductive system	Divine healing power of soul infusion	Deep appreciation of your femininity or your masculinity
Respiratory system	Divine inspiration through the breath	Higher level of honesty and integrity
Sinus	Divine freedom	Love flowing through your sinuses to clear all toxins
Sore throat	Inner stillness and higher creativity	Ability to speak clearly about your deepest desires
Sprains	Divine trust	Compassion for the sprained ankle or wrist
Stroke	Divine inspiration to reverse any damage	Expanded love of life

Healing Colors	Question for Inner Healer	Healing Image
Blue—gentle if intense rash, brighter as rash heals	Ask for creative ways to eliminate toxins—through play, laughter, long walks.	See the angelic healers placing layers of healing colors over your skin.
Orange to purify; green to heal	Ask how to heal and keep this system healthy and in perfect balance with other systems.	See the angelic healers linking your sacral center energy with your throat center to enrich both creative centers.
Orange to clear; sapphire blue or violet to heal	Ask how to purify the air you are breathing and how to clear this system with breath, exercise, sunlight, and food.	Visualize a radiant angelic substance filling the air you are breathing.
Orange to clear and purify; sapphire blue to heal infections	Ask for ways to express all anxieties and find solutions.	See the angels focusing lines of light into your sinuses.
Sapphire blue or electric blue in throat center	Ask how to breathe in colors to heal and how to transfer Solar light to director of respiratory system.	See a healing laser light restoring your perfect voice and throat.
Gold, white, or green around and inside the joint (experiment to choose best color)	Ask for help in creating a new reality in which no sprain happened.	Visualize the angels restoring this area with three layers of colors.
Green, rose, and gold	Ask for ways to restructure thoughts and activities to match soul's rhythm.	Visualize the angels restoring your nerves and muscle and brain connections with beautiful cosmic sounds.

Area to Heal	Solar Angel and Soul Bring	Angels of Divine Love Bring
Thymus gland	Activation of thymus gland through the soul's light	Expanded ability to receive and to give love
Thyroid – hyperthyroid (overactive thyroid)	Divine serenity	Serene acceptance of all that is
Thyroid – hypothyroid (underactive thyroid)	Divine joy and gratitude	Harmonious union of mind, body, and soul
Tumors	Divine comprehension	Compassionate understanding of harmony with the soul
Weight (over)	Divine security	Lifting of illusions to reveal higher purpose
Weight (under)	Divine absorption	Vision to use body as an instrument of the soul

Healing Colors	Question for Inner Healer	Healing Image
Gold or white to help activate this gland to protect you from disease	Ask how to stimulate the director in your heart center to energize your thymus; ask about chanting and singing.	See the angels increasing the spiritual stream of energy that flows into your heart center and thymus gland.
Soft rose hues; clear blue hues	Ask how to experience a balance of inner stillness and joy.	See the angelic healers rebalancing your thyroid with gentle pulses of color.
Golden rays of light in throat center.	Ask about sounding the "O" and A-El-I-O and other healing sounds.	See the angelic healers rejuvenating your thyroid so perfectly that your moods are positive and even.
All cool colors— light green, blue, peach and rose	Ask for help on diet, supplements, homeopathy, or other therapy.	See angelic lights balancing the center and director nearest tumor.
Orange flame to stimulate metabolism; rose as food	Ask about raising your metabolism with exercise, food, and new friendships.	Visualize healing angels on each side of you all day.
Rose and green	Ask for guidance in nutrition and embracing a nourishing lifestyle.	See the angelic healers bringing you nourishment with colors.

Additional Resources: Books and Tapes

The Awakening Life Series

Book I: *Bridge of Light: Tools of Light*
for Spiritual Transformation
By LaUna Huffines
Publisher: H J Kramer

Bridge of Light shows you how to build a Bridge of Light to the vast intelligence and love of your soul. Your Bridge of Light consists of actual streams of spiritual energy that can be directed into any part of your life. You learn to link your Bridge of Light with the power of courage, joy, love, and many other radiant soul qualities that can make your life a wonderful spiritual adventure.

You learn how to bring others on your bridge to heal and enrich your relationships with them, to direct your subpersonalities, and to develop the spiritual trust that dissolves fears. You also learn how to change your future by changing your past, how to use crises as spiritual doorways, and how to find your true teacher. Each chapter contains step-by-step guidelines for creating changes in your life and for making these changes with the grace and poise that enable your family and friends to support and enjoy your emerging spiritual self. *Bridge of Light* is a wonderful companion for *Healing Yourself With Light.*

Healing Yourself With Light *Tape Albums*

Healing Yourself With Light guided journeys on audio-cassette tape help you to make a strong soul connection and to contact the healing angels. They assist you in connecting with your inner healer and the directors of your systems and in creating your healing hologram. They show you how to purify, heal, and evolve your body to hold more light. You learn how to absorb the colors and higher frequencies of light and sound being sent to you. Both the voice and background music carry the energy of the healing angels. Binaural sound frequencies beneath the music silently assist you to synchronize your brain waves and slow them to smooth alpha, theta, and occasional delta rhythms, where the greatest healing and rejuvenation can happen.

Volume I and Volume II
Healing Yourself With Light Tape Albums

(These journeys are similar to the ones in the book; however, they are expanded versions and can take you deeper than written exercises can do. There are eight journeys on four double-sided cassettes in each album.)

Volume I: Your Temple of Angelic Healing ($59.95)
Side 1: A Journey to your Temple of Healing
Side 2: Connecting With Your Solar Angel and Soul

Side 3: Healing With Your Golden Triangle
Side 4: Healing With the Angels of Divine Love
Side 5: Healing With Angelic Colors
Side 6: Healing With Angelic Sounds
Side 7: Learning From Your Inner Healer
Side 8: Creating Your Healing Hologram

Volume II: Healing Your Systems and Cells ($59.95)
Side 1: Regenerating Your Circulatory System
Side 2: Revitalizing Your Nervous System
Side 3: Purifying Your Respiratory System
Side 4: Strengthening Your Immune System
Side 5: Rejuvenating Yourself
Side 6: Raising Cellular Light
Side 7: Raising Your Will to Be Healed
Side 8: Creating Your Highest Healing

(Volumes I and II are $99.95 when ordered together.)

Audiotapes: Angelic Journeys for Healing

(There are four journeys in each set on two double-sided audiocassettes.)

Angelic Healing for Contagious Diseases ($29.95)
If you have colds, flu, sore throats, or other viral illnesses with a rapid onset (or want to protect yourself from contagious diseases), you can get immediate help to accelerate healing and relieve these symptoms, strengthen your immune system, and also protect your body against future infections.

Angelic Protection From Fears and Anxieties ($29.95)
This will help with times of anxiety, dread, discouragement,

or fear about illness, about environmental accidents, or about staying well for yourself or your family or children. Angelic circles of protection create a strong, peaceful center of calm serenity and clear thinking to handle any situation.

Angelic Healing for Pain ($29.95)
If you have pain, stress, or tension in your shoulders, neck, lower back, arms, or legs, you can learn how to use colors and sounds with the angelic healers, how to merge with the angels of divine love, and how to create a powerful healing hologram to reduce or eliminate this kind of pain.

Angelic Healing for Hospitals, Dental, or Surgery ($29.95)
If you are going to the hospital or dental office for surgery, testing, or observation, or if you are receiving any invasive treatments for your body, you can bring the healing angels to protect you, to inspire your physician or surgeon, to accelerate your healing, and to block out harmful frequencies that cause side effects or otherwise obstruct perfect healing.

Angelic Assistance for Autoimmune Diseases ($29.95)
If you have rheumatoid arthritis, AIDS, chronic fatigue, muscular sclerosis, lupus, or any other autoimmune disease, you can accelerate healing with the Solar angels, the angels of divine love, and Solar light to create lifestyle changes and build in finer frequencies to replace all denser frequencies caused by toxic materials or anxiety.

Angelic Assistance for the Endocrine System ($29.95)
Whatever illness you have will be assisted in healing by upgrading your endocrine system. If you want to raise the

frequency of light in your cells and evolve your body, by learning how to work with the angelic healers to purify, develop, and nourish your thyroid, thymus, pancreas, and adrenal glands, you will also strengthen your immune system and encourage the rejuvenation of every system in your body. Use in conjunction with any of the other tape sets on healing.

Angelic Healing for the Digestive System ($29.95)
If you have bloating, indigestion, or other discomfort caused from digestive disturbances, you can work with your inner healer and relieve this system from stress or irritation as the angelic healers infuse your digestive system with a calm and tranquil efficiency.

Angelic Healing for the Muscular and Skeletal Systems ($29.95)
If you want stronger, more flexible, and more supportive muscles and if you want strong bones that last throughout your life, you can learn to strengthen these with angelic sound frequencies and your active participation as shown to you by your inner healer.

Angelic Protection From Environmental Damage ($29.95)
If you are living in a metropolitan area or other environment polluted by pesticides, air, noise, toxins from wood-burning fires, automobiles, or nonorganic food, you will be guided in bringing the angels to purify and build a finer substance to protect you from damage.

Angelic Healing for Accidents ($29.95)
If you have an accident or burn or cut your skin, if you sprain an ankle or arm, break a bone, or bruise your body in a fall,

you are guided through reversing the potential damage immediately with the angelic healers and shown how to call upon the inner healer to assist you further.

Angelic Healing for a Strong Heart ($29.95)
If you have heart disease, arrthymia, angina, low or high blood pressure, or partially blocked arteries, you can learn to accelerate healing with the angels of divine love, the Solar angels, and your inner healer.

Angelic Healing for Allergies ($29.95)
If you have hay fever, sinus problems, asthma, skin rashes, chronic coughs, or bronchial problems, you learn the true causes, how to strengthen your immune system to protect you from environmental oversensitivities, and how to begin working with the angels of healing to regenerate your respiratory system or skin.

Angelic Healing for Cancer ($29.95)
If you fear cancer developing in your body, or if you already have cancer, you can learn how to build a strong will to live, to handle discouragement, to find the right doctor/healer, the right therapy or medication, and how and where to infuse angelic light and colors into your body to build in the healthy cells you need for healing. You also will build a magnetic healing hologram to accelerate your healing with the angelic healers.

All of these Angelic Journeys for Healing can be used in conjunction with Volume I and Volume II, which strengthen your skills in working with your soul and the angelic healers, and strengthen the work of the directors of your systems, especially your immune system.

Healing Journeys on Single Tapes

(The same journey is recorded on both sides so you can replay without rewinding.)

Revitalizing Yourself With the Angels ($9.95)
This tape includes two simultaneous angelic voices, one sounding in each ear.

Angelic Healing for Awakening ($9.95)

Angelic Healing for Sleep ($9.95)

Angelic Healing for Headaches ($9.95)

Angelic Music for Healing

LaUna held a focus for this music to be created with a very sensitive musician and an angel of healing named Thaddeus to supplement your healing processes and bring a profound sense of peace and serenity to you. Each volume has four musical compositions on two double-sided cassettes.

Becoming Your Soul ($29.95)

Angels ($29.95)

Solar Light Transmissions ($29.95)

Please Note!

The taped journeys are not substitutes for a professional diagnosis or treatment of any illness. See your doctor or other health professional when symptoms last for more than a few hours or days to get a diagnosis and choose the best outside intervention if needed.

LaUna does not give references for doctors, therapies, vitamins, or herbal sources. Excellent information is available in libraries, bookstores, and journals. She also does not offer individual sessions in person or by phone. She has found that the most powerful angelic connections occur in a group setting. To provide this setting, LaUna leads seminars that will help each participant bring in the healing angels. Dates and descriptions of current seminars are included in her newsletter, *Choosing Light*.

LaUna welcomes your letters about your experiences with the healing angels. You may write her at the address below. If you would like a free subscription to the *Choosing Light* newsletter, which includes articles, exercises, and a descriptions of tapes on healing, send your name, address, and phone number to:

Choosing Light
P.O. Box 5019
Mill Valley, CA 94941

To order tapes, write or call our order desk at 1 (800) 525-5950, or use the order form at the end of the book.

About the Author

LaUna Huffines has taught spiritual awakening for thirty-five years to therapists, seminar leaders, and other healers in various countries. For the past eight years, she has focused entirely on teaching how to upgrade and heal the physical body through the light of the soul and the healing angels. The author of *Bridge of Light: Tools of Light for Spiritual Transformation* (H J Kramer, 1993), LaUna has produced more than 130 guided journeys on tape for merging into greater light and accelerating healing. She also teaches seminars in the San Francisco Bay Area. She has a master of science degree in counseling and has completed all course work for a Ph.D. in East-West psychology at the California Institute of Integral Studies in San Francisco. LaUna has four sons and currently lives in Mill Valley, California.

Choosing Light Order Form

Qty.	Description	Price

Postage Rates

Up to $35.00: $3.50 shipping charge.
Over $35.00: Add 10% of order up to $10.00.
Canada: Add $5.00 additional postage.
All overseas orders: Add $10.00 additional postage.
(If your order exceeds this postage, we will
notify you.) Orders shipped in 48 hours for an
additional $5.00. Call for rates on air delivery.
Regular orders shipped within 5 to 7 business days.

Subtotal	
CA res. add 7.25% Sales Tax	
Postage	
Priority handling ($5.00)	
Total	

Name _____

Address _____

City _____ State _____ Zip _____

Phone: Home ( ) _____ Work ( ) _____

Visa or MasterCard # _____ Exp. Date _____

Signature as on card _____

Make check payable to Choosing Light.
Mail order form to: Choosing Light, P.O. Box 5019, Mill Valley, CA 94942
For credit card orders call (800) 525–5950.

COMPATIBLE BOOKS

FROM H J KRAMER INC

THE EARTH LIFE SERIES
by Sanaya Roman
*A course in learning to live with joy,
sense energy, and grow spiritually.*

LIVING WITH JOY, BOOK I
*"I like this book because it describes the way I feel
about so many things."*—VIRGINIA SATIR

PERSONAL POWER THROUGH AWARENESS:
A GUIDEBOOK FOR SENSITIVE PEOPLE, BOOK II
"Every sentence contains a pearl. . . "—LILIAS FOLAN

SPIRITUAL GROWTH:
BEING YOUR HIGHER SELF, BOOK III
*Orin teaches how to reach upward to align with the
higher energies of the universe, look inward to expand
awareness, and move outward in world service.*

An Orin/DaBen Book
CREATING MONEY
by Sanaya Roman and Duane Packer, Ph.D.
This best-selling book teaches advanced manifesting techniques.

An Orin/DaBen Book
OPENING TO CHANNEL:
HOW TO CONNECT WITH YOUR GUIDE
by Sanaya Roman and Duane Packer, Ph.D.
This breakthrough book is the first step-by-step guide to the art of channeling.

UNDERSTAND YOUR DREAMS
by Alice Anne Parker
A practical book that offers the key to dream interpretation.

JOURNEY INTO NATURE
by Michael J. Roads
*"If you only read one book this year, make that book
JOURNEY INTO NATURE."*—FRIEND'S REVIEW

JOURNEY INTO ONENESS
by Michael J. Roads
*"With this book, Michael Roads has established himself as an inspired
writer, storyteller, teacher, and radiant being."*—MAGICAL BLEND

COMPATIBLE BOOKS

FROM H J KRAMER INC

BRIDGE OF LIGHT
by LaUna Huffines
Tools of light for spiritual transformation . . . a spiritual classic.

MESSENGERS OF LIGHT:
THE ANGELS' GUIDE TO SPIRITUAL GROWTH
by Terry Lynn Taylor
*A lighthearted look at the angelic kingdom designed
to help you create heaven in your life.*

GUARDIANS OF HOPE:
THE ANGELS' GUIDE TO PERSONAL GROWTH
by Terry Lynn Taylor
*GUARDIANS OF HOPE brings the angels
down to earth with over sixty angel practices.*

ANSWERS FROM THE ANGELS:
A BOOK OF ANGEL LETTERS
by Terry Lynn Taylor
*Terry shares the letters she has received from people
all over the world that tell of their experiences with angels.*

CREATING WITH THE ANGELS
by Terry Lynn Taylor
*A journey into creativity including powerful
exercises and assistance from the angels.*

WAY OF THE PEACEFUL WARRIOR
by Dan Millman
A tale of transformation and adventure . . . a worldwide best-seller.

SACRED JOURNEY OF THE PEACEFUL WARRIOR
by Dan Millman
*"After you've read SACRED JOURNEY, you will know
what possibilities await you."—WHOLE LIFE TIMES*

NO ORDINARY MOMENTS
by Dan Millman
*Based on the premise that we can change our world by
changing ourselves, this book shares an approach to life that turns
obstacles into opportunities, and experiences into wisdom.*

THE LIFE YOU WERE BORN TO LIVE:
A GUIDE TO FINDING YOUR LIFE PURPOSE
by Dan Millman
*A modern method based on ancient wisdom that can help
you find new meaning, purpose, and direction in your life.*